On Monique Wittig

On Monique Wittig

Theoretical, Political, and Literary Essays

Edited by
NAMASCAR SHAKTINI

University of Illinois Press
Urbana and Chicago

∞ This book is printed on acid-free paper.

Library of Congress Cataloging-in-Publication Data
On Monique Wittig : theoretical, political, and literary essays /
edited by Namascar Shaktini.
    p.   cm.
Includes bibliographical references and index.
ISBN 0-252-02984-4 (cloth : alk. paper)
ISBN 0-252-07231-6 (pbk. : alk.paper)
1. Wittig, Monique—Criticism and interpretation.
2. Feminism and literature—France.
3. Lesbians in literature.
I. Shaktini, Namascar, 1939–
PQ2683.I8Z78   2005
843'.914—dc22   2004014401

*This book is lovingly dedicated
to the memory of Monique Wittig
(1935–2003)*

CONTENTS

Preface / ix

Acknowledgments / xv

Introduction / 1

Chronology / 7

PART 1: MONIQUE WITTIG'S MANIFESTO / 13

1. Introduction to "For a Women's Liberation Movement"
   Namascar Shaktini / 15

2. For a Women's Liberation Movement
   Monique Wittig, Gille Wittig, Marcia Rothenberg,
   Margaret Stephenson (Namascar Shaktini) / 21

PART 2: ESSAYS BY MONIQUE WITTIG / 35

3 Some Remarks on *Les guérillères*
   Monique Wittig / 37

4. Some Remarks on *The Lesbian Body*
   Monique Wittig / 44

PART 3: CRITICAL APPROACHES / 49

5. When Lesbians Were Not Women
   Teresa de Lauretis / 51

6. Universalizing Materialist Lesbianism
   Diane Griffin Crowder / 63

7. A New Grammar of Difference: Monique Wittig's Poetic Revolution
   Linda M. G. Zerilli / 87

8. Transformation of Gender and Genre Paradigms in the Fiction of Monique Wittig
   Erika Ostrovsky / 115

PART 4: THEORETICAL APPLICATIONS / 131

9. Quixote's Journey: How to Change the World and Degenderize the Stage
   Jeannelle Laillou Savona / 133

10. The Critical Mind and *The Lesbian Body*
    Namascar Shaktini / 150

PART 5: A NEW GENERATION OF READERS / 161

11. Dialogic Subversion in Monique Wittig's Fiction
    Dominique Bourque / 163

12. Politics and Poetics of Travesty in Monique Wittig's Fiction
    Catherine Rognon Ecarnot / 180

13. Wittig la Politique
    Marie-Hélène Bourcier / 187

Bibliography of Works by Monique Wittig / 199

Selected Bibliography of Monique Wittig Criticism / 203

Contributors / 223

Index / 227

PREFACE

On Monique Wittig: Theoretical, Political, and Literary Essays is a collection of essays written by Monique Wittig and by some of the most important Wittig scholars in the anglophone and francophone worlds. Their rereadings of Wittig's innovative subversion of canonical literature respond to influential misreadings that dismiss her writing as "essentialist," "humanist," and/or "lesbian separatist." The essays were selected for their focus on Wittig's revolutionary epistemological project: to investigate and expose the oppressive relation between gender and subjectivity in our shared language and culture.

These essays are addressed to a broad but educated English-language readership, including academics and students in such fields as literature, women's studies, philosophy, and the social sciences—wherever a radical critical perspective on gender is wanted. Wittig's materialist lesbianism provides such a perspective. This first collection of essays by and on Monique Wittig will politically situate her fiction and theory, making it accessible to anglophone readers. The only other English-language book dedicated exclusively to Wittig is a literary study by Erika Ostrovsky, *A Constant Journey: The Fiction of Monique Wittig* (1991). The following overview of the chapters indicates the range of subjects—three by Wittig herself (and my introduction to Wittig's chapter 2, "For a Women's Liberation Movement") and nine by critics focusing on Wittig's theory, politics, and writing.

Monique Wittig's Manifesto

This collection includes what is probably Monique Wittig's first important work of nonfiction, "For a Movement of Women's Liberation," which was used as a feminist manifesto at the very first action of what was soon to become the Mouvement de Libération des Femmes (Women's Liberation Movement).

Published in May 1970 in the now-defunct leftist monthly *L'Idiot Interna-tional*, the manifesto was never republished during Wittig's lifetime. Follow-ing my introduction to it, "For a Movement of Women's Liberation" appears here in English for the first time with the permission of the *militantes* who collectively signed it with Monique Wittig.

Essays by Monique Wittig

I am also pleased to include two of Wittig's literary essays in which, recount-ing the process of textual creation, she reveals strategic elements of her ma-terialist technique. Wittig wrote the first essay on *Les guérillères* in English and presented it for the first time in 1992 at Florida Atlantic University. A revised French version appeared in *L'Esprit Créateur* in 1994 as "Quelques remarques sur les guérillères" and is the version published here in English for the first time as "Some Remarks on *Les guérillères*" (chapter 3). At my request in 1997, Wittig began "Some Remarks on *The Lesbian Body*" (chapter 4) as a companion piece and sent it to me in 2001 for inclusion in this collection. Although she didn't have a chance to review it for publication, it is preserved in the last form she gave it.

In addition to these precious texts by Wittig, the present volume includes three groups of critical essays by other Wittig critics. Part 3, "Critical Ap-proaches," includes a grouping of general theoretical articles that are often critical of earlier theoretical approaches and even of each other. "Theoretical Applications," Part 4, features essays treating individual works of fiction that warrant specific focus: Wittig's only play, which has been seen by only a hand-ful of people, and her most difficult work, which has been subject to serious misreadings by anglophone critics. Part 5, "A New Generation of Readers," includes essays by three younger critics, an indication of some of the new directions of Wittig criticism.

Critical Approaches

Teresa de Lauretis's theoretical essay "When Lesbians Were Not Women" (chapter 5) offers a tribute to Monique Wittig. De Lauretis acknowledges Wittig's influence on her own decision to write lesbian theory as distinct from feminist theory. She explains Wittig's impact on theory as a shift in historical consciousness: "If de Beauvoir the philosopher had said, 'One is not *born* but *becomes* a woman,' . . . Wittig the writer said: 'one is not born a *woman*' (empha-sis added). Almost the same words, and yet such a difference in meaning."

De Lauretis sees Wittig's "lesbian" as a new conceptual figure, "the subject of a cognitive practice based on the lived experience of one's body, one's desire, one's conceptual and psychical dis-identification from the straight mind, . . . aware of the power of discourse to shape one's social and subjective . . . reality." De Lauretis examines a "curious paradox" in the critical reception of Wittig's work, centered on a book by Judith Butler, important because it brought Wittig to the attention of nonlesbian and nonfeminist readers. "Butler failed to understand the figural, theoretical character of Wittig's 'lesbian' and its epistemological valence." As de Lauretis puts it:

> [Butler] tossed her theory in the dump of surpassed and discarded philosophies: . . . to the reader of *Gender Trouble*, Wittig appears to be an existentialist who believes in human freedom, a humanist who presumes the ontological unity of Being prior to language, an idealist masquerading as a materialist, and most paradoxically of all, an unintentional, unwitting collaborator with the regime of heterosexual normativity. This, in my opinion, may account for the relative disregard or condescension in which Wittig's work has been held in gender and queer studies until now. Until, that is, the renewed attention to Wittig's work on the part of a new generation may perhaps reopen another virtual space of lesbian thought and writing.

Diane Griffin Crowder's "Universalizing Materialist Lesbianism" (chapter 6) elucidates Wittig's work from a lesbian materialist perspective. Her analysis is especially useful for anglophone readers who may not be aware of the French theoretical tradition of materialism. It is the feminist theory developed most notably by Christine Delphy, Nicole-Claude Mathieu, and Colette Guillaumin as well as Wittig, growing out of this tradition, that forms the basis for Wittig's lesbian theory.

From the perspective of materialism, Crowder addresses the misreadings of Wittig's work by Americans who divide feminism into either the essentialist or the social constructionist camps and separate gender from sex. From the perspective of lesbianism, Crowder attacks Ostrovsky's assimilation to heterosexuality of Wittig's concept of "universalism," which, as Wittig shows, can strategically be used as the minority writer's Trojan horse. By viewing Wittig's fiction as a form of political praxis, Crowder provides a corrective to important misreadings. "While Fuss, Butler, and others recognize that Wittig is radically 'constructionist' in her view that social relations alone create 'men' and 'women,' they tend to view her 'lesbian' as . . . having an essence." Crowder argues that "Wittig's *materialist* viewpoint has allowed her to home in on the one thing all lesbians have in common—a rejection of the institution(s) of heterosexuality on at least some level. This rejection of the material services heterosexual women perform for men within those institutions is a political, rather than an essentialist, position."

In "A New Grammar of Difference: Monique Wittig's Poetic Revolution" (chapter 7), Linda M. G. Zerilli, a political scientist, develops her earlier thought on Wittig's "universalism." Zerilli uses the political theory of Immanuel Kant, Hannah Arendt, and Ernesto Grassi in a rereading of Wittig's *Les guéril-lères* to demonstrate how it creates a new space of political freedom, a new social contract. "What *Les guérillères* achieves is an alteration in our sense of reality by means of the archaic language of images. Wittig's text disrupts the heterosexual social contract, whose synchronic or 'always already there' picture of two groups, men and women, holds us captive. . . . And she does so, . . . with the strange use of an ordinary pronoun, *elles.*" Zerilli points out, "What Wittig shows by combining two existing concepts which are normally not related (i.e., the feminine gender and the universal voice) is not a new 'subject,' let alone a hegemonic one, but a new enunciative position, a place from which to speak and act in concert."

Like de Lauretis and Crowder, Zerilli is critical of past receptions of Wittig's work: "Judith Butler's well-known critique of Wittig as a humanist . . . focused exclusively on the question of identity and neglected the problem of freedom (or, at best, redefined it in terms of identity) in Wittig's texts. Butler's reading served for many American feminists as the definitive verdict on Wittig's work, which is stunningly absent in the 1990s feminist debates. This dismissal of Wittig is not reducible to Butler's critique, let alone caused by it, but symptomatic of the dominant problematic of feminism at the time, namely identity." Zerilli concludes, "What defines the work of Monique Wittig is the problem of freedom as a political phenomenon."

Erika Ostrovsky, noted for the authorship of her 1991 book on Wittig's fiction, offers a rereading of that work: "Transformation of Gender and Genre Paradigms in the Fiction of Monique Wittig" (chapter 8). "While a decade or so ago, it seemed certain that *'renversement'* could be considered the key to Monique Wittig's writing," Ostrovsky explains, "a rereading today suggests that, rather than the overthrow or the annihilation of existing literary canons in order to allow new growth to occur, her major accomplishment consists of an action that is far more subtle, yet also more demanding: Transformation, transmutation, transfiguration—actions that indicate various degrees of change and an ascending order of magnitude." Moreover, "A reconsideration of Wittig's fiction shows that, once this new key is accepted, every area of her writing gains in depth and brilliance . . . it is probably the most striking and significant when it comes to the transformation of gender and genre paradigms."

Theoretical Applications

Wittig's work on gender reaches into many genres, including the theater. Her only published play, *Le voyage sans fin* (The Constant Journey) is analyzed in Jeannelle Laillou Savona's essay "Quixote's Journey: How to Change the World and Degenderize the Stage" (chapter 9), which traces the history of the production and reception of Wittig's play and provides a materialist analysis. Published in French as *Le voyage sans fin* in 1985, the play was translated by Sande Zeig, who played Quixote when it was first produced in 1984 at Goddard College and when it was mounted again in 1985 in Paris at the Petit Théâtre du Rond-Point. As Savona points out, "Insofar as the play interpellates its audience on an ideological level, it is obviously addressed to feminists, lesbians and gay men who all have an interest in subverting the notion of gender, but its parable—that of Quixote—appears universal enough to appeal to open-minded, cultured spectators interested in a theatrical modernization of a classical theme through an original combination of Brechtian cinematic techniques and unusual body movements."

In "The Critical Mind and *The Lesbian Body*" (chapter 10), I survey the positive and negative reception of *The Lesbian Body* in North American academic circles, affirming the "more subtle" investigations of Wittig's textual strategies that escape less careful readings motivated by an anxiety to expose "essentialist" discourse. I also develop a constructionist conception of the "lesbian body." Within the universe of Wittig's most misunderstood book, the lesbian body is not an object that precedes a point of view. Therefore, its existence may be denied, and it may be unnameable. When seen through alien eyes it may have monstrous attributes, or in the eyes of a lover it may be idealized and adored. By multiplying the identities of the lesbian and by decomposing and recomposing the body in the 110 prose poems of the book, Wittig shifts attention away from the notion that there is such a thing as a "lesbian body" and focuses instead on how a lesbian body is figured. The issue she raises is less sexual than epistemological.

A New Generation Reads Wittig

A new theoretical approach is brought by Dominique Bourque's "Dialogic Subversion in Monique Wittig's Fiction" (chapter 11). Bourque draws on Mikhail Bakhtin's insight that "when words are quoted in such a way that two distinct perspectives, two different linguistic awarenesses, are perceptible, we are in the presence of an utterance that is double-voiced, or dialogic." Bourque examines the dialogical strategies that allow Wittig to propose a philosophical and social revaluation of the subject. The ethico-political perspective on the world of this new subject transgresses the idealist thought and polarized conceptual categories that support the various occidental discourses, including literature and language. Bourque describes Wittig's work as a "counter-text" that relativizes the canonized discursive and literary corpuses in order to allow the emergence of a dialog between critical and responsible subjects.

Catherine Rognon Ecarnot is the author of the excellent *L'écriture de Monique Wittig à la couleur de Sappho* (2002). Her essay "Politics and Poetics of Travesty in Monique Wittig's Fiction" (published in French in *CLIO: Histoire, Femmes et Sociétés* in October 1999) has been translated for publication here in English for the first time (chapter 12). Ecarnot, taking as her point of departure that "femininity is a travesty," displaces the question of cross-dressing or travesty (*travestissement*) to the metamorphosis of bodies in Wittig's fiction. But the travesty, she points out, is not limited to bodies: "Studded with citations and rich with borrowed personnas, the writing of Wittig pastiches, parodies, travesties anterieur texts more often than sexed representations."

Marie-Hélène Bourcier, the coordinator of *La pensée straight* and the translator of three essays from *The Straight Mind and Other Essays*, presents here for English readers "Wittig la Politique" (chapter 13), a revised version of her French preface. Blending the queer fantastic with her loose interpretation of the "facts," she produces an irreverent parody that readers may find at odds with the otherwise scrupulously academic style of the rest of the volume. As Simonetta Spinelli has put it, "Queer theory claims to have retaken, to have actualized, Wittig's theory. Yet queer theory . . . has navigated itself into varying and conflicting courses, frequently utilizing Wittig's theory in an unabashedly reductive manner."[1]

Bourcier reviews Wittig's political concepts and strategies in the guise of a fictive dialogue/interview between two characters—herself and "Manastabal," the parodic Virgilian character from *Virgile, non.* She brings to the events and theoretical issues of Wittigian politics a view inflected not only by her own queer politics but also by her role as a translator and by her life in both France and the United States. By pointing to the bilingualism of Wittig, she makes us understand that "to be" lesbian is always to be exposed to translation to make oneself understood.

NOTE

1. "La queer theory rivendica di aver ripreso, attualizzandolo, il pensiero di Wittig. Ma queer theory . . . si è diramato in rivoli contraddittori e che spesso utilizzano Wittig operando disinvolte riduzioni." Simonetta Spinelli, "Monique Wittig: Queer or Not Queer?" *Labrys, études féministe,* special issue, Sept. 2003 <http://www.unb.br/in/his/gefem/special/artigos.htm>. Translated by Arthur Tang.

ACKNOWLEDGMENTS

I gratefully acknowledge the personal support of my loving family; my French friends in the Mouvement de Libération des Femmes for helping me raise my consciousness and change my life's direction in 1970; Roland Barthes for encouraging my studies when I might have abandoned them; and Beth, Shari, and especially Sally for loving support of my work on Wittig over the years.

I want to acknowledge the institutional support of the Center for the Study of Women and Society at the University of Oregon for a research grant; the Dorothy F. Schmidt College of Arts and Letters at Florida Atlantic University for partial summer research support; the Archives Lesbiennes and the Bibliothèque Marguérite Durand in Paris for their kind assistance and permission to copy lesbian and feminist photographs and documents; Carlos Nelson for assistance at the Florida Atlantic University Library; and Marie-Lynn Raymond for secretarial support.

I offer sincere thanks for the collaborative support of many people: Gille Wittig, Suzette Robichon, and Louise Turcotte for reading and contributing to the chronology; Diane Crowder for significant contributions to the critical bibliography; the anonymous reviewers for helpful suggestions on the manuscript; Joan Catapano for editorial support; the anonymous movement photographers of the 1970s for leaving us a photographic record; Babette Mangolte for the frontispiece and cover photograph; Colette Geoffrey for contributing three photographs; Jacquelene Ambrose for contributing skillful photo restoration; and, finally, Sande Zeig, executor of the Monique Wittig estate, for carefully correcting many versions of the manuscript and for contributing precious photographs.

I especially appreciate my students, with whom I continue to learn. Sabrina Draï and Victoria Kopcik have provided translations from the French. Arthur

Tang has provided translations from both French and Italian and has created the index. Catherine Olson and Yamaya Kauri-Alecto have contributed to the critical bibliography.

INTRODUCTION

Namascar Shaktini

Many of us were shocked by Monique Wittig's sudden death on January 3, 2003. The international response to her unexpected disappearance was a measure of the widespread feeling of loss.[1] Attacking oppression through her social theory, her literary praxis, and her political organizing, she made a difference. She made us see what we had not seen before—that heterosexuality is a political régime, that the categories of sex, man and woman, are inherently oppressive, and that the masculine appropriation of the "universal" is a criminal act.

It was as a writer that Wittig first became known, although her theory and politics were always inseparable from her fiction. Marguerite Duras and Nathalie Sarraute were on the jury that awarded the prestigious Prix Médicis (one of the top literary awards in France) for her first novel, published in 1964. Duras described *L'opoponax* (The Opoponax) as written according to an iron rule, a comment that could be extended to Wittig's second and third novels as well. All three are characterized by an iron discipline. They compose what I call her "pronoun trilogy," a systematic experiment with pronouns, narrative subjectivity, and gender. *The Opoponax* was probably the first major novel of education written from a generic child's point of view. This was followed in 1969 by *Les guérillères*, an epic from a feminist point of view. In 1974 her most deconstructive work appeared: *Le corps lesbien* (The Lesbian Body), where the female body is figuratively taken apart and reconceptualized from a lesbian point of view. The trilogy was followed by three significant rewritings, the first of the dictionary *Brouillon pour un dictionnaire des amantes* (Lesbian Peoples: Material for a Dictionary), which Wittig coauthored with Sande Zeig in 1976; the second a play rewriting *Quixote* by Cervantes, *Le voyage sans fin*

(The Constant Journey), first performed in 1984 and starring Sande Zeig; and in 1985 the third, *Virgile, non* (Across the Acheron), a rewriting of Dante's *Divine Comedy.*

When Wittig began writing it was generally believed that women are naturally inferior to men. It was natural that they should be oppressed. It was natural that they should be victims. No serious challenge to women's oppression had been mounted. Even Beauvoir's pioneer focus on the *Second Sex,* although a brilliant interdisciplinary analysis of the feminine condition, did not suggest action leading to change, and Beauvoir did not consider herself a feminist when her book was published in 1949.

Wittig's theory was revolutionary from the start, as evident in her May 1970 essay "For a Movement of Women's Liberation," published here in English for the first time. Using a materialist approach, she began by analyzing the situation of women in terms of political economy. She took as her point of departure Karl Marx's concept of the sexual division of labor in the family, but she refuted his assumption that it was natural. She built on Simone de Beauvoir's theory that the concept of woman is cultural rather than natural but went on to identify women as a political class.

Women, according to Wittig's analysis, are a political class, like serfs in feudal times. Just as serfs were tied to the land for labor, women are tied to the house for labor. When male serfs, with the historic shift to a capitalist mode of production, were liberated from feudal ties to become proletarians, female serfs could not completely make the change to the new class of workers. Unlike the oppression of capitalism, that of feudalism was personified. The feudal service the serf owed was to his lord as a person. If that lord were killed in battle, his army of serfs, having sworn to give military service to him as a person, could quit fighting and go home. The proletarian is not tied to a person; he is free to exchange his labor for money on the market of capitalism.

But where male serfs were liberated by capitalism from feudalism, women were not—or not completely. A woman remained tied to the home, obligated to provide the domestic service of housework and childcare, a service owed personally to her husband as head of the family. Although this service is a socially necessary production, it has no exchange value. Wittig calls it "servile labor." A woman entering the world of paid labor carries the burden of a prior obligation to fulfill her responsibilities to her family, causing her value to be less to the employer and causing her to have double the work. Wittig argues that it is unjust that a whole category of people, because of their sex, have to work without being paid. She uses citations from Fredrick Engels's *Origin of the Family* to call into question the so-called natural division of labor in the family and attacks it as the only form of serfdom surviving into modern capitalist times. This division of labor rests on the concept of sexual difference, a concept that Wittig would target in later essays.

Her 1970 essay also refers to the movement just underway in the United States. It introduces into French the American term *male chauvinism* and decries the exploitation of women's bodies as merchandise. Citing Bobby Seal, it draws a parallel between the struggle against male chauvinism and that against racism. Her conclusion echoes the Black Panthers: "All power to the people." Wittig, however, first had to make a case that "we are the people."

Wittig mentions in her manifesto an idea she had just demonstrated in *Les guérillères*—that of appropriating the universal: "Like racism, sexism is so well implanted in ruling class ideology that only a radical seizing of power can destroy it—a political takeover to represent, in our turn, our interest as being the universal interest. That is necessary for the first phase, the end goal of all seizure of power by the people being an abolition of domination in general. Our interest is that of the people. We are the people." The idea is taken from Marx, who observed that "every class which is struggling for mastery, even when its domination, as is the case with the proletariat, postulates the abolition of the old form of society in its entirety and of domination itself, must first conquer for itself political power in order to represent its interest in turn as the general interest, which in the first moment it is forced to do."[2]

But where Marx argues that the main conflict of interest is between the (male) proletariat and (male) capitalist class, Wittig shines a new theoretical light on the interest of women as a class. Although she argues for the necessity of economic and political struggle, especially on the front of the family, the war she wages as a writer is epistemological, as she made explicit a decade later: "There is room for so-called minority writers to enter the privileged (battle) field of literature, where attempts at constitution of the subject confront each other."[3]

Beauvoir had showed that "He is the Subject, she is the Other," but her point only gave rise to an academic discussion in the realm of philosophy. Wittig reframed the issue of gender and subjectivity by focusing on language in her literary experiments and politics. A pioneer, she confronted head on the pseudo-universal (masculine) subject or, as people would refer to it once the term was coined in 1975, "phallogocentrism." Of course, our goal was to raise the issue not just with intellectuals but with the public and create a political movement to fight against the oppression of women in society.

We distributed Wittig's article at the first action of what was soon to be called in France the Mouvement de Libération des Femmes (MLF). In May 1970, eighteen of us organized the first French demonstration about women's oppression at the new leftist campus of the University at Vincennes. The movement, quickly gaining momentum, was followed three months later by a now-famous action, the first public, media-covered demonstration of the MLF at the Arc de Triomphe on August 26, 1970. In solidarity with the strike of American feminists commemorating the fiftieth anniversary of woman suffrage, ten activists—Cathy Bernheim, Monique Bourroux, Julie Dassin, Christine Delphy, Emmanuèle de Lesseps, Christiane Rochefort, Janine Sert, Margaret Stephenson (Namascar Shaktini), Monique Wittig, and Anne Zelensky—laid a wreath on the Tomb of the Unknown Soldier in the name of "the one more unknown than the unknown soldier, his wife." Christine Delphy carried the wreath, and eight others carried the four banners. I brought up the rear, distributing leaflets explaining our action.

The feminist movement became widespread in France, and in 1978 Wittig collaborated on the Editorial Collective of *Questions Feministes;* Simone de Beauvoir gave her name as editor of the journal. In 1980 Wittig published in it an important theoretical essay, "La pensée straight." The conclusion: "Les lesbiennes ne sont pas des femmes" (Lesbians are not women). A schism within the eight-member editorial collective on the lesbian question ended the journal.

Wittig began the second phase of her theory, during which she no longer identified herself by the terms *woman* or *feminist.* In 1980 editors Mary Jo Lakeland and Susan Ellis Wolf invited Wittig to be advisory editor of a new journal, *Feminist Issues.* Wittig's "The Straight Mind" appeared in the first issue, and "One Is Not Born a Woman" in the second. Most of her other theoretical essays of the 1980s were published in the journal: "The Category of Sex," "The Trojan Horse," "The Mark of Gender," "On the Social Contract," "Homo Sum," and "The Point of View: Universal or Particular?" They were collected and republished in *The Straight Mind and Other Essays* (1992) along with another essay, "The Site of Action," a study of the "unlimited power over the other granted by language" in the work of her good friend Nathalie Sarraute.[4]

Language, its power, its role in constructing the genderized world, and its role in constructing the subject was the constant focus of Wittig's work, whether in literature, theory, or politics. For Wittig, a materialist, the revolution will take place only if it is an epistemological revolution. "Consciousness of oppression is not only a reaction to (fight against) oppression. It is also the whole conceptual reevaluation of the social world, its whole reorganization with new concepts, from the point of view of oppression."[5]

Among the words of Monique Wittig's coinage, two appear in the 2001 edition of the *Grand Robert* dictionary: "bourreleuse" and "cyprine." "Bourreau," torturer, executioner, from "bourrer" ("frapper," to strike), entered the French language in 1319 and remained as a masculine word with no feminine form (or feminine concept). The synonym, "bourreleur," from the literary form "bourreler," entered the French in 1554. In 2001 a feminine form, "bourreleuse," was attributed to Wittig: "J/e suis la bourreleuse forcenée galvanisée par les tortures et tes cris m//emportent d'autant plus m/a plus aimée que tu les contiens."[6]

"La bourreleuse" makes its first appearence in line 18 of Poem 2 of *Le corps lesbien* as the tenth of ten repetitions of Wittig's "j/e suis" (slashed *I* plus *am*). This first part of her poem rewrites the sixth quatrain of Baudelaire's "L'héautontimorouménos" (One's Own Executioner), a poem that problematizes the conventionally accepted subject-object dichotomy. Baudelaire's "je" assumes multiple identities on both sides of the subject-object split.

"Cyprine" currently has no English equivalent. According to the *Grand Robert,* "cyprine" (classified as "didactique") entered the French language during the 1970s. The word is attributed to Monique Wittig: "Une agitation trouble l'écoulement de la cyprine eau fluide transparente."[7] The citation is from the eleventh prose poem of the French original of *The Lesbian Body,* which celebrates "cyprine" as the theme. *Le corps lesbien* includes occurrences of "cyprine" in other prose poems as well—Poems 29, 45, 51, 93, and 102.[8] "Cyprine" is the first of the attributes of the lesbian body to figure in the list of *Le corps lesbien.*[9] David Le Vay, the English translator, had recourse to words such as *juice* to translate the poetic French "cyprine," derived from Aphrodite's surname.[10] (*Semence,* of course, has an English equivalent: semen.) I propose that we bring "cyprine" into the English language.

Instead of a genderized world (one seen through the lens of phallogocentrism), Wittig has created a lesbianized world within the universe of her writing. It is from the point of view of lesbianism that Wittig speaks: "A new personal and subjective definition for all humankind can only be found beyond the categories of sex. . . . Lesbian is the only concept I know of which is beyond the categories of sex (woman and man), because the designated subject (lesbian) is not a woman, either economically, or politically, or ideologically. For what makes a woman is a specific social relation to a man, a relation that we have previously called servitude." The quotation is from an article published in *L'Idiot International* (May 1970), whose original title was "Pour un mouvement de libération des femmes" (For a Women's Liberation Movement).[11]

NOTES

1. Monique Wittig's ashes were placed in Père-Lachaise Cemetery, Paris. Memorials were held in Paris, Toulouse, Tucson, Milan, New York, and Berlin, and obituaries were

published in *Le Monde, Libération*, the *New York Times*, the *Los Angeles Times, Humanité*, and *Le Devoir*, among others. Dozens of obituaries appeared on the Internet (where Wittig is mentioned on more than 4,800 sites).

2. Karl Marx, *The German Ideology, Part 1* (A. Idealism and Materialism, note 2). Wittig is referring in her note to the text published here in English for the first time.

3. Monique Wittig, *The Straight Mind and Other Essays* (Boston: Beacon Press, 1992), 61.

4. The collected essays, with some changes, were translated and published in French as *La pensée straight* (Paris: Balland, 2001). The French edition does not include Wittig's discussion of *The Lesbian Body* in "The Mark of Gender" and does not include "The Site of Action," but it does include an essay that is not included in the English version of the collected essays: "Paradigm," which was translated into English by Georges Stambolian and, to my knowledge, was the first of Wittig's essays to be published in English. Georges Stambolian and Elaine Marks, eds., *Homosexualities and French Literature* (Ithaca: Cornell University Press, 1979).

5. Wittig, *The Straight Mind,* 18.

6. "Ɨ am the mad tormentor galvanized by torture and your cries intoxicate m/e m/y best beloved the more that you restrain them" (Monique Wittig, *Le corps lesbien* [Boston: Beacon Press, 1973], 16). In the author's note to the Le Vay translation, Wittig explains why she puts a slash through the first-person signifiers in *The Lesbian Body*: "J/e is the symbol of the lived, rending experience which is m/y writing, of this cutting in two which throughout literature is the exercise of a language which does not constitute m/e as subject" (10).

7. "An agitation bothers the flow of the cyprine water transparent fluid" (my translation). Wittig, *Le corps lesbien,* 20.

8. Ibid., 49; Monique Wittig, *The Lesbian Body* (Boston: Beacon Press, 1986), 50, 76 (Minuit), 72 (Beacon Press), 87 (Minuit), 80 (Beacon Press), 157 (Minuit), 139 (Beacon Press), 172 (Minuit), 151 (Beacon Press).

9. Ibid., 22 (Minuit), 28 (Beacon Press).

10. For a concordance of *Le corps lesbien* (produced by Sally Douglas), see Namascar Shaktini, "The Problem of Gender and Subjectivity Posed by the New Subject Pronoun 'J/E' in the Writing of Monique Wittig," Ph.D. diss., University of California, Santa Cruz, 1981, appendixes C, D, and E.

11. Monique Wittig, Gille Wittig, Marcia Rothenburg, and Margaret Stephenson, "Combat pour la libération de la femme: Par delà la libération-gadget, elles découvrent la lutte des classes" (For a Women's Liberation Movement), *L'Idiot International* 12 (May 1992): 13–16 and Wittig's note 102.

CHRONOLOGY

July 13, 1935 Monique Wittig, novelist, poet, social theorist, and activist, born in Dannemarie (Alsace) France. Mother, born Maria Doppler into a family of Alsacian peasants; father, Noël Wittig, the son of Alsacian workers who took refuge in the Franche Comté during the War of 1870. Parents married in Alsace in 1934. Sister, Gille Wittig, born in Alsace in 1938.

1938–44 When Alsace comes under German control, family moves to Audin-court (Franche Comté), birthplace of Noël Wittig, where Monique Wittig attends primary school.

1944–50 Family moves to Rodez and surrounding countryside. Monique and Gille Wittig attend Pension Jeanne d'Arc.

1950 Family moves to Paris, where Monique Wittig will later take courses (Sorbonne, Langues Orientales).

1964 Monique Wittig publishes first novel, *L'opoponax* (Éditions de Minuit), which is translated into a dozen languages and awarded the Prix Médicis, one of the top literary awards in France).

1965 Publishes "Banlieues" in *Nouveau Commerce*.

1966 *The Opoponax* is translated by Helen Weaver (Simon and Schuster).

1966 Publishes "Lacunary Films" in *New Statesman* (July 15).

1967 Publishes "A propos de Bouvard et Pécuchet" in *Les Cahiers Madeleine Renaud–Jean Louise Barrault* (59).

1967 Publishes "Voyage: Yallankoro" in *Le Nouvelle Commerce.*

1968 Translates as *L'homme unidimensionnel* (Éditions de Minuit) *One Dimensional Man* by Herbert Marcuse.

May 1968 Participates in events.

1969 Publishes second novel, *Les guérillères* (Éditions de Minuit).

May 1970 Publishes, with Gille Wittig, Marcia Rothenburg, and Margaret Stephenson (Namascar Shaktini), "Combat pour la libération de la femme" in *L'Idiot International* 6 (May 1970): 13–16. As submitted to the editor, the title was "Pour un mouvement de libération des femmes." Copies of article distributed in May at University of Paris at Vincennes at first demonstration of what was to be the MLF in France.

August 26, 1970 Participates in first public, media-covered demonstration of the Mouvement de Libération des Femmes (MLF) at the Arc de Triomphe. In solidarity with the strike of American feminists commemorating the fiftieth anniversary of woman suffrage, ten activists, Cathy Bernheim, Monique Bourroux, Julie Dassin, Christine Delphy, Emmanuèle de Lesseps, Christiane Rochefort, Janine Sert, Margaret Stephenson (Namascar Shaktini), Monique Wittig, and Anne Zelensky, lay a wreath on the Tomb of the Unknown Soldier in the name of "the one more unknown than the unknown soldier, his wife." Wittig helps carry banner reading "One Man Out of Two Is a Woman."

1970 Publishes "Une partie de campagne," *Le Nouveau Commerce* (26).

April 5, 1971 Signs "Notre ventre nous appartient," Manifeste des 343, published in *Le Nouvel Observateur.*

1971 English version of *Les guérillères* is translated by David Le Vay (Peter Owen).

1972 Writes radio plays, *Le grand-cric-Jules, Récréation,* and *Dialogue pour les deux frères et la soeur,* for Radio Stuttgart.

1972 Publishes "Un moie est apparue" in *Le Torchon Brûle* (no. 5 [July 1972]: 3) and *Revue Minuit* ([1972]: 43–46).

1973 Publishes third novel, *Le corps lesbien* (Éditions Minuit).

1974 Translates (with Evelyne le Garrec and Vera Prado) *Novas cartões Portuguesas* by the Three Marias (Isabel Barreno, Teresa Horta, and Fatima Velho Da Costa) as *Les nouvelles lettres Portugaises* (Éditions Minuit).

1975 *The Lesbian Body* is translated by David Le Vay (Peter Owen).

1976 Publishes with Sande Zeig *Brouillon pour un dictionnaire des amantes* (Éditions Grasset).

1976 Moves to United States with Sande Zeig.

1976–89 Holds teaching positions at the University of California, Berkeley; University of Maine; New York University; University of Southern California; University of California, Davis; Duke University; Vassar College; and SUNY, Buffalo.

1978 Collaborates on the Editorial Collective of *Questions Feministes,* to which Simone de Beauvoir lends her name as editor.

1978 Publishes "Un jour mon prince viendra" in *Questions Feministes* (2).

1978 Affirms "lesbians are not women" in the conclusion of a paper, "The Straight Mind," presented to the Modern Language Association in New York.

1979 Publishes "Paradigm" in *Homosexualities and French Literature,* edited by Elaine Marks and George Stambolian (Cornell University Press). Defines woman: "Insofar as the virtuality 'woman' becomes reality for an individual only in relation to an individual of the opposing class—men—and particularly through marriage, lesbians, because they do not enter this category, are not 'women.'"

1979 Publishes with Sande Zeig *Lesbian Peoples: Material for a Dictionary* (Avon Books).

1979 Presents "One Is Not Born a Woman" at "The Second Sex, Thirty Years After" conference in New York. When during the conference Hélène Cixous declares that, in France, the word *lesbian* is not used because it has negative connotations, Wittig exclaims from the back of the hall, "Which France? This is a scandal."

1980 Publishes "La pensée straight" in *Questions Féministes* (7). The conclusion: "Les lesbiennes ne sont pas des femmes." A schism occurs within the eight-member editorial collective on the lesbian question. Attempts prove unsuccessful to find a way of sharing the publications between the two ideological positions, feminist and radical lesbian. Therefore, the editorial collective signs an agreement to terminate the journal. Despite this agreement, Christine Delphy and two others publish a new journal, *Nouvelles Questions Feministes,* which is incorrectly assumed to be a continuation of *Questions Feministes.* Wittig begins second phase of her theory, where she no longer identifies herself using the term *feminist.*

1980 Publishes "The Straight Mind" in *Feminist Issues* (1, no. 1). Editors Mary Jo Lakeland and Susan Ellis Wolf invite Wittig to be advisory editor of the new journal.

May 1980 Publishes "On ne naît pas femme" in *Questions Feministes* no. 8, the final issue of the journal.

1981 Publishes "One Is Not Born a Woman" in *Feminist Issues* (1, no. 2).

1982 Translates (with Avant-Note) as *La passion* (Éditions Flammarion) Djuna Barnes's *Spillway.*

1983 Publishes "The Point of View: Universal or Particular?" in *Feminist Issues* (3 no. 2).

1983 Publishes "Les tchiches et les tchouches" in *Le Genre Humain* (6).

1983 Publishes "Les questions féministes ne sont pas des questions lesbiennes" in *Amazones d'Hier, Lesbiennes d'Aujourd'hui* (2, no. 1 [Montreal]).

1984 Publishes "The Trojan Horse" in *Feminist Issues* (4, no. 2).

1984 Publishes "Le lieu de l'action" in *Digraphe* (32, on Nathalie Sarraute).

1984 Premiere performance of *The Constant Journey* with Sande Zeig at the Haybarn Theater, Goddard College, Plainfield, Vermont.

1985 *Le voyage sans fin* with Sande Zeig performed at the Petit Théâtre du Rond-Point, Paris (and published as a *Supplément* to *Vlasta* [no. 4]).

1985 *Vlasta* publishes special issue (no. 4) on Monique Wittig.

1985 Publishes "Paris-la-politique" and "Le cheval de Troie," Marthe Rosenfeld's translation of "The Trojan Horse," in *Vlasta* (no. 4).

1985 Publishes *Virgile, non* (Éditions Minuit).

1985 Publishes "The Mark of Gender" in *Feminist Issues* (5, no. 2).

1986 Translates "The Place of the Action" (on Nathalie Sarraute) in *Three Decades of the French New Novel* edited by Lois Oppenheim (University of Illinois Press).

1986 Receives doctorate from the École des Hautes Études en Sciences Sociales, Paris.

1987 *Across the Acheron* is translated by David Le Vay in collaboration with Margaret Crosland (Dufour Éditions/Peter Owen).

1989 Publishes "On the Social Contract" in *Feminist Issues* (9, no. 1).

1990 Appointed tenured professor in the department of French and Italian at the University of Arizona, Tucson, where she will also teach in women's studies.

1990 Publishes "Homo Sum" in *Feminist Issues* (10, no. 1).

1992 Publishes *The Straight Mind and Other Essays* (Beacon Press).

March 1992 Presents first version of paper on *Les guérillères* in English at Florida Atlantic University.

1994 Publishes "Quelques remarques sur *Les guérillères*" in *L'Esprit Créateur.*

April 1994 Organizes the Nathalie Sarraute Conference at the University of Arizona, Tucson.

1995 Delivers the Curtin Lesbian, Alternative, and Gay (CLAG) Collective's fourth annual David R. Kessler Lecture, CUNY.

Summer 1996 Publishes papers from Nathalie Sarraute Conference in *L'Esprit Créateur.*

June 1997 Participates in a colloquium on gay and lesbian studies at the Centre Georges Pompidou, organized by Didier Eribon.

June 23, 1997 Publishes interview in *Libération.*

1998 Publishes "Sur le contrat social" in *Études gay et lesbiennes* edited by Didier Eribon (Éditions du Centre Georges Pompidou).

1999 Publishes *Paris-la-politique et autres histoires* (P.O.L. Éditeur).

2001 *Le Grand Robert de la langue Française* admits two new words into the French language, "bourreleuse" (8) and "cyprine" (20), which it attributes to Monique Wittig, citing *Le corps lesbien* (Éditions Minuit).

2001 *La pensée straight* (Éditions Balland).

2001 *The Girl*, a film by Sande Zeig and adapted from an unpublished short story by Monique Wittig, scenario by Wittig and Zeig.

June 2001 International colloquium around the work of Monique Wittig at Columbia University in Paris. Standing-room crowd overflows Reid Hall as Wittig and Zeig talk about *The Girl*. Wittig reads excerpts from her work in progress, "Le chantier littéraire."

Dec 2002 Organizers Marie-Hélène Bourcier and Suzette Robichon publish the papers presented at the colloquium as *Parce que les lesbiennes ne sont pas des femmes* (Éditions Gaies et Lesbiennes).

January 3, 2003 Wittig dies from heart attack in Tucson, Arizona. Ashes placed in Père-Lachaise Cemetery, Paris. Memorials held in Paris, Toulouse, Tucson, Milan, New York, and Berlin, and obituaries published in *Le Monde, New York Times, LA Times, Humanité, Libération*, and *Le Devoir*, among others. Dozens of obituaries appear on the Internet, where Wittig is mentioned on more than 4,800 Internet sites.

PART 1

MONIQUE WITTIG'S MANIFESTO

Introduction to "For a Women's Liberation Movement"

Namascar Shaktini

Nous, les femmes (we, women) is the subject of Monique Wittig's feminist manifesto. She wrote this subject as she was in the midst of her most systematic literary experiment—the pronoun trilogy. This *nous* came out in print in May 1970, exactly two years after the revolutionary events of May 1968 in France and just a few months after the *elles* ("they," f.) appears with the publication of *Les guérillères* in 1969. But where the *elles*, like the *on* ("one," "you," "they," "people," "we," "I"; indeterminate subject pronoun) of *The Opoponax* before it, and the *j/e* (I, ł) of *The Lesbian Body* that was to be published three years later, are the subjects of present-tense narration, each existing only within a limited fictional universe, the *nous, les femmes* is the subject of real political action.

The manuscript of the manifesto, as we presented it to Jean-Edern Halier, the editor who was to publish it in the leftist monthly *Idiot International,* which is now defunct, had been entitled by Wittig: "Pour un mouvement de libération des femmes" (for a women's liberation movement). Her text was signed by four of us: Monique Wittig, Gille Wittig, Marcia Rothenberg, and me, Margaret Stephenson (Namascar Shaktini). The editor changed the title, which appeared in print as *Combat pour la liberation de la femme* (Combat for the Liberation of Woman), and he added his own subtitle: *Par-delà la libération-gadget, elles découvrent la lutte des classes* (Beyond Gadget Liberation, They Discover the Class Struggle).

But he left the text alone (although he forgot to put in three little notes). And we distributed the article at the first action of what was to be called in France the Mouvement de Libération des Femmes. In May 1970, eighteen of us, wearing tee shirts introducing into France the new women's symbol, organized this first French demonstration about women's oppression at the new leftist campus of the University at Vincennes.

At first, we were greeted by about two hundred males chanting *à poil à poil!* (strip, strip!). And we had great difficulty getting the crowd of young men to leave so we could meet with women students. The idea of women meeting without men present was new in France. Finally, after much loud discussion where we were often shouted down, a tall black activist stood up and said he supported our attempts to meet among ourselves, and when he walked out most of the other men followed. But a handful of white male leftists refused to leave, insisting on giving unsolicited advice about our liberation as we were trying to meet with the small number of women students attending. Christiane Rochefort and a few other demonstrators took notes, and the humorous account they wrote collectively of this first meeting was published in *Le Nouvel Observateur.* It featured a list of remarks by the males, followed by our retorts. I remember one. They said, "Nous voulons vous soutenir" (we want to support you). We said, "Nous en avons assez des souteneurs" (we're fed up with pimps), *souteneur* meaning both "supporter" and "pimp." At this first demonstration at Vincennes, the *nous* of Wittig's text became in reality a political subject. Monique Wittig and other activists were photographed at the May 1970 demonstration at Vincennes .

In France, where intellectuals knew Marxist theory and people were more politicized than in the United States, the "woman question" couldn't be dealt with as an ahistorical single issue. To introduce it into the movement of 1970, it had to be integrated by a historical, theoretical analysis that took as its point of departure Marxist assumptions. Wittig did this. She addressed political and economic history. She highlighted women whose revolutionary roles during the French Revolution and the Paris Commune had been ignored. She referred to the historical change in the mode of production in France. She addressed the struggle between the productive classes in relation to the owners of the means of production, addressing the ideology of the family in relation to capitalist ideology and basing her political argument on the feudal nature of the personal relation of a woman to her husband within the family.

Drawing on Fredrick Engels's *Origin of the Family,* Wittig challenged Karl Marx's claim in the *German Ideology* that the sexual division of labor in the family is "natural." She analyzed unpaid housework as servile labor, serflike labor, a vestige of serfdom persisting from feudal to modern capitalist times. "Man is the bourgeois, woman the proletarian," said Engels. Yes, said Wittig, there is an analogy, but only up to a point. Woman is not free like the proletarian to sell her labor on the market. She is tied like the serf. Where the serf was tied as laborer to the land, woman is tied as laborer to the house. If she tries to sell her labor on the market, she brings with her the prior obligation of housework and child-rearing. Employers know she must first provide this unpaid labor at home, so she has less value on the market than a male worker.

There is another difference. The proletarian's oppression is not tied to any one person, but the serf's obligation is to his lord personally. If the lord is killed in battle, his army of serfs, who owe him military service, can quit fighting. Similarly, the woman's obligation of service is to her husband personally. She has a relation of personal dependency to him. This relation, these obligations of service, define woman just as the serf's relation to his lord, his obligations of service, define him. Wittig's analysis shows that women (not a natural class) are a political class, like serfs. We will see this idea developed later in Wittig's theoretical essays.

Wittig's text engages with quotations and other texts, often opposing what "they say" with what "we say." Two sources that she integrates into the core of her analysis are Margaret Benson's work on the politics of housework and Bobby Seale's statement that the class struggle against racism and that against male chauvinism are closely tied. She echoes the black power movement in her conclusion: "All power to the people."

Blacks and women have been reduced, epistemologically speaking, to their differences from white males, whose point of view is at the center of the current symbolic order. The white male point of view has marked blacks in terms of color and has marked women in terms of sex. But the white male has reserved the categories "white" and "male" as unmarked. The white male point of view is, for the current symbolic order, universal. It goes without saying. Wittig focuses on that ideological assumption in this text, as she had in *Les guérillères:* "Like racism, sexism is so well implanted in ruling class ideology that only a radical seizing of power can destroy it—a political takeover to represent, in our turn, our interest as being the universal interest. That is necessary for the first phase, the end goal of all seizure of power by the people being an abolition of domination in general. Our interest is that of the people. We are the people."

Wittig mentioned to me more than once that she got her idea of appropriating the universal from Marx. Although the concept of markedness is indeed an aspect of grammar, as the Harvard linguistics department informed Emily Culpepper when she raised the issue of sexism in language, markedness carries inestimable political power. Which group will be unmarked and thus universal? Which group will be marked and thus specific? Wittig's strategy is that women and other minorities appropriate in our turn the universal.

White people are not by nature more universal than people of color. Men are not more universal by nature than women. We are all in specific groups, and appropriating the universal is a political takeover. But how can this silent takeover be made visible? Appropriating the universal point of view in order to make it visible is one of the central political objectives of Wittig's work, but it has not always been understood by the critics.

"For a Women's Liberation Movement" introduced ideas new to the social theory of France in 1970. Some Wittig had just introduced in 1969 in fictional form in *Les guérillères*. Others were seeds to be developed in subsequent theoretical essays that would be collected and published in English in 1992 and in French in 2001. For more than three decades the social theory of Monique Wittig developed in a consistent direction.

May 1970: Monique Wittig, far left, was an organizer of the first demonstration for women's liberation in France. The event was held at the University of Paris at Vincennes, where her manifesto, "For a Women's Liberation Movement," was distributed. (Anonymous movement photograph courtesy of the Estate of Monique Wittig)

August 26, 1970: Monique
Wittig, right, was an organizer
of the first publicized action
of the MLF at the Arc of
Triumph. Her banner, "Un
Homme sur Deux est une
Femme" (one man out of
two) targeted the
pseudogeneric "he." (Anonymous movement photograph
courtesy of the Archives Lesbiennes, Paris; photo restoration
by Jacquelene Ambrose)

The point, however, went over
the heads of the police who arrested us. The one who booked
me (right) looked at my pass-
port and said, in French, "You
American women think that
half the men in France are
effeminate." (*Lectures pour
Tous,* Nov. 1970, 34, courtesy
of the Bibliothèque Marguérite
Durand, Paris)

En 1970,
pour le législateur,
les employeurs
et même les compagnies
d'assurances, une
femme ne vaut pas un homme.
Pour obtenir l'égalité
les Françaises
seront-elles
obligées
de descendre
dans la rue?

Le 26 août 1970 quelques néo-fémi-
nistes françaises ont tenté de dé-
poser une gerbe sous l'Arc de
Triomphe en hommage ironique à
« la femme inconnue du soldat ».

JUST
POUR LES

Monique Wittig, Gille Wittig, Marcia Rothenberg, and Margaret Stephenson (Namascar Shaktini)

Translated by Namascar Shaktini

Serf: Under feudalism, person who did not have complete personal liberty. . . , was struck with various incapacities and subjected to certain obligations.

Servitude: State of total dependence of a person subject to another. ex: The servitude in which man holds woman.
  —Maurois, *Dictionnaire Robert*

The overthrow of mother right was the great historic defeat of the feminine sex; the social revolution it provoked, one of the most radical that History has known.
  —Engels, *Origin of the Family*

We, from time immemorial, live like a people colonized within the people, so well domesticated that we have forgotten that this situation of dependence doesn't go without saying. It's for man that we are nourished and raised, it's by man that we live; he can buy our body and when he is sated, he can get rid of it.

Farewell Pont-Neuf Samaritaine
Butte Saint-Roch Petits-Carreaux
Where we spent such good days.
We are going to the islands
Since we are no longer wanted in the cities.

It's the song that we, the girls of Paris, sang on the road to la Rochelle, when, shackled, we set out on the road to deportation. We were accused of prostitution by a hypocritical society that profited from our poverty. The children we have, we have for our masters. And if we ever have children on our own, they are the object of ostracism. "Bastard," child without a father, it's one of the worst insults in our society. Man can speak with impunity a master's language: "I take you, I possess you, you have given yourself to me." He can, as a master, mock us, treat us like objects, vilify us: "If you go to the women, don't forget the whip" (Nietzsche). He can, with the pretense of scientific thought, reduce us to our ovaries, as he reduces a black person to the color of their skin (Freud: "Anatomy is destiny"). Will he make rulings, decide, think for us long? No. "The dreams of Freud are the nightmares of women" (graffiti of an English activist). We're beginning to revolt and it's not in a dream.

"Slavery with a hoarse voice, doesn't speak loudly" (Shakespeare). False. Slaves today shout their shame and their humiliation. It's the moment in history when they have risen up, when their fists are raised, when they declare loudly indeed that they're ready to die rather than live in slavery. We women are truly the serfs of history. As far back as we go in the past, it is subjected, under guardianship, in dependence that we find ourselves. Women kneeling, chained to their carts in the nineteenth-century mines, under the guardianship of fathers and husbands. Until 1965 we needed the authorization of our husbands to work. These arrangements are so familiar they no longer shock us.

> The first class opposition that manifested itself in History coincides with the development of the antagonism between man and woman in conjugal marriage; and the first class oppression, with the oppression of the feminine sex by the masculine sex.
> —Engels

We are the class that has been oppressed for the longest time. As such, we want to begin the fight against the power that maintains this oppression. We, the oppressed sex, are the only humans to be just sex, *sex itself,* "the prey and the servant of the collective voluptuousness," says Marx. American women, who have begun their fight for liberation, call the segregation in which we are held "sexism." Like racism, sexism is so well implanted in ruling class ideology that only a radical seizing of power can destroy it—a political takeover to represent, in our turn, our interest as being the universal interest. That is necessary for the first phase, the end goal of all seizure of power by the people being an abolition of domination in general. Our interest is that of the people. We are the people.

Ruling-class ideology that perpetuates sexism and draws multiple and sundry benefits from it is, at this moment of History, that of the capitalist class and its accomplices: all males who consciously or unconsciously, with more or less violence according their interests, use the situation of class in which the capitalist society placed them in relation to us. The Americans in struggle call this supremacy, this class attitude that characterizes the male, "male chauvinism." Male chauvinism holds sway everywhere. In the factories, the workers, those that the system oppresses as much as us, our true allies, have let themselves be corrupted by the ruling class. Very often they treat us as it does, like sex objects. Yes, in the factories, as if Proudhon's slogan "housewife or courtesan" had profoundly marked the collective unconscious of the working class itself, we are prostitutes. Either we are, for the supervisors and the bosses, the whores of the workers, or else we are, for the workers, the whores of the supervisors and bosses. We are told when we enter the factory, "watch out which side you go to" but it's always as a virtual prostitute.

A long time ago, working women, ardent feminists, wrote in the first political journal for women: "The moment is near when woman and the people, shaking hands, cross together the barrier of inequality."

At the national meeting of women at Oxford, which gave its impetus to the women's liberation movement in England, an activist said: "My husband oppresses me when he gets home because he has been oppressed all day by his boss."

That's how the masters have always found weapons against us, even among the poorest of the poor; they have made the worker think he wasn't the lowest of men because there was someone *beneath* him, someone to oppress—his wife. That's how the ruling class corrupts our relations with the rest of the people, that's how it divides the people.

Sexual Exploitation

Male chauvinism rages everywhere. When we walk on the street we are whistled at, yelled at, touched, we are judged appreciatively or critically by looks. We are always forced into abject complicity with those who have made simple sex objects out of us. If we resist we are prudes, bitches, shrews, or hysterical feminists. We don't walk on the street like individuals free to meet the looks. We are objects in or out of service. When our eyes, in all innocence, rest on billboards, we see images that humiliate us and constantly remind us that we are objects of sexual exploitation. We see clearly how the capitalist system uses our bodies as publicity for all the products it distributes to its markets. We are always consumable. A brand of beer promotes a new product: "Drink a big blond" and at the same time as its product, the image offers a tall young blond woman. To attract attention to the quality of its tobacco, a brand of cigarettes offers this invitation: "Taste a redhead for a change." The brands of lingerie, bras, and corsets pin us up on the walls of our cities, in the newspapers, naked, half-naked, or encorseted, trying to seduce us by representing us as objects; they repeat that we are made to be naked, half-naked in a bed, in the street where all the looks undress us as perpetual sex objects.

And that is quite natural, "housewife or courtesan." The only second function that is conceded to us in the society in which we live, that of housewife, is also recalled with machiavelic cruelty. "Three generations of women use the iron to iron such-and-such." Paic gets you out of *your* kitchen faster." "Moulinex liberates woman," "Hoover looking for women who are exacting customers." We are always reminded that we are sex objects or else that we are, by our "nature," housewives, sacrosanct function. In the most advanced capitalist societies, where the standard of living is high enough to permit it, we have the right to combine both functions. That's what the system calls "liberation" of women. And then we see on the billboards perfect sex objects who press the button of a washing machine with a gloved finger.

> The modern conjugal family is founded on the overt or covert domestic slavery of woman and modern society is a mass exclusively composed of conjugal units.
> —Engels

In reality, what we are condemned to by capitalist society is solitude. Each one of us in the family unit or in the "couple" lives in solitude, in isolation, unique in the history of humanity. Unlike Blacks, we don't have ghettos where we are together and assembled. If we work only at home, we must wait for the return of our husbands to have human contact. Fed up with ourselves, cut off from the world, we destroy ourselves. We have no relation with the world in which men live. We have no hold on it; by our activity, we do not transform it. For us society is the family. We wear ourselves out on servile tasks with no benefit, without the support of any sort of comradeship or friendship that would be a weapon against the solitude that our dependence within the couple imposes on us. Having children—that ought to be for us a socially important production. In the context where this production is inscribed, we cannot perceive it that way. Pregnant, we are discredited, "knocked up," we don't "produce" a child, it grows in our stomach as if we were still for males the eternal vases spoken of in the Bible.

Menial Work, Woman's Work

When we work outside the home, our solitude is barely lessened. We can't easily speak of activity that transforms the world since we are given the most menial tasks, those that men do not want. There are only a few work hands, but thousands of maids (for a man, this sort of work is menial, for a woman, housework). In the factories we are on the same level as immigrant laborers, unskilled workers. In the offices, typists, secretaries, we are the domestics of the executives. In the hospitals, nurses, we are the servants of the doctors. The list is open. We are not, as workers, liberated of our—oh so natural!—menial tasks. That's even what condemns us to the worst of solitudes. We don't have the time to make ties of comradeship between workers. We have to hurry; we run as we leave the factory, the office; there are errands to run, children to pick up at school, meals, laundry, dishes to do, etc. We have the total responsibility of caring for children. If they are sick, we stop working (our bosses know this well and that permits them to maintain us in subservient positions). Educating them is completely our responsibility. When we have children, it is far from being a socially necessary production, it's a handicap; we can never advance in our job, put in the wrong as we are by this biological function. And in spite of this combination of particularly unfavorable conditions for us, we represent 34 percent of French workers, 36 percent counting moonlighting. If we are lucky enough to be married to nonchauvinists, we have better relations with our husbands than those among us called "housewives." But very often our husbands—mindless chauvinists—on the pretext that we are more exploited than they, that we do double work and we earn less money than they because of the discrimination of which we are the object, scorn us more or less openly.

> Half of humankind is mentally deficient—women.
> —Nietzsche

No doubt, it is indecent to speak of these things, we might chase off the men (following the advice of the inestimable magazine, *ELLE*). The law that we must obey: "Be beautiful and be quiet." Have we ever had the right of free speech? How long have we been quiet?

Yet we were the ones, the women of Paris, the women of les Halles, who shouted the loudest at the beginning of the French Revolution. We were the ones that the bourgeois historians designate by the name populace. We were the ones who, with cries of "we want bread, the baker, the baker's wife, and the baker's son," began the first revolution of this country. We were at the Bastille on July 14, 1789. We were the people. Among the people we fought to overthrow royalty. We, the people, have been had!

Yet we said proudly through the voice of Olympe de Gouges in 1791: "We have the right to mount the rostrum since we have the right to mount the scaffold." We constituted, with Pauline Léon, legions of female citizens, with Claire-Rose Lacombe, unions of republican revolutionaries. We demanded "education and work *to be able to live.*" We believed firmly that the revolution was going to liberate us "like the slaves and the Blacks." The chauvinist Robespierre indeed put an end to our illusions. He dissolved our societies, prohibited us from speaking in public, had Rose-Claire Lacombe imprisoned, and promulgated a law on the "natural organization" which specifically applied to us and which made us "inapt" for public functions. In 1848, it was the same story. The minority in power—chauvinist—systematically repressed feminist activists and imprisoned them; it forbade us access to political organizations, dissolved feminine clubs, and prohibited us from appearing and speaking in public. We were indeed absent when, in the discussion of our right to vote, the issue was knowing with whom we should be assimilated: with the insane, with convicts, with the bankrupted, or with minors. In the Commune, however, we rose up again, on the barricades, and we were the ones that a bourgeois writer calumnied thus: "Females who are only women when they are dead" (Alexandre Dumas). We, the shopkeepers, artisans, petites bourgeoises of Paris, moved by a great surge of solidarity for the Communards that were butchered under our eyes in the streets of our city, came out of our houses to die at their side. In 1914 we discovered brusquely, in the throes of this inter-imperialist war, the political power that maternity conferred on us. Grouped in union as women, we went on strike against the production of children.

> Woman and worker have this in common: they are oppressed.
> —Bebel

Unite. Assemble. Unite. From the beginning, the first of us insisted on this necessity. Flora Tristan, who went from one factory to another to persuade workers to form unions, asked the workers to make ties with women. Jeanne Deroin, a few years later, did the same political work uniting men and women workers, which was difficult at this time when men reproached women for *stealing* their work. But very soon she had to deal with male chauvinism. Her political program for the union of workers' associations, which prefigured the great federations of labor (she succeeded in making a federation of 104 associations of men and women workers), succeeded so well that she became rivals with males. In prison where she is incarcerated with some male comrades they asked her, "in the name of the masculine associations," not to acknowledge before the tribunal that she was the *author* of the project and of the act of Union. Jeanne Deroin, who certainly didn't want to reinforce male chauvinism, was, however, obliged to comply, for what she wanted even less was to "provoke a confrontation between socialists in the presence of our enemies." Exemplary but unilateral.

> Man is the bourgeois, woman, the proletarian.
> —Engels

To all the bourgeois, all the reactionaries who say to us, But what are you talking about, all that is past, now women are "emancipated"? we reply: no. To all the bourgeois, to all the reactionaries who ask us, What do you want? We reply: we want our liberation, we are ready to fight for it. We reply by this long quote from Engels: "In the family, man is the bourgeois, woman plays the role of the proletariat. But in the industrial world, the specific character of economic oppression that weighs on the proletariat only manifests itself in all its rigor after all the legal privileges of the capitalist class have been abolished and the complete legal equality of the two classes has been established. The democratic republic does not abolish the antagonism between the two classes; on the contrary, it is democracy that first furnishes the terrain on which the outcome of their combat will be decided. And in the same way the particular character of the predominance of man over woman in the modern family, as well as the necessity and manner of establishing a true social equality between the two sexes, will only show themselves in full daylight once man and woman will have absolutely equal legal rights."

The historic moment has indeed come for us to begin the struggle against male chauvinism. We know well that in 1789, when the bourgeois class seized power and liberated the serfs from serfdom, it was to be able to exploit them freely. Juridically, on paper, serfs had become free to sign contracts with the ruling class. But what is the freedom of free men when they are obliged for survival to exchange their labor power for a salary with a class that possesses all the means of production? They are free, in effect, to become "wage slaves," as Lenin said. Free to sign contracts, they were free for exploitation by the bourgeois class that needed workers for its expanding industry. It's then and only then, when two kinds of free classes are face-to-face, that the antagonism appears, that it becomes evident that freedom for some doesn't at all resemble freedom for the others, some are free to make a profit from those who are free to be exploited by them. Then and only then begins the class struggle between them.

> I was taken by the great words: emancipation of the people, emancipation of women. . . . My emancipation consists in serving him after I get home from work while he reads or while he "thinks." While I skin the vegetables, he skims *Le Monde* and reads works about Marxist economy. Liberty exists only for the well-off and in the present society, the well-off are men.
> —Letter of a woman, published by *France Soir*

The struggle is beginning for us. Juridically, we have the same rights as men. (Capitalism reserves a last bastion: it prevents us from disposing freely, on the same basis as man, of property at the level of the family. But we don't want to fight for property rights because we want to destroy private property.) As for the rest of our rights within the family, through parental law, we have just legally conquered an autonomy we were far from having. Marriage becomes an association more than a seizure of power by one individual of another. What does that mean in reality? It means that, finally, "the particular character of the predominance of man over woman appears in plain daylight." Indeed, the liberty of the one, as for the proletarian and the bourgeois, has nothing to do with the liberty of the other. What appears clearly is that from this first class antagonism, based on the first division of labor, we have never escaped. This antagonism, this division of labor, is built on sexual difference. All the ruling classes that History has known have always perpetuated it in terms of their ideology and their culture. Whatever the development of the productive force in the society in general, this division of labor, that engendered servile labor at the level of the family, has always persisted. Through *serfdom,* through *capitalism,* in the city, in the country, in all classes of society, the family reproduces this model. Now that we have theoretically the same rights as men, what appears to us clearly now is this monstrosity: In modern societies there is a kind of work that has no exchange value, it's the work that we do at home. It represents an enormous mass of socially necessary production. "Each time a soup is made, a button sewed on clothes, that represents a production, but it's not a production for the market" (Mandel). What we call this work is servile labor.

A Division of Labor Never Put into Question

It seems to us totally, absolutely unjust that, side-by-side with clauses and contracts that regularize work between exploiters and exploited, a vestige of implicit feudal right survives requiring that a whole category of individuals must, by virtue of their sex, work without being paid: us. (At the women's days organized by the French Communist Party, the issue of providing child-care centers is raised, to lighten women's work. But the division of labor between men and women is never questioned.) "Classes," Lenin said, "are groups of men in which one can appropriate the work of the other as a result of the difference of place they hold in a given system of social economy." In the family, man is the bourgeois, woman the proletarian; man appropriates our work (in return, he provides protection and nourishment as feudal lords did previously for serfs). There is truly an antagonism between him and us. And if, as Marx says, the proletarian is the one who is free to exchange his labor power on the market, we cannot be, like men, proletarians. Born into the category of women, our principal responsibility is domestic work and child-rearing. That's why they marry us. And if we work outside the home, it's not that we are "free to exchange our labor power on the market," it's shackled to this domestic labor that we participate in production and uniquely on this condition: free to be responsible for double work. "If woman fulfills her *duties* in the private service of the family, she is excluded from social production and cannot earn anything. Besides, if she wants to participate in public industry and earn for herself, it is impossible for her to accomplish her family *duties*. It's the same for woman in every branch of social activity, in medicine and law, in the factory. The modern conjugal family is founded on the domestic slavery, acknowledged or veiled, of woman, and modern society is a mass exclusively composed of conjugal units" (Engels, *Origin of the Family,* our emphasis).

As a result, we, who work for nothing, are worth less than men when we participate in social production. Yet there is a law that decrees "equal pay for equal work." And in reality, this is the amount of difference in salaries for men and women: for the population as a whole, 36 percent; for upper management, 38 percent; for middle management, 31 percent; for employees, 24 percent; for workers, 36 percent. And since the Grenelle Accords this difference tends to grow. The definition of a serf in the dictionary is: "person who does not have complete personal liberty . . . under feudalism." If we think that until July 13, 1965, women in France could not work outside the home without the husband's permission, it's that the law itself attributed to us the status of serf, of a person without complete personal liberty. In the same way, the law that prevented us from choosing our domicile, reserving this right for husbands, was in complete contradiction with the Declaration of the Rights of Man, which reserved for the citizen complete freedom of movement and domicile. (In principle, parental law finally grants us freedom of movement.)

Let the antagonism appear in the light of day: we say, after eight hours of work in the factory, our workday begins at five. We say that, we, women workers, are particularly the objects of discrimination. We don't have professional training. In general, les Certificats d'Aptitude Professionelle are reserved for men; this fact emphasizes the transitory aspect of our nondomestic work. We are always at the bottom of the ladder, and at the first crisis, at the first reduction of personnel, we are affected more than men. If our work doesn't have the character of necessity it has for man, it's by virtue of the fact that we are an underdeveloped sex, good to work for nothing, to do the work that indeed was formerly done by slaves (they shared it, by the way, with "free" women).

> The struggle against male chauvinism is a class struggle. . . . It is closely tied
> to racism . . . and perpetuated in the United States by the ruling classes. The
> white man has taken a dame, he has stuck her up on a pedestal and given her
> a torch to hold. I say give her a machine gun in the other hand.
>   —Bobby Seale

We well understand that sexual difference alone— like racial difference—is not sufficient to create class antagonism. We know now that there were and are societies where men and women do not have antagonistic relations. But we see clearly that all despotic, autocratic governments, all totalitarian regimes (Incan Empire, Mayan Empire, Confucian China, Nazi regime) used the difference between the sexes—among other elements of division—to create an antagonism between man and woman at the level of the family. The schema is the following: The State is like a big family where the head governs the woman and children. In this way the reality of the class struggle and levels at which it is situated are obfuscated. The fact of absolute domination is presented like a phenomenon just as natural as the absolute domination of woman by man.

It's Not in the Interest of the Capitalist Bourgeoisie to Free Us

We know the role played in our enslavement at the level of the family as economic unit by private property and the appropriation of the means of private production by man. We see clearly that when the capitalist bourgeoisie appeared it did not have an interest in freeing us from the serfdom imposed by our familial function—as it did in freeing the other serfs. In fact ours is the only form of serfdom that continues in modern industrial society. The family is the frame in which we furnish children to the bourgeois State. It's also the frame in which we work as unpaid domestic employees. It's the frame in which labor power renews itself at no cost for the benefit of the bourgeois State since it's in their families that proletarians eat, rest, and renew their labor power without costing their employers anything; for it's the workers who pay to maintain this unit. We understand clearly that to survive, capitalist society needs an enormous quantity of work to be done for nothing. The work we do for nothing at home increases the profit of the employers. No man would be able to work for a low salary if we, at home, didn't do a lot of work for nothing. But it is "natural" that we do this sort of work, just as it's "natural" that the employers don't have to raise the salary of "heads of family" for them to be able to pay us, the servants of their houses. (In this situation, we represent a reserve labor force for social production, we are ready to accept the lowest salaries when there is an increase in production.)

We understand how male chauvinism turns against men themselves. They are much more exploited than they realize. Indeed, they are paid for two, them and us, which considerably reduces the value of their labor power, or rather their exchange value. It's against their interest that men practice male chauvinism in the proletarian classes where exploitation is the greatest.

Transform a Relation of Weakness into a Relation of Strength

We know that in the present state of things, if the bourgeois State had to pay for the work we do for nothing, it couldn't deal with the redistribution of wealth that this would imply, as Margaret Benson has said. For us, this means that even when we don't participate directly in production we represent a political force dangerous for the capitalist system. When we complain that we are discriminated against at the level of salaries, one can always say, "It's not your true work, your true work is at home." Therefore we must struggle at the very level of our oppression, in the family. Following the law of contraries, what makes our weakness also makes our strength: We can turn the weapons used to keep us in slavery against the enemy. We say that it's in the family of which we are the pillars that our political strength is great. Without us, there is no family. If we refuse to assure through our servile labor the survival of the family, or if we refuse under the present conditions to produce children for the bourgeois State—there is no more family. Deprived of its economic base, the multiple family units that serve its domination, the bourgeois State falls. We know well which side the virtuous censors are on—those who defend the family, women and children, who rise up against contraception. They are indeed aware what arms contraception has given us women for the first time in history to use against them. That we have an economic function, that our servitude in the family has an economic function, and that this economic function constitutes our strength has always been hidden from us since we could threaten the established order.

Oppressed ideologically, economically, and politically, we know that we have the means to struggle against this triple oppression. We say, like the first feminists, we must first unite. Sexism has poisoned society as a whole, giving advantages only to the class in power. It sells our body and reduces us to the condition of merchandise, it puts us below the working class in order to divide the people. It persuades some of the people that they have the right to oppress us, the people; that they have the right to have a political role that we do not have; that they have the right to have higher salaries (a working man said one day, "And *that,* is it a man's pay?"); that they have the right to constantly devalorize us, to call us bitches if we aren't in the mood to be their sex objects; that they have the right to appropriate our work power in the bosom of the family.

To all the reactionaries who say and who write that there will not be a revolt of women in France, as in the USA and in Holland, we say that as long as there is in this country an oppressed woman, serf in her family, victim of discrimination in her public job, we women will not be liberated, and it's for all women that we want freedom.

> The struggle of American women is more and more integrated with that of workers and African-Americans; it strikes increasingly heavy blows against the domination of the bourgeoisie in the cities.
> —*China News Agency,* March 8, 1970

To the revolutionaries who claim we're putting the cart before the horse, that it's only *after* the overthrow by the proletariat that the "problems" (so small in truth) of women will be resolved, we reply: All power to the people. We are the people, and we want to participate in the overthrow in order to represent our own interests. We say that it is a male chauvinist point of view to want to prevent us from participating in the overthrow except as the aides and auxiliaries we have always been.

To those that tell us to begin our struggle within already existing revolutionary organizations, we reply by several points:

Our principal front is the struggle against the system that perpetuates male chauvinism. We must therefore encounter bourgeois ideology directly, without intermediary, in a movement of women. Why? Revolutionary organizations that already exist are directed by men. Male chauvinism holds sway there as everywhere. We always hear there that our struggle is a "secondary problem." Rare are those that attribute to it as much importance as the struggle of Blacks in the US or immigrant laborers here. When we are the issue in question, the concepts that account for people's oppression lose all their meaning, as if by enchantment. Mentioning our oppression always provokes embarrassment and malaise, even very often among some of us. Our oppression is such an intimate and continuous part of our lives (contrary to that of workers who find respite when they leave the factory) that, if it becomes visible, continuing our lives as in the past becomes impossible. Our total existence is put into question. Men—revolutionary activists, for example—have all participated in our oppression at one time or another, they have all been accomplices with male chauvinism at one time or another, they are all suspect. Besides, what does our struggle seem like to them? Domestic struggle, prosaic struggle, struggle of serfs, it doesn't have the appeal of that of the Palestinians or the Afro-Americans.

But we are tired of fighting against our revolutionary comrades to put forward our oppression. We don't want to waste our energy and strength struggling against male chauvinism inside the already existing organizations. The time is past when we asked men—even if they are revolutionary activists—for permission to revolt. No one can liberate another, one must liberate oneself. We know that we are part of the vast revolutionary movement that since May 1968 has changed the aspect of struggles in France, of which the goal is the overthrow of capitalism and the takeover of power by the people. We are the people.

> It will be the great merit of French women in this second half of the twenti-eth century to denounce the paternalism of the parties toward them and to stop mystifying themselves and their companions into thinking that salvation is obtained thanks to parties instead of taking one's own destiny in one's own hands.
> —Geneviève Texier and Andrée Michel

To those who accuse us of provoking division among the workers, we reply that not we but the bourgeoisie in power perpetuates this division. At the beginning of the worker's movement, the bourgeoisie divided men and women by making their interests contradictory. The bourgeoisie developed male chauvinism to the extreme, benefiting from the poverty in which we found ourselves. At the threshold of industrialization men were the first to enter industry, taking all the work, because it was harder for us women, artisans and peasants, than for them to leave the family to go to the cities and look for work in the factories. The capitalist class paid us ridiculously low salaries then. Thus, the bourgeoisie systematically maintained division within the people: men called us "scabs," accusing us of stealing *their* work, of cheapening *their* work. We say that in fighting against male chauvinism we fight against the class interests of the bourgeoisie.

To those who say to us that we cannot constitute the major front because of our relation to production, we ask if they have ever taken the trouble to analyze our relations with the means of production and the system that controls them. We ask: major front in relation to what? As oppressed people, we are our own major front, it's on the major front of our oppression—the family—that we want to fight. We want to fight for our interests like the rest of the people.

To those who tell us there are presently two types of contradiction in so-ciety: the principal contradiction between workers and the capitalist class and secondary contradictions, those between men and women being a secondary contradiction, we say that there is one principle contradiction between the class that oppresses and the ensemble of oppressed people, among whom there are also contradictions. When we are considered a secondary contra-diction we are not understood. We are suspected of having in mind a war of the sexes. We indeed want to fight against male chauvinism within the people (secondary contradiction), but we want above all to fight against the ideology that produces male chauvinism and the system that benefits from it (principal contradiction). For we know our true enemy: the system that makes men its accomplices to oppress the people. All men, when they are chauvinists, we call puppets.

To those who tell us at this time the weakest link to push on is that of immigrant laborers and not us, women, we say yes, it's true that immigrant laborers are a weak link, very weak, on which it is necessary to push. But we ask in what way that excludes women from also being a weak link of the system. We say to them that in raising immigrant laborers' consciousness of their class interests they are not afraid of creating a division among workers, although manifestly their class interests can enter momentarily in contradiction with those of French workers. We say that one cannot send us back to our country, we can take big risks in the struggle. Besides, we have many interests in common with immigrant laborers. In the factories we are discriminated against on the level of salaries and that of our persons. Like them we know sexual misery and exploitation.

To the women who say: I am carrying on the fight as a revolutionary activist and not as a woman, we reply that they are putting themselves above classes and practicing Christian, petit-bourgeois altruism. No woman is above women. We are all involved.

To the men who say your fight is just, we support it, we ask them to educate and persuade the chauvinists. We say to them, and to everybody: All power to the people!

PART 2

ESSAYS BY MONIQUE WITTIG

Monique Wittig, Paris, 1985. (Copyright © 1985 Colette Geoffrey, all rights of reproduction reserved)

3   *Some Remarks on* Les guérillères

Monique Wittig

Translated by Namascar Shaktini

A book should be able to do without any commentary on the part of the one who wrote it since the elements for reading it are incorporated in the text. However I would like to give some precisions on *Les guérillères* in the margin of the interpretations that have already been made.

In the movement of revisiting a text on which I will not work any more I situate myself in what I call the critic's point of view, the point of view of afterwards. But this critical point of view is not completely the same as that of the critic who hasn't written the book. For it shares after the fact the point of view of before, when there was only the blank page. And therefore the writer's is a double critical movement: when s/he writes s/he is in the before working the material, sometimes cut off apparently from everything, facing the unknown, but from time to time in the course of the work emerging to bring a critical look at what s/he is in the process of doing, a look of afterwards. It's a sort of back and forth that is difficult to keep track of except for those who keep working notebooks. Then after the book has reached a limit of work, when it is published, when it is discussed, in short the writer no longer completely disposes of the text, but can look at it with this double critical movement, this time backwards.

If I were asked how to describe *Les guérillères,* I would say it's an epic poem, it's a collage, that you can't assign a genre to it outside of the epic movement given by the rhythm, the action, and the characters. And in this regard I would like to recall that Brecht, at war against classical dramaturgy, "Aristotelian" as he called it, introduced to the theater an epic "revolutionary" dimension that the theater had never had and that seems contrary to all dramatic art but that has the advantage of presenting to the spectator an open, incomplete form on which s/he can immediately exercise her/his critique, and act. I would also like to recall the reflection of the filmmaker Jean-Marie Straub on what he describes as "lacunary" art with a homology drawn from *Littré,* a term from mineralogy: "Lacunary body, body composed of agglomerated crystals that leave intervals among themselves." He uses this term à propos of cinematographic writing. Applied to literary writing this designation indicates for me the fact of creating intervals, putting holes in the sentence at the grammatical level, of destabilizing the conventional order of discourse.

In terms of literature, intertextuality, as we currently say today, following Kristeva, is for my work the intertext created by the writers of the New Novel. Naming them together, one mustn't forget that their processes are very different and that there are as many poetic arts as writers. What's important is that each one of them tried to create new forms of the novel at a time when, in France, the novel seemed destined to die. So much so that when Sartre wrote a preface for *Portrait of an Unknown Man* he called this novel an anti-novel, while Sarraute worked at renewing the forms of the novel. Sarraute, Beckett, Butor, Pinget, Ollier, Robbe-Grillet, Simon have changed the form of the French novel. It's a matter of the chronology of the novels, characters, plot, subject, descriptions, and narrative forms. And these are the writers who taught me my craft.

An epic movement and dynamic, a lacunary writing, inscribed in their historic context, are what first appear in *Les guérillères.* The book is composed of fragments distributed in three parts; each part is preceded by a thick circle in the center of a white page. There is also a list of first names, written in capital letters, which appear every five pages, always on the righthand page and situated like the circles in the middle of a white page. This list is opened and closed by a poem written in the same letters. Finally, the title of the book is a neologism.

After this general description, a little dry, I must transport myself to a space where the book doesn't yet exist. It's a matter of the blank page, a space that I call the literary workshop by homology with what one calls the workshop of the painter. That's where the point of view of before confronts the point of view of afterward. On one hand it's the strangeness produced by the prolonged sojourn in the literary workshop, an experience shared by all writers. On the other the library, that is, the company of books that one likes. There are also those that one doesn't. Like all my books but more perhaps than any other, *Les guérillères* is completely composed of heterogeneous elements, fragments of all sorts, taken from everywhere, that had to be held together to form a book.

The constitutive element is the pronoun, the plural personal pronoun of the third person, **elles.** It is utilized like a character. Ordinarily, a character of a novel represents a singular entity. But here from the start a collective entity developed in the literary workshop and took over all the space of the narrative.

The form that this **elles** imposed was for a longtime linear in my work although it was composed of fragments. And this first series of fragments fell out at the time of the last montage of *Les guérillères.* It's what I call a parasite text.

I needed a new start. What was left in the workshop was just the collective entity **elles** and a momentum comparable to the "si parfaite fureur," the red band announced on the book of Francis Ponge, *Pour un malherbe.* This fury, this movement, was the motor of the still-inexistent book, and at each stage of the work I tried to maintain it, for example in the rhythm of the book. In this emptiness of the workshop the material form of the object helped me. A book is made of two sides, the page on the right and the page on the left that can be in a dialectical relation. In this case the fold of the book, to the extent that it unites them, serves as dialectical copula. The page on the left became for me the page where my own text could develop, and the page on the right became the page of history. Thus, each page had to be written in parallel but at the same time, each in conflict with the other on either side of the fold.

A chaotic period of writing followed where the righthand page devoted to history was submerged by all sorts of texts (of Lacan, Freud, Lévi-Strauss, and a lot of others that I've forgotten). The tension between the righthand page and the lefthand page where the text per se was supposed to develop was so strong that I had to quit the whole enterprise. I therefore tried to maintain otherwise the momentum that was necessary for me. I wrote the sentence "this order must be broken" to make a running title at the top of the pages on the left and the right. It would have had the function of producing each fragment of text. Again a fruitless effort.

Once again the emptiness of the workshop. Only my angry **elles** remains and the memory of an epic song that I cited at length in *The Opoponax:* "In the great palace with the paved hall, Lady Guibourc had donned her shirt of mail, laced on a helmet and girded a sword; there was no woman who was not armed that day." It's the "Song of William of Orange." There are also labyrinths in circular form that I design as new consitutive elements. I imagine **elles** lost in these concentric labyrinths (it's this uncertainty of their moves that is going to correspond to the first part of *Les guérillères*). And little by little the circle empties itself of its labyrinth to become a simple circular line. This experimentation with a collective heroic character, the "Song of William of Orange" and the circular geometrical form led me toward the epic genre, that is to say toward the cycle of *Les guérillères:* "CYCLE: Lat. *cyclus,* fr. Gr. *kuklos* . . . (1839). Lit. Series of epic or fabulous poems taking place around a single subject and where one finds more or less the same characters" (*Petit Robert*). "*Oeuvres* . . . grouped around a single action, a unique hero" (*Petit Larousse*). The epic form that now imposes itself on me suddenly gives a shape to my project but also a force. I have the hero, **elles;** I also have the action that I will speak of later. **Elles** has taken on a new dimension, **elles** is put in motion, **elles** is activated by this form.

From that moment, I write very fast what I already know to be the last part of the text. It's the last part because an element until then absent intervenes, a pronoun as collective entity, a pronoun that cannot be present at the beginning of the book, since indeed I play on its absence to give to **elles** its heroic dimension and as such its universal dimension. This last part concerns the war, or rather the guerrilla warfare between **elles** and **ils.** And I must write it first because it's the most violent part of the text. It permits me to take the measure of the pronoun **elles** as a collective character. I try to give it a textual force so it can topple over the pronoun **ils** as general, with masculine connotation, and steal its universality, at least in the space of this text.

There is one textual reason for writing the war part first, and that is also a question of measure. That has to do with the already mentioned fact proper to the epic, that is to say *la geste*. Here it's the overthrow as it is said in the last poem: "WHICH IS TO WRITE VIOLENCE . . . ACTION OVERTHROW." For this *geste*, for this deed, a rhythm must be found, a vocabulary and even a certain kind of rhetorical figure that will motivate the course of the whole book. (A work in reverse.) The rhythm contributes above all to the way in which the text is fragmented. Here there is no fluidity, no link between the sequences. The desired effect is short-winded rapidity, as in a battle, as when numerous feet strike the ground. The vocabulary must be concrete, precise. The emphasis is on technical terms as needed. For example, anatomical terms that describe the sexual organs taken from medical textbooks. The words are equally chosen for their aspect, for their sound. For me they must be heavy, rude. And another factor comes into play, it's the way they behave once they are associated. Indeed, this arrangement can be at the origin of the effect of shock, of surprise that the reader has a right to expect from every new book.

As for the rhetorical figures, I indicate in passing their poetic/political importance. In the before on the blank page they are chosen blindly and recognized as such in the after, that is to say this critical point of view of the writer, already detached from her/his work, that I mentioned above. For example, while writing *The Opoponax,* I tried to put holes in the sentence, to obtain this effect described by Jean-Marie Straub. Litotes in all their possible forms give form to this book, including the choice of foreign texts that are incorporated in it. There are no litotes in *Les guérillères.* On the other hand there are very numerous paraleipses, especially in the second part, such as: "They do not say that the vulvas are like black suns in the shining night" (58).

Or, they do not say that vulvas with their elliptical shape are to be compared to suns, planets, innumerable galaxies (61). It's an ironic way to undo the feminaries of the first part. These ambiguous feminaries where all the terms describing vulvas are listed no longer serve now, in this second part, except to inform and amuse the little girls. Nevertheless the text tries to retain some poetic luster from its own negations, gleanings suitable for endowing the hero **elles,** like on another level the play on the goddesses. The paraleipses also function to put the reader on guard against a linear reading of the text. The circle also has this function. As well as certain fragments of text: "They say that even without the feminaries they can recall the time when . . . they made war" (53). The war is already made in this second part. However it has yet to come in the text. For in a text of fiction one can be, as here, at once in the present, the future, and the past.

To come back to the generative text, this section of *Les guérillères* written first—it becomes the last part of the text, the textual end of the book. But chronologically it constitutes the start of the action and the beginning of the narrative because the book is written back to front. It must therefore be read back to front, hence the importance of the circle as a modus operandi (it turns on itself to rejoin the beginning of the text). The sentence of Pascal and of Marie de Gournay situated in the second part of the book gives a general description of its aspect: "It's virtually that infinite sphere whose center is everywhere, circumference nowhere" (69). (The circle appears three times in *Les guérillères* and indicates how the book develops chronologically and formally. It also serves to divide the book in three parts. And its meaning changes each time. The first circle corresponds to the emergence out of the labyrinth, out of the old culture; the second gives the manner of functioning of the text; the third is that of the action, of overthrow, of the epic poem.)

Why such a composition where the end of the text is the beginning of the action? Is it just a device to disconcert the reader? No, it's a matter of necessity, of textual strategy. My goal was to make **elles** come as a shock for the reader, as a surprise; since **elles** holds the whole story, a sort of disorientation should follow from it. The reader enters the book and finds her/himself confronted with an **elles** that is not familiar, not ordinary and that is new and heroic. In any case it's what guided me along with the hope that this **elles** could situate the reader in a space beyond the categories of sex for the duration of the book. (This is perhaps the utopia.)

In the first part **elles** has already turned the world upside down. The war belongs to the past. **Elles** tries to make its way across the labyrinth of a dead culture of ancient signs, of representations—across stories, facts, history, ancient symbols. **Elles** exalts itself in some of the "feminaries"; **elles** is caught in the trap of narcissism or self-admiration. But **elles** continues and transcends itself. In the second part **elles** destroys the feminaries and replaces them with the "great register," always open and in which **elles** can at any moment write facts, names, dates, stories. It's the book-within-the-book, which puts *Les guérillères en abyme*. This second part is an intermediate part not just through its situation but through its function: it goes back and forth from the future to the past while maintaining its own story. At the same time it prepares the reader for the war that has already taken place chronologically but not textually and it describes the modification of the naïve conceptions of the guérillères such as they were just after the war, that is to say in the first part. One can say that there is the story from back to front as I indicated and through the intermediary of this part an underlying story that indicates a counter-chronology, that is to say here the projection of a linear development, that of the text. And in this part there are unstable, free, floating sequences that could indeed also situate themselves in the first part or in the last part. This intermediate part is not the center of the book since "it is everywhere."

In the ancient epic songs there was always a surreal, supernatural dimension with appearances of legendary characters. This device is called the Christian fantastic. It has a poetic function that is to aggrandize the heros of the fable. *Les guérillères* would not have been an epic without its own element of the fantastic. But here it's a pagan fantastic, with the apparition of goddesses who have therefore a decorative function. They also have, as in the Christian fantastic, the poetic function of adding a dimension to the heroines of the fable who glean some glory not from the possibility of goddesses but from their description; for as in painting it adds another layer to the story. However the denigrating, ironic sequences, that make you want to laugh, are humorous enough to warn the reader that s/he has paper goddesses to deal with.

Before the book took on the aspect it now has, I literally had to spread out all the cut-up fragments of the text on the floor and give myself up to a pitiless montage during which I almost, once again, lost it. That's when the above-mentioned parasite text fell out (it was published later under the title "Une partie de campagne" in the journal *Commerce*). Everything fell into place after this surgical operation. The page on the right, the page of history that had had many reincarnations (including one that saluted Brecht with his stage placards), simplified itself at the end with a succession of names every five pages, a procession that crosses the book, representing the guérillères as coming from throughout the world.

I cannot finish this description without mentioning a rather complicated process that took place at the moment of writing: the embedding in *Les guéril-lères* of a great number of foreign texts, effected in such a way that the reader can't recognize them. There are also simple references to Nerval, Rimbaud, Hegel, Mallarmé, for example.

I wanted to describe certain aspects of the construction of the book to show that I wrote it as a modern epic. One might be surprised that this article appears in a special issue of a journal on utopia.[1] But I don't see any essential contradiction. I am not in a position to say if an epic can be at the same time a utopia. But granted that the book doesn't happen anywhere and that the action described never took place, it's an open question. I leave it open for the specialists of utopia.

NOTE

1. Monique Wittig, "Quelques remarques sur *Les guérillères*," *L'Esprit Créateur* 34, no. 4 (1994): 116–22.

Some Remarks on The Lesbian Body

Monique Wittig

With *The Lesbian Body* I was confronted with the necessity of writing a book totally lesbian in its theme, its vocabulary, its texture, from the first page to the last, from title page to back cover. I was thus located in a double blank. The blank that all writers have to face when they begin a book. The other blank was of a different nature. It was the nonexistence of such a book till then. I never lived a more challenging time. Would I do it? Could I do it? What was it going to be? I kept the manuscript six months in a drawer before showing it to my publisher.

There were no lesbian books except Sappho; at least that's how I saw it then. (I did not know Djuna Barnes yet.) Sappho was with Pindar one of the great lyric poets five centuries before Christ.

So I started writing fragments in this virgin territory with only Sappho at the horizon. These fragments were lost. They did not work. I remember that in the next step one of the formal possibilities was to use all of Sappho's work and write around it—use Sappho as the main text, write around it, in its margins. Later on I saw another possibility, which was to annex Sappho's text and intratexualize it into my work. It didn't work because Sappho's poems were too far away, they were referring to a place, a time, and to characters I did not know anything about.

Very few verses have been left from one of the greatest poets of all time. The longest fragment we have has often been imitated as a model of lyricism, for example by Louise Labé, a sixteenth-century poet, and by Boileau, a seventeenth-century poet who wrote *Poetical Art*. Sappho was able to express passion in very economical terms but with an extreme potency. "When I see you I become green like grass," thus evoking the role of organs like the liver and gall bladder in carnal passion, or rather the revulsion of the organs to the extreme point of almost dying under the violence of passion.

Most of the Sapphic fragments include one or two verses, sometimes only two words. And in these, violence is not expressed or perceptible. On the contrary, one can imagine that these persons were evolving in a world deprived of violence. And no where can one imagine in these poems that there exists an oppression of women by men. Later Sappho was compared by historians to Plato, and her school on Lesbos was compared to the Socratic school. She has left us in total mystery. She is an enigma.

If I speak at such length about Sappho's work it's because this idea of taking it as the *TEXT*, the Bible, *le livre* and of writing around it is a recurrent idea for me. But it never works. So I am always left with the blank space of the page, a space I call the literary workshop. I can't insist too much on this space that may at any time become an abyss for all writers, an abyss from which one always risks not to rise.

Trying to find a new form, trying to write about that which doesn't dare to speak its name, trying to write about it forcefully, that was the dilemma I had to face. It so happens that violence was doubly at the nexus and the core of this undertaking. It's necessary to talk about violence in writing because it is always the case with a new form: it threatens and does violence to the older ones. You do it with words, with words that you must charge through your work with a new form and therefore with a new meaning. You do it with words that must bring a shock to the readers. If the readers don't feel the shock of words, then your work is not done. That is true for any work of literature you are producing. So from the start there is a violence to the reader. And a good reader could be blasted in the process. (As I felt when I was on the street reading *Tropisms* by Nathalie Sarraute for the first time. After that writing and reading were never the same.)

The second kind of violence I felt I had to express in that book that had no existence yet was the violence of passion. The passion that dares not speak its name—lesbian passion. Now I must say, to explain why my book *The Lesbian Body* had to be so cryptic and realistic in its expression, that lesbian love in literature existed only as the mildest kind of love—best expressed by the writer Colette—as the association of two beings victimized by men, trying to find together a kind of association. In my literary context Colette was the best-known writer. And in this context the two poor women had to help each other—out of compassion—to pass over the peak of passion—that is orgasm—as a sister of charity helps a dying man.

Literature about lesbians started with Baudelaire, who invented the term; his book *Les fleurs du mal* was at one time going to be called *The Lesbians*. Later Verlaine wrote *Parallèlement*. It was a very rich time for lesbianism as a literary paradigm while gay men were hiding their homosexuality under fictive lesbians. Not that I want to blame them. Where would I be without them? When I was fifteen they told me everything I needed to know.

So let's go back to my literary workshop, where I am with fire between my teeth and still nothing but my blank page. Suddenly giving me a big laugh (for one can laugh even in anguish) two words came in: *Lesbian Body.* Can you realize how hilarious it was for me? That is how the book started to exist: in irony. The body, a word whose gender is masculine in French with the word *lesbian* qualifying it. In other words "lesbian" by its proximity to "body" seemed to me to destabilize the general notion of the body. It's a good way for me to make you understand that a writer writes word by word, each word being a material entity as well as a conceptual one. From these two words the whole book *The Lesbian Body* unraveled. Not in one piece, but little by little as one describes an armour. First the helmet, then the shoulders, then the breastpiece etc. Such was my "Lesbian Body," a kind of paradox but not really, a kind of joke but not really, a kind of impossibility but not really.

Anyway because of these two first words, everything that I would say would be transformed. If I used the anatomical vocabulary to design the human body then I would appropriate it for my purpose. The whole vocabulary of the fiction *The Lesbian Body* is thus derived from a rigid anatomical vocabulary. Thus I acquired a precise set of words with which to talk about the body without metaphors, staying practical and pragmatic without sentimentality or romanticism.

It fit an old idea I had that the reader should be acquainted in advance with the words the writer would use. On my blank page I could start building. The anatomical vocabulary is a primary layer in the construction. I have it piercing the book from part to part, showing thus its instrumentality. From this strict vocabulary I was able to lesbianize the whole map of love as it is known. (My model is Proust in *A la recherce du temps perdu—Remembrance of Things Past.*) Then layer after layer I could add multiple references to carnal love, and they would all mingle to create what I named lesbian passion.

This anatomical vocabulary is cold and distant and I used it as a tool to cut off the mass of texts devoted to love. At the opposite end of the scale there was for me the necessity of textual violence as a metaphor for carnal passion.

The texts I have borrowed and intertextualized, thrown together are from Ovid (The Transformations), from Du Bellay, Genet, Baudelaire, Lautréamont, Raymond Roussel, Nathalie Sarraute, from the New Testament, from The Song of Songs, from the Homeric poems etc. I could borrow from these texts on the condition they were assimilated into the reader's mind with violence. These texts could become pliant to my idea of a tension between the "you" and the "I," that is, the protagonists of *The Lesbian Body*. The whole project is an impassible description of lesbian passion; I attempted to leave behind Baudelaire, Lautréamont, and Verlaine.

For what is total ecstasy between two lovers but an exquisite death? A violent act (here in words) that can only be redeemed by an immediate resuscitation. For the great lovers of heterosexual culture (Don Juan, Othello, even Orpheus, the sweet one) are the first a rapist, the second, a murderer, and the third is brainless. Now on the contrary, when the lovers of *The Lesbian Body* kill, they resuscitate. Thus illustrating the poetical sentence from the Bible that love is stronger than death. We are still in irony somehow.

Also I wanted to talk about lesbian love from a carnal point of view, where sentiments, abandon, tears, all these social signs could be annexed only from that carnal point of view, a momentary one. Here there are not couplings forever or a reassuring love that can lead the reader to a "being-happy-forever." I am just describing a moment, a state of being that can happen to everyone and that cannot last. It's not the foundation for a mode of life. It has nothing to do with social life. For poems are not a representation of real life. And when there is a coincidence between the two, the text of life and the text of the book, it can only be inexplicable flashes as with such verses from Rimbaud that obsess me and still shock me:

Au bois il y a un oiseau
Son chant vous arrête et vous fait rougir.

(By the wood there's a bird
Its song stops you and makes you blush.)

As I said in my book *The Straight Mind*, personal pronouns are part of the subject matter. Sometimes I consider *The Lesbian Body* as a reverie about the beautiful analysis of the pronouns *je* and *tu* by the linguist Émile Benveniste. The bar in my j/e is a sign of excess. A sign that helps to imagine an excess of 'I,' an 'I' exalted in its lesbian passion, an 'I' so powerful that it can attack the order of heterosexuality in texts and lesbianize the heroes of love, lesbianize the symbols, lesbianize the gods and the goddesses, lesbianize Christ, lesbianize the men and the women." This 'I' and this 'you' are interchangable. There is no hierarchy from 'I' to 'you' which is its same. Also the 'I' and the 'you' are multiple. One could consider that in each fragment they are different protagonists.

As for *Les guérillères*, I used for *The Lesbian Body* a technique of montage (of editing) as for a film. All the fragments were spread flat on the ground and organized. The book has been constructed according to this principle. The final organization produced an asymmetrical symmetry. By this I mean that each fragment has been duplicated in a slightly different form and meaning.

The book is thus formed in two parts. It opens and falls back on itself. One can compare its form to a cashew, to an almond, to a vulva.

PART 3

CRITICAL APPROACHES

5   *When Lesbians Were Not Women*

Teresa de Lauretis

There was a time, in discontinuous space—a space dispersed across the continents—when lesbians were not women. I don't mean to say that now lesbians are women, although a few do think of themselves that way, while others say they are butch or femme; many prefer to call themselves queer or transgender; and others identify with female masculinity—there are lots of self-naming options for lesbians today. But during that time, what lesbians were was that one thing: not women. And it all seemed so clear, at that time.

It would be perhaps appropriate, in contributing to this book of essays on Monique Wittig, to mourn her passing and honor her memory with a story, a fiction in the style of *Les guérillères,* an allegory after *Paris-la-politique,* or an epic poem remade like *Virgil, non.* Wittig herself is something of a legend now. But I will not tell you a story—or, not exactly a story. I will reflect on what her work meant for me in the 1980s when I was working in feminist and lesbian studies and how it still intersects with the critical questions that concern me now.

In the 1980s, it was reading Wittig, and the few but wonderfully intense conversations I had with her in northern California, that first started me on the project of writing lesbian theory as distinct from feminist theory. The distinction became clear in my mind only after I read three crucial texts: "The Straight Mind," "One Is Not Born a Woman," and *The Lesbian Body.* In retrospect, it seems to me that a new figure—a conceptual figure—emerged from those works and was encapsulated in the statement "lesbians are not women."[1] Generally misunderstood and criticized from many quarters, nevertheless that statement did fire the imagination and, indeed, from the vantage point of today has proved to be prophetic. As I said a moment ago, today's lesbians are many other things—and only rarely women. But at that time the statement "lesbians are not women" had the power to open the mind and make visible and thinkable a *conceptual* space that until then had been rendered unthinkable by, precisely, the hegemony of the straight mind—as the space called "the blind spot" is rendered invisible in a car's rear-view mirror by the frame or chassis of the car itself. Wittig's writing opened up a conceptual, virtual space that was foreclosed by all discourses and ideologies left and right, including feminism.

In that conceptual virtual space, a different kind of woman appeared to me, if I may say so, after the title of a book we read at that time.[2] I called her the "eccentric subject."[3] For if lesbians are not women and yet lesbians are, like me, flesh and blood, thinking and writing beings who live in the world and with whom I interact every day, then lesbians are social subjects and, in all likelihood, psychic subjects as well. I called that subject "eccentric" not only in the sense of deviating from the conventional, normative path but also eccentric in that it did not center itself in the institution that both supports and produces the straight mind, that is, the institution of heterosexuality. Indeed, that institution did not foresee such a subject and could not contemplate it, could not envision it.

What characterizes the eccentric subject is a double displacement: first, the psychic displacement of erotic energy onto a figure that exceeds the categories of sex and gender, the figure Wittig called "the lesbian," and, second, the self-displacement or disidentification of the subject from the cultural assumptions and social practices attendant upon the categories of gender and sex. Here is how Wittig defined that figure:

> Lesbian is the only concept I know of which is beyond the categories of sex (woman and man), because the designated subject (lesbian) is *not* a woman, either economically, or politically, or ideologically. For what makes a woman is a specific social relation to a man, a relation that we have previously called servitude, a relation which implies personal and physical obligation as well as economic obligation ("forced residence," domestic corvée, conjugal duties, unlimited production of children, etc.), a relation which lesbians escape by refusing to become or to stay heterosexual. (20)

To refuse the heterosexual contract, not only in one's practice of living but also in one's practice of knowing—what Wittig called a "subjective, cognitive practice"—constitutes an epistemological shift in that it changes the conditions of possibility of both knowing and knowledge, and this constitutes a shift in historical consciousness.[4]

> Consciousness of oppression [Wittig wrote] is not only a reaction to (fight against) oppression. It is also the whole conceptual reevaluation of the social world, its whole reorganization with new concepts, from the point of view of oppression . . . call it a subjective, cognitive practice. The movement back and

forth between the levels of reality (the conceptual reality and the material reality of oppression, which are both social realities) is accomplished through language. (18–19)

The work of language in that movement back and forth is inscribed in the very title of Wittig's 1980 essay, "On ne naît pas femme." If de Beauvoir the philosopher had said, "One is not *born* but *becomes* a woman" (and so, in his way, had Freud), Wittig the writer said, "One is not born a *woman*" (emphasis added). Almost the same words and yet such a difference in meaning—not to say such a sexual difference. In shifting the emphasis from the word *born* to the word *woman*, Wittig's citation of de Beauvoir's phrase invoked or mimicked the heterosexual definition of woman as "the second sex," at once destabilizing its meaning and displacing its affect.

Such a shift entails displacement and self-displacement: leaving or giving up a place that is known, that is "home"—physically, emotionally, linguistically, epistemologically—for another place that is unknown, that is not only emotionally but also conceptually unfamiliar, a place from which speaking and thinking are at best tentative, uncertain, unauthorized. But the leaving is not a choice because one could not live there in the first place. Thus all aspects of the displacement, from the geopolitical to the epistemological and the affective, are painful and risky for they entail a constant crossing back and forth, a remapping of boundaries between bodies and discourses, identities and communities. At the same time, however, they enable a reconceptualization of the subject, of the relations of subjectivity to social reality, and a position of resistance and agency that is not outside but rather eccentric to the sociocultural apparati of the heterosexual institution.

I remember thinking at that time that the possibility to imagine an eccentric subject constituted through disidentification and displacement was somehow related to one's geographical, linguistic, and cultural dislocation—Wittig's, from France to the United States; my own, from Italy to the United States. Only later did I find that a similar conception of the subject was emerging in postcolonial theory and would be subsequently articulated in Homi Bhabha's notion of cultural hybridity and the recent studies on the transnational subject.[5] However, already back then, in the 1980s, I noted the kinship of Wittig's "lesbian" with other figures of eccentric subjects that emerged from the writings of women or lesbians of color such as Trinh T. Minh-ha, Gloria Anzaldúa, Barbara Smith, and Chandra Mohanty. I would argue, therefore, that Wittig's critical writings anticipated some of the emphases of today's postcolonial feminism.

With de Beauvoir and with other feminists of our generation in France, Italy, Britain, and the Americas, Wittig shared the premise that women are not a "natural group" whose oppression would be a consequence of their physical nature but rather a social and political category, an ideological construct, and the product of an economic relation. Most of us, at that time, shared a Marxist understanding of class and a materialist analysis of exploitation, although in Europe that understanding preceded feminism whereas in anglophone America it often followed and resulted from the feminist analysis of gender. I need not tell you about the theory of materialist feminism, because others have done so.[6] I will only say that the definition of gender oppression as a political and subjective category—one arrived at from the specific standpoint of the oppressed, in the struggle, and as a form of consciousness—was distinct from the economic, objective category of exploitation. And that redefinition was also shared by others in North America, such as the black feminist group the Combahee River Collective, for whom gender oppression was indissociable from racist domination.[7]

But Wittig went further: If women are a social class whose specific condition of existence is gender oppression and whose political consciousness affords them a standpoint, a position of struggle, and an epistemological perspective based in lived experience, then what Wittig saw as the goal of feminism was the disappearance of women (as a class). A curious paradox has occurred in the history of feminism since the 1970s in relation to this idea. I will come back to it in a moment, but first allow me to continue with my account of the argument.

In order to imagine what female people would be like in such a classless (i.e., genderless) society, Wittig did not offer a myth or a fiction but referred to the actual existence of a "lesbian society," which, however marginally, did function in a certain way autonomously from heterosexual institutions. In this sense, she claimed, lesbians are not women: "The refusal to become (or to remain) heterosexual always meant to refuse to become a man or a woman, consciously or not. For a lesbian this goes further than the refusal of the *role* 'woman.' It is the refusal of the economic, ideological, and political power of a man."[8] Well, the phrase "lesbian society" had everyone in an uproar. They took it to be descriptive of a type of social organization, or a blueprint for a futuristic, utopian, or dystopian society like the amazons of *Les guérillères* or the all-female communities imagined in Joanna Russ's science fiction novel *The Female Man.* They said Wittig was a utopist, an essentialist, a dogmatic separatist, even a "classic idealist." You cannot be a Marxist, people said, and speak of a lesbian society. You can speak of lesbian society only in the liberal political perspective of free choice, according to which anyone is free to live as they like, and that, of course, is a capitalist myth.

In effect, Wittig mobilized both the discourse of historical materialism and that of liberal feminism in an interesting strategy, one against the other and each against itself, proving them both inadequate to conceiving the subject in feminist materialist terms.[9] To this end, she argued, the Marxist concept of class consciousness and the feminist concept of individual subjectivity must be articulated together. Their joining is what she called a "subjective, cognitive practice," which implies the reconceptualization of the subject and the relations of subjectivity to sociality from a position that is eccentric to the institution of heterosexuality and therefore exceeds its discursive-conceptual horizon: the position of the subject lesbian. Here, then, is the sense in which Wittig proposed the disappearance of women as the goal of feminism.

Critiques came from all quarters of feminism, including many lesbian quarters; for example, those lesbians who wanted to reclaim femininity for women and rehabilitate its traits of nurturing, compassion, tenderness, and caring as equal in value to so-called masculine gender traits; these were the same critics who indicted Wittig's already famous book *The Lesbian Body* for what they called its violence. Critiques came from those who wanted to promote a women's culture, conceived not as a class but as a community of woman-identified women, and from those who favored the idea of a "lesbian continuum" to which any woman who, for whatever reason, had refused or resisted the institution of marriage could rightfully belong—and be considered a lesbian regardless of sexual choice, behavior, or desire. And critiques also came from those who, on the other hand, considered sexuality and desire central to lesbian subjectivity while on the other maintained that heterosexuality necessarily defines homosexuality and dictates the very forms of lesbian and gay sexualities, however subversive or parodic they may be.

These critiques mainly failed to see that Wittig's "lesbian" was not just an individual with a personal "sexual preference" or a social subject with a simply "political" priority but the term or conceptual figure for the subject of a cognitive practice and a form of consciousness that are not primordial, universal, or coextensive with human thought, as de Beauvoir would have it, but historically determined and yet subjectively assumed—an eccentric subject constituted in a process of struggle and interpretation; of translation, detranslation, and retranslation (as Jean Laplanche might put it); a rewriting of self in relation to a new understanding of society, of history, of culture.

Similarly, her critics did not understand that Wittig's "lesbian society" did not refer to some collectivity of gay women but was the term for a conceptual and experiential space carved out of the social field, a space of contradictions in the here and now that need be affirmed and not resolved. When she concluded, "It is *we* who historically must undertake the task of defining the individual subject in materialist terms," that "we" was not the privileged women of de

Beauvoir, "qualified to elucidate the situation of woman."[10] Wittig's "we" was the point of articulation from which to rethink both Marxism and feminism; it was, or so it seemed to me, the term of a particular form of feminist consciousness which, at that historical moment, could only exist as the consciousness of a something else; it was the figure of a subject that exceeds its conditions of subjection, a subject in excess of its discursive construction, a subject of which we only knew what it was not: not-woman. Reread the second sentence of *Le corps lesbien:* "Ce qui a cours ici, pas une ne l'ignore, n'a pas de nom pour l'heure."[11]

There is, as I said, a curious paradox in the history of feminism since the 1970s with regard to Wittig's call for the disappearance of women. In a certain sense, women have disappeared from the current lexicon of feminist studies, at least in the anglophone world. It began in the late 1980s, in the wake of identity politics and with the increasing participation of women of color, lesbians and straight, in academic studies, when the word *women* came to be subjected to the same critique that had dismantled the notion of Woman (capital W, *la femme*) by the early 1980s.[12] In the 1990s, then, to speak of women without racial, ethnic, or other geopolitical modifiers was to take for granted a common and equal oppression based on gender or sex, which disregarded concomitant forms of oppression based on racial, ethnic, class, and other differences.[13] The notion of sexual difference was especially targeted and discarded—not without good reasons—as inadequate, insufficient, Eurocentric, and class-centered. Moreover, in the version of poststructuralist feminism that has become popular in academic feminist and queer theory (where the term *poststructuralist* references almost exclusively the influence of the early Foucault and Derrida), women are understood to be simulacra of the social imaginary, with no inherent physical or psychic substance. Women, like gender, sexuality, the subject, and the body itself, according to this view, are all discursive constructs, sites of convergence of the performative effects of power. In this perspective, a concept such as Wittig's "subjective, cognitive practice" and the notion of lived experience, which was central to feminist theory in the 1970s and 1980s, have been dismissed as essentialist, naturalizing, ideological,[14] or, worse, as humanist—which, in the context of the "posthumanist" or postmodern vogue of the 1990s, was definitely a derogatory word. So, in a way, one could say that women *have* disappeared.[15]

The paradox is this: Wittig, who had first proposed the disappearance of women, was herself cast in the essentialist, passé, or humanist camp. In the words of one poststructuralist feminist philosopher, "Wittig calls for a position beyond sex that returns her theory to a problematic humanism based in a problematic metaphysics of presence."[16] The phrase *metaphysics of presence,* a sign of the influence of Jacques Derrida's early work, recurs several times in Judith Butler's *Gender Trouble* (1990), the book that brought Wittig to the attention of nonlesbian and nonfeminist readers, and for this reason will be briefly referred to here. Marketed as a feminist intervention in the field of French philosophy, the book was widely cited and translated and became an authoritative text of gender studies and queer theory. Its extensive discussion of Wittig's work in the disciplinary context of philosophy effectively mainstreamed Monique Wittig as a French feminist theorist (next to the two others whose names circulated widely in North American universities, Luce Irigaray and Julia Kristeva). Butler, however, objected to Wittig's radical stance, which she mistook for what she called a "separatist prescriptivism"—as if Wittig had been arguing that all women should become lesbians or that only lesbians could be feminist.

Like the other critics, Butler failed to understand the figural, theoretical character of Wittig's "lesbian" and its epistemological valence. The subject of a cognitive practice based in the lived experience of one's body, one's desire, one's conceptual and psychical disidentification from the straight mind, Wittig's "lesbian" was well aware of the power of discourse to shape one's social and subjective (and, I would add, psychic) reality: "If the discourse of modern theoretical systems and social science exert[s] a power upon us, it is because it works with concepts which closely touch us," Wittig had written in "The Straight Mind" (26–27). Butler, however, referred to Wittig's lesbian subject as the "cognitive subject," endowing it with strong Cartesian connotations, and tossed her theory in the dump of surpassed and discarded philosophies. To the reader of *Gender Trouble,* Wittig appears to be an existentialist who believes in human freedom, a humanist who presumes the ontological unity of Being prior to language, an idealist masquerading as a materialist, and, most paradoxically of all, an unintentional, unwitting collaborator with the regime of heterosexual normativity.[17] This, in my opinion, may account for the relative disregard or condescension in which Wittig's work has been typically held in gender and queer studies until now. Until, that is, the renewed attention to Wittig's work on the part of a new generation may perhaps reopen another virtual space of lesbian thought and writing.

The conceptual originality and radical import of Wittig's theory are inscribed in her fiction prior to *The Straight Mind.* In *Les guérillères*, the figure of the lesbian as subject of a cognitive practice that enables the reconceptualization of the social and of knowledge itself from a position eccentric to the heterosexual institution is figured in the practice of writing as consciousness of contradiction ("the language you speak is made up of words that are killing you"), a consciousness of writing, living, feeling, and desiring in the noncoincidence of experience and language, in the interstices of representation, "in the intervals that your masters have not been able to fill with their words of proprietors."[18] And it is also already there in the first page of *Le corps lesbien.*

One of the first to grasp this was Elaine Marks, who in "Lesbian Intertextuality" (1979) wrote: "In *Le corps lesbien* Monique Wittig has created, through the incessant use of hyperbole and a refusal to employ traditional body codes, images sufficiently blatant to withstand reabsorption into male literary culture."[19] Indeed, the thematic topos of the voyage in Wittig's fiction corresponds to her formal journey as a writer. Both are voyages without fixed destination, without end, more like a self-displacement that in turn displaces the textual figurations of classical and Christian mythologies, the Homeric heroes and Christ, in Western literary genres and reinscribes them otherwise: *The Divine Comedy* (*Virgil, non*) and *Don Quixote* (*Voyage sans fin*), the epic (*Les guérillères*), the lyric (*Le corps lesbien*), the Bildungsroman (*L'opoponax*), the encyclopedic dictionary (*Brouillon pour un dictionnaire des amantes*), and later the satire (*Paris-la-politique*), the political manifesto and the critical essay (*The Straight Mind*).

In *Le corps lesbien,* the odyssey of the lesbian subject *j/e* is a journey into language, into the body of Western culture, a season in hell. "Ce qui a cours ici, pas une ne l'ignore, n'a pas de nom pour l'heure."[20] *Ici* refers at once to the events described in the diegesis and to the process of their inscription, the process of writing. The dismemberment of the female body limb by limb, organ by organ, secretion by secretion, is at the same time the deconstruction term by term of the anatomical female body as represented or mapped by patriarchal discourse. The journey and the writing ignore that map, exceed the words of the masters to expose the intervals between them, the gaps of representation, and trespass into the interstices of discourse to reimagine, re-learn, and rewrite the body in another libidinal economy. And yet the journey and the writing do not produce an alternative map, a whole, coherent, healthy female body or a teleological narrative of love between women with a happy ending, till death do us part. On the contrary, death is assumed in the lesbian body, inscribed in it from the beginning. "Fais tes adieux m/a très belle." "Ce qui a cours ici" is death, the slow decomposition of the body, the stench, the worms, the open skull. Death is here and now, because it is the inseparable companion and the condition of desire.

Time and again, over the years, I have returned to this extraordinary text that will not let itself ever be read at one time or "consumed" once and for all. That the book is about desire (nonphallic desire, to be sure) was always clear to me. If Virginia Woolf's *Orlando* has been called the longest love letter in history (to Vita Sackville-West), *Le corps lesbien,* I thought, might be called the longest love poem in modern literature. But what has become clear to me only lately is that *Le corps lesbien* is not about love. It is an extended poetic image of *sexuality,* a canto or a vast fresco, brutal and thrilling, seductive and awe-inspiring.

Let me be clear: I do not mean sexuality in Foucault's sense of a technology that produces "sex" as the truth of proper bourgeois subjects. I mean it in the sense of Freud's conception of sexuality as a psychic drive that disrupts the coherence of the ego; a pleasure principle that opposes, shatters, resists, or compromises the logic of the reality principle. The latter is none other than the symbolic logic of the name of the father, the family, the nation, and all the other institutions of society that are based on the macroinstitution, and the presumption, of heterosexuality. Freud saw these two forces, the pleasure principle and the reality principle, as active concurrently in the psyche and at war with each other. When he later reconfigured them on a scale beyond the individual, he named one Eros and the other death drive. But it is the latter, the death drive and not the Platonic Eros, that is the agent of disruption, unbinding, negativity, and resistance that he had first identified in the sexual drive. It is the death drive, and not Eros, that is most closely, structurally associated with sexuality in Freud's metapsychology, his theory of the psyche.[21]

This warring of two psychic forces is what I now see in Wittig's text: its inscription of the enigma of sexuality and of nonphallic, non-Oedipal desire. And this is perhaps what has always provoked my fascination with *Le corps lesbien* and the urge to return to it time and time again: the enigma that it poses and the enigma that it is.

NOTES

1. Monique Wittig, "The Straight Mind" (1980) in *The Straight Mind and Other Essays* (Boston: Beacon Press, 1992), 32. Subsequent page citations will appear in the text.

2. Renée Vivien, *A Woman Appeared to Me* (1904). Renée Vivien, née Pauline Tarn, was an Anglo-American poet and friend of Colette, living in France.

3. Teresa de Lauretis, "Eccentric Subjects," *Feminist Studies* 16 (Spring 1990): 115–50; "Soggetti eccentrici" in de Lauretis, *Soggetti eccentrici* (Milano: Feltrinelli, 1999), 11–57; and "Sujetos excéntricos" in de Lauretis, *Diferencias: Etapas de un camino a través del feminismo* (Madrid: Editorial Horas y HORAS, 2000), 111–52.

4. A similar point is made by Namascar Shaktini: "Wittig's reorganization of metaphor around the lesbian body represents an epistemologoical shift from what seemed until recently the absolute, central metaphor—the phallus." "Displacing the Phallic Subject: Wittig's Lesbian Writing," *Signs: Journal of Women in Culture and Society* 8, no. 1 (1982): 29.

5. See Homi K. Bhabha, *The Location of Culture* (London: Routledge, 1994).

6. The text that circulated in the anglophone world was Christine Delphy, *Close to Home: A Materialist Analysis of Women's Oppression,* trans. and ed. Diana Leonard (Amherst: University of Massachusetts Press, 1984).

7. See "The Combahee River Collective Statement" in *Home Girls: A Black Feminist Anthology,* ed. Barbara Smith (New York: Kitchen Table: Women of Color Press, 1983), 272–82.

8. Monique Wittig, "One Is Not Born a Woman," in *The Straight Mind and Other Essays* (Boston: Beacon Press, 1992), 13.

9. First she deployed the Marxist concepts of ideology, class, and social relations against liberal feminism. She argued that to accept the terms of gender or sexual difference, which constructed woman as an "imaginary formation" on the basis of women's biological-erotic value to men, makes it impossible to understand that the terms *women* and *man* "are political categories and not natural givens," and thus prevents one from questioning the real socioeconomic relations of gender. Second, however, Wittig claimed the feminist notion of self as a subject who, although socially produced, is apprehended and lived in its concrete, personal singularity, and this notion of self she held against Marxism, which denied an individual subjectivity to the members of the oppressed classes. Although "materialism and subjectivity have always been mutually exclusive," she insisted on both class consciousness and individual subjectivity at once. Without the latter, "there can be no real fight or transformation. But the opposite is also true; without class and class consciousness there are no real subjects, only alienated individuals" ("The Straight Mind" 19).

10. Simone de Beauvoir, *The Second Sex,* trans. H. M. Parshley (1949, repr. New York: Vintage, 1974), xxxii.

11. "No one is unaware of what takes place here, it has no name as yet" (my translation). Monique Wittig, *Le corps lesbien* (Paris: Éditions Minuit, 1973), 7.

12. Teresa de Lauretis, *Alice Doesn't: Feminism, Semiotics, Cinema* (Bloomington: Indiana University Press, 1984).

13. Robyn Wiegman, "Object Lessons: Men, Masculinity, and the Sign Women," *Signs: Journal of Women in Culture and Society* 26, no. 2 (2001): 355–88.

14. Joan W. Scott, "The Evidence of Experience," *Critical Inquiry* 17 (Summer 1991): 773–97. The notion of *expérience vécue* has now become central to postcolonial and critical race theory stemming from the rereading of Frantz Fanon, while the concept of experience is now being revaluated in the writing of Foucault, which was formerly read as the staunch basis of the social-constructionist position against the essentialist position allegedly represented by "the evidence of experience."

15. A move to replace academic programs in women's studies with gender studies has met with very few objections. Leora Auslander, "Do Women's + Feminist + Men's + Lesbian + Gay + Queer Studies = Gender Studies?" *differences* 9, no. 3 (1997): 1–25. The author's answer to the question in her title is an enthusiastic yes.

16. Judith Butler, *Gender Trouble: Feminism and the Subversion of Identity* (New York: Routledge, 1990), 124.

17. Here are some typical passages from *Gender Trouble:*

Wittig's radical feminist theory occupies an ambiguous position within the continuum of theories on the question of the subject. On the one hand, Wittig appears to dispute the metaphysics of substance, but on the other hand, she retains the human subject, the individual, as the metaphysical locus of agency. (25)

In her defense of the "cognitive subject," Wittig appears to have no metaphysical quarrel with hegemonic modes of signification or representation; indeed, the subject, with its attribute of self-determination, appears to be the rehabilitation of the agent of existential choice under the name of the lesbian. (19)

As a subject who can realize concrete universality through freedom, Wittig's lesbian confirms rather than contest the normative promise of humanist ideals premised on the metaphysics of substance. (20)

Clearly her belief in a "cognitive subject" that exists prior to language facilitates her understanding of language as an instrument, rather than as a field of significations that preexist and structure subject-formation itself. (154n27)

Wittig's radical disjunction between straight and gay replicates the kind of disjunctive binarism that she herself characterizes as the divisive philosophical gesture of the straight mind. (121)

Lesbianism that defines itself in radical exclusion from heterosexuality deprives itself of the capacity to resignify the very heterosexual constructs by which it is partially and inevitably constituted. As a result, that lesbian strategy would consolidate compulsory heterosexuality in its oppressive [as opposed to "volitional or optional," 121] forms. (128)

Wittig's materialism . . . understands the institutuion of heterosexuality as the founding basis of the male-dominated social orders. "Nature" and the domain of materiality are ideas, ideological constructs, produced by these social institutions to support the political interests of the heterosexual contract. In this sense, Wittig is a classic idealist for whom nature is understood as a mental representation. (125)

Very similar statements appear in Rosi Braidotti, *Metamorphoses: Towards a Materialist Theory of Becoming* (Oxford: Polity Press, 2002), which attributes to Wittig "a naïve social constructivism which paradoxically works with an idealist position on language and social changes" (35) and damns her as "a humanist who is still caught in the metaphysics of substance" (102). Remarkably, Braidotti follows almost verbatim Butler's assessment of Wittig in the context of a critique of Butler, for the project of *Metamorphoses* is to challenge U.S. poststructuralist feminist philosophy as represented by Butler with a French poststructuralist feminist philosophy based in Deleuze and Irigaray.

18. Monique Wittig, *Les Guérillères,* trans. David Le Vay (Boston: Beacon Press, 1985), 114.

19. Elaine Marks, "Lesbian Intertextuality," in *Homosexualities and French Literature,* ed. George Stambolian and Elaine Marks (Ithaca: Cornell University Press, 1979), 375.

20. As I pointed out elsewhere, the linguistically impossible subject pronoun *j/e* may be read in several theoretically possible ways that go from the more conservative (the slash in *j/e* represents the division of the Lacanian subject) to the less conservative (*j/e* can be expressed by writing but not by speech, recalling Derridean *différance*), to the radical feminist ("*j/e* is the symbol of the lived, rending experience which is *m/y* writing, of this cutting in two which throughout literature is the exercise of a language which does not constitute m/e as subject" (Wittig, quoted in Margaret Crosland's introduction to *The Lesbian Body* in the paperback edition I own [Boston: Beacon Press, 1986]. The play of *j/e-tu* also suggests the butch-femme double subject of lesbian camp performance envisaged by Sue-Ellen Case. Teresa de Lauretis, "Sexual Indifference and Lesbian Representation," *Theatre Journal* 40 (May 1988): 155–77, translated as *Differenza e indifferenza sessuale: Per l'elaborazione di un pensiero lesbico* (Florence: Estro, 1989), *Film in Vidno* (Ljubljana: SKUC, 1998), and "Diferencia e indiferencia sexual" in de Lauretis, *Diferencias: Etapas de un camono a través del feminismo* (Madrid: horas y HORAS, 2000).

21. Jean Laplanche, *Life and Death in Psycho-Analysis,* trans. Jeffrey Mehlman (Baltimore: Johns Hopkins University Press, 1976), ch. 6; see also Laplanche, "La pulsion de mort dans la théorie de la pulsion sexuelle," in *La pulsion de mort* (Paris: PUF, 1986).

6

Universalizing Materialist Lesbianism

Diane Griffin Crowder

Revolutionary thinkers, those who transform the ways in which we conceptualize the world, are inevitably utopian in the sense that they have a new vision of how things are or ought to be. Their ideas may seem odd, even incomprehensible, at first. But slowly they undermine our old ways of seeing. In the process they risk being misunderstood. Monique Wittig is one such thinker, and she has described the process of literary revolution thus: "Any important literary work is like the Trojan Horse at the time it is produced. Any work with a new form operates as a war machine, because its design and its goal is to pulverize the old forms and formal conventions. It is always produced in hostile territory. And the stranger it appears, nonconforming, unassimilable, the longer it will take for the Trojan Horse to be accepted."[1] She goes on to argue that a writer who has a particular position as a historically determined subject must universalize that individual point of view. She concludes that it "is the attempted universalization of the point of view that turns or does not turn a literary work into a war machine" (*SM,* 75).

Critics generally acknowledge Wittig's status as an innovative writer of fiction and drama who has transformed our way of reading. But certain key ideas reflected in her philosophical essays and fiction have provoked controversy. Her concepts of sex, gender, and sexuality rest finally on a "materialist lesbian" theory that places new importance on the definitions of the concepts of lesbianism, the universal, and the project of envisioning a world where oppressions are eliminated. My aim is to elucidate these ideas, to further understanding of how Wittig's Trojan Horse operates.

In her foreword to *The Straight Mind,* Louise Turcotte rightly observes, "It is impossible to locate Wittig's influence entirely in literature, politics, or theory, for her work in fact traverses all three, and it is precisely from this multidimensionality that the great importance of her thought derives" (*SM,* vii). Wittig exemplifies in all her work the principle that form and meaning cannot be separated, and her oeuvre is remarkably unified. Yet in order to fully comprehend the revolutionary nature of her fiction it is useful to trace the complexities of Wittig's philosophy of "materialist lesbianism," the term she uses to describe her approach to politics and theory (*SM*, xiii).

If American feminists have not always understood Wittig's thought it is perhaps because they lack the tradition of materialist feminism developed in France by Wittig, Christine Delphy, Nicole-Claude Mathieu, Colette Guillaumin, and others. These social scientists, emerging from a French Marxist/socialist tradition, conceptualize society in terms of concrete relations among groups of people. The relationships between men and women rest on the material exploitation of women's labor—including reproductive and sexual labor—by men. Wittig's debt to Marxist theory is evident from her earliest essays. Like the other French materialist feminists, however, Wittig recognizes that Marxism is inadequate to the needs of feminist analysis. She criticizes it—especially in "On the Social Contract" and "Homo Sum"—because it rests upon a fundamental binarism that always fails to resolve itself into the desired synthesis. Further, women cannot be compared directly to the proletariat because women's economic and social condition is premodern, more comparable to a feudal relation between lord and serfs.

As the only literary writer among this group of thinkers, Wittig also contends that the symbolic order, which Marxism relegated to the superstructure, is itself a material force in society. Expanding upon the insight of Simone de Beauvoir that men are the One and women the eternal Other within all social realms including language, Wittig maintains that the symbolic order is as much a fundamental political category as economics or other concrete social relations. For Wittig, words and works of fiction are material objects that can shape not only the mind but also the social and physical bodies of humans. Her fiction demonstrates how language maintains and perpetuates the physical exploitation of women and how it can be changed.

Despite the existence of a socialist feminist branch in the United States, mainstream American feminism has historically tended to divide into either essentialist or social constructionist theories. Diana Fuss has defined the former as the concept of a "pure or original femininity, a female essence, outside the boundaries of the social and therefore untainted (though perhaps repressed) by a patriarchal order."[2] Social constructionism "insists that essence is itself a historical construction." It rejects the "idea that any essential or natural givens precede the processes of social determination. . . . For the constructionist, the natural is itself posited as a construction of the social."[3] Another way of describing these two perspectives is that used by Naomi Schor, who groups

American and French feminisms into "difference" and "equality" feminists. The former believe in an "inalienable female difference," whereas the latter see femininity as "a male construct."[4] Fuss typifies Wittig as the extreme example of social constructionism, and in a certain sense that is true.[5] Yet although Wittig certainly rejects vehemently any suggestion of a female (or male) essence, her materialist approach is based on a different conception of the relationship between social structures and the complex of behaviors that defines men and women.

American feminists have also tended to separate gender from sex and to see the latter as the natural base upon which society constructs the mental and physical behaviors that compose gender identity. Further, in constructionism there is separation between the material and the mental or ideological, with greater emphasis placed on the latter. Despite some exceptions in the 1990s (such as Judith Butler and the emergent transsexual/transgender movements) the physical division of humans into two anatomical sexes is generally not questioned per se, only the imposition of different-and-unequal genders upon these physical groups. Thus, if we can change attitudes or gender roles, we can liberate women from the oppressive effects of sexism. Gender differences are often seen as arbitrary, susceptible to change if enough people decide the oppressive effects of gender roles demand it.

For a materialist like Wittig, gender is not at all an arbitrary set of roles or expectations superimposed on biological sex. Rather, these roles and expectations follow logically and inevitably from material exploitation of the class "women" by the class "men." That exploitation, and the material benefits men derive from it, determines both sex and gender, the former being used (as black skin was used by slave owners) as a convenient "naturalizing" excuse for imposing the latter. To summarize briefly the differences among essentialism, social constructionism, and materialism, Colette Guillaumin uses the example of women's fearfulness. An essentialist would say that women are by nature more fearful and emotional than men and would provide a biological (or psychoanalytical) explanation. A constructionist would say that women have been taught to be fearful, and if the way young women are raised was changed, they would not be more fearful than men. A materialist would say, as Nicole Mathieu has so clearly articulated, that women are fearful because men punish women in order to keep them exploited.[6]

If, for Fuss, social determinism is as bad as biological determinism because, in each case, the subject is a passive victim of preexisting forces, that argument cannot apply to materialist feminism.[7] Mathieu demonstrates that women do not passively consent to domination, nor are men unconscious transmitters of biological/social aggression. Rather, the complex range of psychological and social traits we associate with sex and gender are, from a materialist point of view, explicable without recourse to deterministic thinking if we comprehend that men dominate women in order to appropriate women's labor and that women develop survival strategies under conditions of extreme physical and psychological violence. Colette Guillaumin has demonstrated that the female body itself is shaped by male dominance.[8]

Wittig's development of her philosophy of materialist feminism follows logically from the premises she laid out, in characteristically blunt and brief terms, in one of her earliest articles, "The Category of Sex" (1976) (*SM*, 2). In a sense, all her later articles are glosses on the principles articulated there. Wittig begins with the premise that "social differences always belong to an economic, political, ideological order."[9] For Wittig, any system that sets up social categories of difference does so in order to create distinct groups, which, on the basis of these perceived differences, can then be placed into a relationship of inequality or social conflict. At the root of this system is economic exploitation of one group by another. It is therefore no accident that this article uses the analogy of the master/slave relationship in which economic exploitation is the obvious motivation behind the creation of the two groups in the first place.[10] For Wittig, it was evident that human societies *create* categories of difference and that these differences divide in order to conquer.

The process of creating social categories is "an operation of reduction, by taking the part for the whole," as in color or sex (*SM*, 8). If Wittig's analogy to slavery is not new, dating as it does to the American nineteenth-century feminist movement, her insistence that the biological marker (color, sex) is created by the need to invent social differences is much more radical. For Wittig, "There is no sex. There is but sex that is oppressed and sex that oppresses. It is oppression that creates sex and not the contrary," for "there are no women without men" (*SM*, 2).

The idea that sex is an artificial creation of social oppression has proven a stumbling point for Wittig's readers. Feminist readers are quite willing to follow her indictment of the oppression of women, but the notion that women and men do not exist outside the relation of oppression flies in the face of common sense. So ingrained is the belief in the naturalness of the genetic/biological differences between the sexes that critics have hardly commented on this baldly stated proposition. It therefore merits attention as a foundation of Wittig's argument.

We know that, in a racist society, physical traits attributed to a given race become signs of social caste or group. Within that society, appurtenance to one race or the other is obvious and "natural," a question of genetics. Even the most enlightened member of such a society is likely to intone that "we are all the same under the skin," after all, thus preserving the difference of the skin color as essential if perhaps irrelevant. Similarly, profeminist thinkers might say that men and women are basically the same despite obvious anatomical differences, which are maintained as biological givens even if irrelevant to the question of, say, admittance to law school. If modern genetic science has largely abandoned the idea of genetic racial differences, it is still frantically searching for all possible evidence of genetic sexual difference.[11] Americans must still often categorize themselves by race. If information about one's race is sometimes optional, one's sex is, as Wittig points out, still mandatory, at least on a birth certificate (*SM*, 8).

Yet just as the concept of race has been proven social rather than biological, the concept of sex as a natural division among persons is at least as untenable. Judith Butler has demonstrated how the search for the "master gene" of sex is so tainted by cultural presumptions about what constitutes a male and a female body that the research is literally circular (as well as sexist in its assumption that it is the male gene that determines sex, the female being defined as the absence of the male gene).[12] If the majority of individuals in a given society fit the physical definitions "male" or "female," that does not disprove the social nature of the definitions, as the existence of anomalous individuals indicates. Indeed, the arbitrary and socially determined nature of physical sex is revealed most starkly by the medical interventions practiced routinely on intersexed infants.[13] What defines male and female is not the physical body itself but that body placed into a relationship of comparison and contrast with another body, and this relationship is, by definition, a social relationship. Although bodies do in fact differ, that difference has no meaning—it does not define people as members of a particular category—until those differences are codified as relevant within a given social relationship.

Thus, for Wittig, men and women exist only in relation to one another and not as ontological categories at all. The mark of sex is imposed by that relationship. "What we believe to be a physical and direct perception [of physical features] is only a sophisticated and mythic construction, an 'imaginary formation,' which reinterprets physical features (in themselves as neutral as any others but marked by the social system) through the network of relationships in which they are perceived" (*SM,* 11–12).

The relationship that defines these two groups is that of dominance. For Wittig, the fact of male dominance is so self-evident that in nonfiction essays she rarely develops examples, simply listing in a sentence or two the most egregious aspects of oppression. "It is the fate of women to perform three-quarters of the work of society (in the public as well as in the private domain) plus the bodily work of reproduction according to a pre-established rate. Being murdered, mutilated, physically and mentally tortured and abused, being raped, being battered, and being forced to marry is the fate of women" (*SM*, 3).[14]

In her fiction, however, especially *Les guérillères*, *Virgile, non*, and such short stories as "Les tchiches et les tchouches" and "Le jardin," Wittig employs the full power of her art to render oppression vivid.[15] In "Le jardin," mutilated people become "les corps" (the bodies) and others become "les tres" (the beings) in order to defamiliarize behaviors of oppression that are so familiar to us between men and women that we cease to see them as oppressive or exploitative. The "milking" competitions of the corps, the sadistic beatings and rapes that the tres consider an amusing part of their festivities, are clearly intended as analogies to relations between men and women, yet Wittig forces the reader to find the appropriate analogies and thus to look at human behavior in a new light. Similarly, in "Les tchiches," classes of oppressors and oppressed are based on the natural division between larger and smaller individuals. That she must resort to such defamiliarizing strategies is an indication of how ingrained the acceptance of male dominance is.

The occultation of the material reality of the exploitation of women is a subject to which Wittig returns in all her essays. Why, if the concrete economic and political oppression of women is so brutally evident, do women and men fail to see it, and why is this gross disparity considered so natural? If Wittig was able to give a concise and lucid explanation in a brief space in her first major article in 1982 ("The Category of Sex"), by 1990 and the publication of "Homo Sum" she had to develop consistently more elaborate explanations of her rejection of the idea that sex is a natural category. Her conception of the problem did not change radically during this fifteen-year period, but she was forced to react to changes within and without feminism during this time.

Wittig begins, in "Category," by setting up a distinction between "social oppositions" and "so-called natural differences." It is in the interests of masters to create differences between themselves and slaves in order to justify exploitation (*SM*, 2). If something is natural (biological, essential), then there is no use fighting it. Until slaves begin to question the naturalness of these differences, they accept the situation. This questioning is extremely difficult for two reasons. First, "The primacy of difference so constitutes our thought that it prevents turning inward on itself to question itself" (*SM*, 2). Every aspect of the social order is constructed on the primacy of difference, impressing on women and men alike three axioms that are so interwoven that they form a "tight network that affects everything, our thoughts, our gestures, our acts, our work, our feelings, our relationships" (*SM*, 4).

These three axioms Wittig summarizes as "metaphysical," "scientific," and "Marxist." Whether it is the ontological division into two sexes, their biological

differences, or the social division of labor within the family, each approach
locates difference and the existence of the two sexes as presocial, natural, and
inevitable. In her later articles Wittig takes up the philosophical problems of
each of these approaches in detail—the ontological in "One Is Not Born a
Woman" and "On the Social Contract," the scientific in "The Straight Mind,"
and the Marxist in "Homo Sum." But in each case society is so constructed
that it is very difficult to call into question the "naturalness" of "difference."

The second reason that women (and men) do not question the naturalness
of the categories of sex results from the occultation of material exploitation
with layers of social myth. Wittig's fictions repeatedly cite the legends, myths,
and "great books" of Western culture, rewriting them in unfamiliar contexts
in order to reveal their role in disguising the social and economic bases of
the oppression of women. I will return to this point later in my discussion of
Virgile, non.

For Wittig, then, what defines men and women is a social relationship of
domination. The law upon which culture is founded is not Lacan's (Wittig is
in no sense a Lacanian).[16] The law that perpetuates oppression is obligatory
heterosexuality, which dictates that "'you-will-be-straight-or-you-will-not-be'"
(*SM*, 28). This law is internalized so as to become invisible *qua* law, and the
first step in a liberatory movement is to render both the law and its enforce-
ment mechanisms visible.

Wittig cites the notion articulated by the Russian formalists (especially
Shklovsky) that literary language should "defamiliarize" the familiar, to force
readers to see anew what has become so familiar that it is not seen anymore.
But she stresses that what the writer forces the reader to attend to is words
rather than things (*SM*, 72). Wittig uses many techniques to create a new
language that can enable a reader to see the laws of heterosexuality and understand how they function, first within language and then within society. Her
novels and her play attack different aspects of the functioning of gender in
order to make it unfamiliar and therefore comprehensible anew.[17]

One dramatic way to illuminate the operations of imposed heterosexuality
is to disobey that law. Wittig's most startling statement is that lesbians are not
women. "Lesbian is the only concept I know of that is beyond the categories
of sex (woman and man) because the designated subject (lesbian) is *not* a
woman, either economically, politically, or ideologically. What makes a woman
is a specific social relation to a man, a relation that we have previously called
servitude" (*SM*, 20). It is in this essay that Wittig introduces an important analogy she will develop much more fully in *Virgile, non:* A lesbian is a runaway
slave and an outlaw.

Wittig's notion of the lesbian as not-woman has provoked a great deal of controversy in recent years. On the one hand, critics associated with postmodernist theories have frequently followed the lead of Diana Fuss and Judith Butler, who claim that Wittig rejects feminine essentialism but substitutes a naive lesbian essentialism instead. On the other hand, some critics tend to downplay the importance of lesbianism in Wittig's work. Both groups have fundamentally misapprehended Wittig's conception of the social group "lesbians."

Although Fuss, Butler, and others recognize that Wittig is radically constructionist in her view that social relations alone create men and women, they tend to view her lesbian as some kind of third gender and having an essence that exists outside or beyond social relations. It is ironic that these postmodernist critics would accuse Wittig of the heresy of essentialism given that her essays promulgating a purely social construct of sex *and* gender predate their work by almost ten years. Yet Butler goes so far as to impute to Wittig totalitarianism and an "imperialist strategy . . . to lesbianize the entire world."[18] Despite Wittig's explicit denunciation of idealism (*SM*, 73), she is accused of both humanism and idealism.[19] Catherine Nelson-McDermott also refers to Wittig's "totalitarian Utopian society" (in *Les guérillères*) and reiterates another argument, that Wittig somehow places the lesbian on the margin, or outside society as Annemarie Jagose puts it.[20] Judith Roof continues this line. Althoughs she, like Butler, acknowledges that Wittig's works constitute a "perceptive critique of the ideology of gender," she claims Wittig has a "very traditional reliance on the originary existence of a subject outside ideology."[21] Further, they maintain that Wittig's definition of lesbian as "not-woman" depends on the categories of heterosexuality that Wittig is criticizing. According to such critics, this reifies those categories rather than contests them. It is as if Wittig was advocating a simplistic lesbian separatism based on a romanticized notion of a lesbian essence that preexists and is only repressed by male dominance. Such interpretations fundamentally misread Wittig, who invariably locates her concept of the lesbian within history, as when she says, "Lesbianism provides *for the moment* the only social form in which we can live freely" (*SM*, 20, emphasis added).

Other critics, typified by Erika Ostrovsky, seek to rescue Wittig from a sort of lesbian ghetto.[22] Ostrovsky relies on the concept of "universalizing" presented in "The Trojan Horse." She argues that Wittig's works have universal appeal, but it is clear from numerous passages that Ostrovsky equates "universal" with "heterosexual." She concludes her chapter on *L'opoponax*, for example, by observing that the work is universal, despite the fact that desire is depicted as "not heterosexual," because most people feel same-sex attraction in adolescence. Moreover, the text depicts "young love itself"; one could just as well substitute a boy's name for one of the girls' names; and quotations from male poets add "a heterosexual dimension, thus making it more universal."[23]

Both groups appear to rely upon a definition of "lesbian" that is the current popular one—a woman who loves women—but is at odds with Wittig's purpose. She wants to eliminate the categories *women* and *men* in order to eliminate compulsory heterosexuality. In her fiction, she avoids the words *women* and *men* almost entirely, and her essays make it clear that a "woman-loving woman" is not at all her definition. Indeed, in the dictionary she cowrote with Sande Zeig, the "lesbian peoples" reject the word *woman* (*femme*).[24]

Wittig repeatedly typifies the lesbian as one who has broken the social contract that is heterosexuality. Lesbians escape the category of "woman" "by refusing to become or to stay heterosexual" (*SM*, 20). Moreover, "The situation of lesbians here and now in society, whether they know it or not, is located philosophically (politically) beyond the categories of sex. Practically they have run away from their class (the class of women), even if only partially and precariously" (*SM*, 47). In addition, she defines the "point of view of a lesbian" in her writing as the suppression of gender (*SM*, 61). Her analogy is that lesbians are "escapees from our class in the same way as American runaway slaves were when escaping slavery and becoming free" (*SM*, 20).

Thus, it is not desire or sexual practice that defines a lesbian, but a political, social, economic, and symbolic action of refusing the myriad institutions that comprise heterosexuality. "If we, as lesbians and gay men," she observes, "continue to speak of ourselves and to conceive of ourselves as women and as men, we are instrumental in maintaining heterosexuality" (*SM*, 30). Nowhere does Wittig posit a preexisting "essence" of lesbianism or any definition other than a social one. She believes that humans are social creatures, and there is no humanness outside society: "The category of sex does not exist a priori, before all society" (*SM*, 5). It is always located within history, and hence is a political concept.

Some of her most cogent definitions appear in "Paradigm," where she makes it clear that heterosexuality *and* homosexuality are social constructs that go beyond any consideration of desire. "Heterosexuality is a cultural construct designed to justify the whole system of social domination based on the obligatory reproductive function of women and the appropriation of that reproduction."[25] Homosexuality is more than just the desire for one's own sex. It is the desire to resist that norm of dominance. For Wittig, truly liberated desire would have nothing to do with a division of people into two sexes. All such divisions are political, designed to allow one group to exercise power over another. Lesbianism, as a concept, is therefore much more than homosexuality. "Lesbianism opens onto another dimension of the human (insofar as its definition is not based on the 'difference' of the sexes)" ("P," 117). For gay men and lesbians, she says, there are as many sexes as there are people ("P," 109). It is a statement that anticipates postmodernist calls for multiple genders and refutes the notion that Wittig wants to impose a totalitarian sameness on humanity. She concludes this important essay by rejecting unequivocally the "woman-loving woman" definition: "And it is not 'women' (victims of hetero-sexuality) that lesbians love and desire, but lesbians (individuals who are not the females of men)" ("P," 121).

If the lesbian is a runaway slave or an escapee, that does not mean lesbians are outside society or can somehow avoid dealing with the "straight mind." Wittig stresses that, as runaways, "there is no escape (for there is no territory, no other side of the Mississippi)," and those who break away from the "political regime" of heterosexuality must still "renegotiate daily, and term by term, the social contract" (*SM*, xiii). But renegotiation alters, bit by bit, the social contract. In her essay "On the Social Contract," Wittig analyzes the pervasiveness of heterosexual relations in all cultures and does not minimize the extent to which the categories *men* and *women* structure all aspects of society. But she also finds in the concept of a social contract the possibility that a new contract can be forged. "Is this a mere utopia?" she asks rhetorically. Her answer: "If ultimately we are denied a new social order, which therefore can exist only in words, I will find it in myself" (*SM,* 45).

Wittig's fictional treatment of lesbians provides another element that belies the "essentialist" accusation made by some critics. In *Les guérillères,* the collective hero *elles* fight a revolution against *ils* and, having vanquished male-dominant society, proceed to create a new civilization. It is clear that if they are tempted to valorize the female body early in this process they quickly reject that approach and burn the feminaries (books exalting the vulva). Indeed, all such passages proceed by negation, as in this typical example:

> Elles ne disent pas que les vulves dans leurs formes elliptiques sont à comparer aux soleils, aux planètes, aux galaxies innombrables. Elles ne disent pas que les mouvements giratoires sont comme les vulves. Elles ne disent pas que les vulves sont comme des formes premières qui comme telles décrivent le monde dans tout son espace, dans tout son mouvement. Elles ne créent pas dans leurs discours des figures conventionnelles à partir de ces symboles.

> (Elles do not say that vulvas with their elliptical shape are to be compared to suns, planets, innumerable galaxies. They do not say that gyratory movements are like vulvas. They do not say that the vulva is the primal form which as such describes the world in all its extent, in all its movement. They do not in their discourses create conventional figures derived from these symbols.)[26]

Not only do the *guérillères* eschew glorification of the female body, but they also incorporate into their society those males who do not find their language of revolution too extreme.[27]

Characters in *Le corps lesbien* literally dismember and reconstruct themselves. In this passage that evokes the Isis/Osiris myth, the power of a lover to give life to a lesbian body is apparent:

> Elles m//attirent jusqu'à tes morceaux dispersés, il y a un bras, il y a un pied, le cou et la tête vont ensemble, tes paupières sont fermées, tes oreilles déchirées sont quelque part, tes globes occulaires ont roulé dans la boue. . . . j/e prononce que tu es là vivante quoique tronçonnée, j/e cherche en toute hâte tes morceaux dans la boue . . . j/e retrouve ton nez une partie de ta vulve tes nymphes ton clitoris . . . j/e te rassemble bout à bout, j/e te reconstitue . . . toi alors m/on Osiris m/a très belle tu m/e souris défaite épuisée.

> (The women [*sic*] lead m/e to your scattered fragments, there is an arm, there is a foot, the neck and head are together, your eyelids are closed, your detached ears are somewhere, your eyeballs have rolled in the mud. . . . *I* announce that you are here alive though cut to pieces, *I* search hastily for your fragments in the mud . . . *I* find your nose a part of your vulva your labia your clitoris . . . *I* assemble you part by part, *I* reconstruct you. . . . then you m/y Osiris m/y most beautiful you smile at m/e undone exhausted.)[28]

Namascar Shaktini points out that the text is also a voyage from Gehenna, or hell, to a community of lesbians. The narrator must become one of the new society through a process of discovery.[29] Again, Wittig seems to stress that the lesbian is made, not born.

It is in her last novel, *Virgile, non,* that Wittig paints her most detailed portrait of lesbians and articulates most clearly the relationship between them and the class "women." It is also the most telling example of Wittig's suppression of gender. In this rewriting of Dante's *Divine Comedy,* a character named "Wittig" (in quotation marks to distinguish her from the author Wittig) visits hell, limbo, and paradise but not in that order. All three spaces are in San Francisco. Those in hell are referred to as the *âmes damnées* (lost souls), who are tormented not by demons but by *ennemis* (enemies).[30] Wittig carefully avoids using words such as "men" or "women"—it is only the grammatical gender of the feminine "âmes" and masculine "ennemis" that determines their pronouns (elles and ils, respectively). Their gender is thus totally linguistic, and Wittig makes it clear in one circle of hell, where people are so self-effacing that they are two-dimensional playing cards, some kings are mixed in with the queens and lesser cards (*VN,* 58). Only rarely does she refer to anatomical features recognizably male or female: breasts and mutilated female genitals in the parade sequences, *pendantifs* (danglers) and *couilles* (balls) in another passage set in a brothel (*VN*, 113–14).

"Wittig" will see in hell only what can be seen every day on the streets, according to her guide, Manastabal (*VN*, 9). Each circle of hell defamiliarizes heterosexual life by showing it from a lesbian point of view. For instance, the fact that mothers are constantly physically and psychologically attached to their families is transformed by referring to family members as "annexes" who pull at souls or hold them back.[31]

> Dans la rue dans les magasins sur les places dans les jardins publics dans les voitures sur les trottoirs dans les autobus et même dans les cafés, partout où elles sont, elles ont leurs annexes. . . . En effet leurs figures ne brillent pas et leur démarche n'est pas alerte. Elles portent un sourire sans éclat mais perma-nent car il est leur étoile jaune. Elles ont les bras au corps, les épaules serrées, elles trainent les pieds et elles sont souvent arrêtées dans leur progression ou ralenties, tirées en arrière par les mouvements désordonnés de leurs annexes. . . . Mais pendant ce temps elles disent:
> (Je les adore.)
> Ou encore:
> (Je ne sais pas ce que je ferais sans.)
> Et c'est vrai que, quand elles se trouvent par hasard délestées de leurs annexes, elles tombent à plat ventre par terre à tout moment dans leur désorientation, ne sachant plus où aller.
>
> (In the street in the stores on the plazas in the public parks in the cars on the sidewalks in the buses and even in the cafes, everywhere they are, they have their annexes. . . . In fact their faces don't shine and their movements are not alert. They wear a smile that lacks luster but is permanent because it is their yellow star. Their arms are tight to the body, their shoulders hunched, they drag their feet and they are often stopped in their progression by the disorderly movements of their annexes. . . . But all this time they say:
> [I adore them.]
> Or again:
> [I don't know what I would do without them.]
> And it's true that, when they find themselves by chance freed from their an-naxes, they fall down flat on the ground at every moment in their disorientation, not knowing any more where to go.) (*VN*, 51–52 [Fr. ed.])[32]

"Wittig" comments that any soul not thus encumbered "must be a dyke" (in English in the text). In another instance the way some men parade their women, holding them around the neck or waist while soliciting envious glances from other men, is depicted by enemies who put souls on leashes (*VN*, 51, 28).

The souls in some circles see their plight as not only ordinary but also desirable. In other cases they accept the most horrible tortures because they see the alternative, lesbianism, as even more fearsome. The latter passages are among the funniest in a darkly funny novel. Wittig shows how myths about lesbians function to keep women trapped in heterosexual hell. The first circle of hell "Wittig" visits is a laundromat full of souls influenced by Anita Bryant's "Save the Children" campaign against homosexuality. These souls believe lesbians are taking over the world by kidnapping, drugging, and raping straight women. When "Wittig" takes off her shirt to show she is just like them, they cry "rape" and tell her she is covered with hair. Astonished, "Wittig" looks down and sees that her body has magically grown thick, shiny hair. Another soul yells that she is covered with scales, and, indeed, the hair turns to iridescent scales, which "Wittig" finds beautiful. Finally, they point to her clitoris, remark it is as long as a finger, and threaten to cut it off, at which point Manastabal saves her from the furious mob (VN, 17–18). In a later passage, in which "Wittig" shoots enemies forcibly marrying souls, the souls hesitate to leave hell because beyond hell are fearsome lesbians, here described by one soul "Wittig" wants to save:

> Je lui demande si elle a entendue parler des lesbiennes. Mais elle:
> (Allons donc, étrangère, je vois bien que tu te moques de moi! C'est chez ces monstres qui ont des poils sur tout le corps et des écailles sur la poitrine qu'on est déporté si malgré le dressage on résiste. Mais pour le lieu, je l'ignore.)
> Et comme je lui demande dans l'étonnement où m'ont plongée ses nouvelles ce qu'il advient de celles qui ont été déportées, elle répond sans aucune hési-tation:
> (Eh bien, puisque tu me le demandes, on n'entend plus parler d'elles, soit qu'elles sont dévorées par les lesbiennes qu'on affame sur leurs terres, soit qu'il leur pousse poils et écailles à leur tour.) (VN, 105)

> (I ask her if she has heard of lesbians. But she:
> [Go on, stranger, I see that you are making fun of me! It is to these monsters who have hair all over their body and scales on their chests that one is deported if, despite the taming process, one resists. But as for the place, I don't know where it is.]
> And as I ask her in the astonishment that her words have plunged me what happens to those who have been deported, she answers without hesitation:
> [Well, since you ask me, we don't hear anything more about them, whether they have been devoured by the lesbians who are starved on their lands, or whether they have grown hair and scales in their turn.])

Wittig opposes these myths of the monstrous lesbian to the reality of those souls who have left hell and inhabit limbo. Limbo is a lesbian bar, complete with pool tables and dancing. Manastabal and "Wittig" repair to limbo to recuperate from the horrors of hell. It is in these passages that the two characters discuss the nature of lesbian society. The inhabitants of limbo are outlaws and runaway slaves who have escaped hell but have not arrived

in paradise. Manastabal makes it clear to "Wittig" that life in limbo, although
certainly superior to that in hell, is a hard one. These souls are always hungry
and must become criminals, stealing crumbs from the dominant society. While
Manastabal and "Wittig" admire their courage and beauty, the latter laments
that they can save other souls only one at a time and at that rate it will take a
hundred years to save all the souls in hell (VN, 46).

The souls in limbo must arm themselves and their lovers and fight a constant battle for survival in a hostile world. "Wittig" comments that places such
as the bar are not only "precious and necessary" but also "precarious and rare"
(VN, 108). The strength of the inhabitants is developed by hard apprentice-
ships in warfare and running constantly, but in circles. Manastabal reiterates
to "Wittig" that there is no river one can cross and be free. They are few to
arrive because there is no place at which to arrive. Further, one cannot maintain relationships with the souls in limbo. As Manastabal says, "On les croise.
On les connaît à peine. On leur parle peu. On les laisse passer" (One crosses
their path. One barely knows them. One speaks little to them. One lets them
pass by.) (VN, 109).

As this last quotation illustrates, the pronouns change in limbo. The *on*
contrasts sharply with the ils and elles of the hell passages. It is both impersonal
and inclusive because on is conversationally used to mean "we." "Wittig" and
Manastabal may be only passing through limbo for a brief respite, but they
identify with the souls found there.

Further, it is in limbo that "Wittig" comes slowly to understand her relationship to the souls in hell and those in limbo. "Wittig's" journey is an intellectual and emotional one as well as a physical voyage. Early in the book the
character is alternately naive, frustrated, enraged, and condescending toward
the souls in hell. She rails at the impassive Manastabal, whose superlative
patience makes her seem distant and cold. Manastabal teaches "Wittig" that
she must develop "la passion active," which alone leads one out of hell. This
passion has no name, although it is usually called "compassion," a word too
weak for the violent and powerful emotion Manastabal feels. It is related to
sexual desire:

> La passion qui conduit à ce lieu tout comme l'autre coupe les bras et les jambes,
> noue le plexus, affaiblit les jarrets, donne la nausée, tord et vide les intestins,
> fait voir trouble et brouille l'ouïe. Mais aussi tout comme l'autre elle donne
> des bras pour frapper, des jambes pour courir, des bouches pour parler et des
> facultés pour raisonner. (VN, 108)

> (The passion that leads to this place [Limbo] like the other [passion] stuns one,
> knots the plexus, weakens the ankles, causes nausea, twists and empties the
> intestines, troubles vision and muddles hearing. But also, just like the other

one, it gives one arms to strike with, legs for running, mouths for speaking and faculties for reasoning.)

It is only after this lesson that "Wittig" is allowed to witness the passage of the lesbians of limbo into paradise.

"Wittig" and Manastabal arrive magically in paradise six times before the final passages, in which they enter definitively. "Wittig" must earn a place in paradise if she is to rejoin her beloved among the angels. Each paradise segment represents a new step in "Wittig's" understanding of her place among the souls of hell, limbo, and paradise. More important, "Wittig" can remain in paradise only if she can find the necessary words. Manastabal tells her in the first paradise sequence that one lands in paradise via compassion, but that word is too hackneyed to describe paradise fully. "Wittig" is stunned that no one has already found the needed words and that the task is left to her. It is clear, then, that the writer Wittig must create a new language, a new vision of paradise. It will end by being an opera—*The Beggar's Opera* is invoked by Manastabal (*VN*, 47).[33] "Wittig" must struggle to find the language of the angels, and Manastabal tells her it must be a literal and not a figurative one. It is in deepening her empathy with the souls in hell and coming to understand how heterosexuality functions to keep them there that "Wittig" can win a permanent place with her beloved.

The first paradise segment is one of the few places where anatomical sex is mentioned.

(Dis-moi, Manastabal mon guide, depuis quand les anges ont-ils un sexe?[34] On m'a toujours dit pourtant qu'ils n'en avaient pas. Je peux d'ici même distinguer clairement leurs vulves quoiqu'on ne m'ait pas appris à le faire dans mon jeune âge et que par la suite on ait voulu me faire croire qu'elles étaient invisibles.)
Et comme je me suis mise à crier (c'est un miracle, Manastabal mon guide) une série de dykes ont apparu, nues sur leurs motos, leur peau brillant, noire ou dorée et l'une après l'autre elles ont sauté la colline, disparaissant dans un buisson de fleurs. (*VN*, 21)[34]

([Tell me, Manastabal my guide, since when do angels have a sex? They always told me that they didn't have one. I can even from here distinguish clearly their vulvas even though no one taught me to see them when I was young and even later they wanted to make me believe they were invisible.]
And as I cried out [it's a miracle, Manastabal my guide] a series of dykes appeared, nude on their motorcycles, their skin shining, black or golden, and one after the other they jumped the hill, disappearing into a hedge of flowers.)

"Wittig's" amazement at seeing their vulvas is contrasted with the invisibility of female genitalia imposed in her childhood and by the religion in which she was raised. Paradise is thus a coming out, as illustrated by the invocation of the traditional Gay Pride parade led by Dykes on Bikes. This massive demonstration of solidarity and defiance of the isolation of the closet is echoed at the end. Paradise is not attained alone. "Wittig" enters it amid a vast crowd of souls, marching out of hell to be welcomed by an equally large crowd of angels. The final paradise passage is not numbered (it would be the seventh heaven, to which "Wittig" had referred in an earlier visit to paradise). It depicts a huge picnic on the hills of San Francisco. "Wittig" has found the words and revels in long lists of sounds, colors, foods, utensils, and musical instruments. Paradise is an overflowing of words, celebrating the coming together of all these souls in that quintessential institution of lesbian community, the potluck supper.[35]

As this discussion of *Virgile, non* demonstrates, Wittig's lesbian is defined as an outlaw—one who breaks the laws of compulsory heterosexuality. Those laws rule in hell, and Wittig shows the multiple ways lost souls are forced or induced to remain there.[36] But her lesbians do not escape to somewhere outside the system, as the precarious and hazardous life in limbo illustrates. Further, the lesbian characters, including "Wittig," cannot separate themselves from the souls in hell. Indeed, "Wittig" must learn painfully to understand the mechanisms of hell and try to rescue as many souls as possible or risk never attaining paradise. Butler's statement that "Wittig's lesbian-feminism appears to cut off any kind of solidarity with heterosexual women" and constitutes a "separatist prescriptivism" would appear to run counter to the evidence in the novel.[37]

It is also evident that lesbian communities as presently constituted are not the goal of Wittig's revolutionary feminist theory. If paradise has some elements in common with that community, it also is a magical place populated with angels and cherubim. It is up to the reader to imagine paradise—just as the character "Wittig" must invent her own. What is certain from the paradise passages in *Virgile, non* is that paradise can be definitively reached only by first taking the terrible risk of leaving hell and taking along as many souls as possible.

Further, it is not absolutely clear that one must be anatomically female to arrive in Wittig's paradise. Although she does say the angels have vulvas, this is in the very first visit, and "Wittig" is hopelessly naive at that point, provoking Manastabal's derision. In the final passages Wittig refers to the *anges* (a masculine noun) with the feminine pronoun *elles* in one sentence. But given the usage of elles as a universal pronoun in *Les guérillères*, can one infer that the angels are biologically female? Or is Wittig implying that only lesbians—those who break the laws of heterosexuality—arrive in paradise? Given her constant reiteration in her essays that she envisions a new social contract in which the categories of sex have been abolished, I think she intends to exclude from her vision of paradise only those who want to keep those categories: the ennemis and those âmes damnées who collude with them to keep hell functioning.

Given Wittig's repeated insistence in both essays and fiction that it is the division of humanity into men and women bound by obligatory heterosexuality that creates an oppressive relation of exploitation, it is hard to explain Ostrovsky's justification of Wittig as a universal writer based on her potential appeal to readers who identify as heterosexual. Although I agree with Ostrovsky that Wittig's fictions and dramas are great works of literature worthy of the detailed attention Ostrovsky has paid them, I believe she has misinterpreted the passages in "The Trojan Horse" and elsewhere that discuss the universalization of the (minority) writer's point of view. That is because Ostrovsky, like some other critics, uses the terms *lesbian* and *heterosexual* to refer to individual sexual tastes or object choices, whereas Wittig's project is to view them as material, social categories based on whether one accepts the laws of patriarchal society or breaks them, becoming the "outlaw lesbian."

It is in her essays on writing that Wittig articulates her theory of the universalization of a writer's point of view. Typically, her style here is both deceptively simple and philosophically complex. In order to understand what she means by "universalization," we must first explore her conceptions of language, of the nature of literature, and finally of the role of the writer in relation to social realities.[38]

Wittig's apprenticeship as a writer came under the powerful influence of the *nouveau roman* of the 1950s and 1960s, a movement that renewed the novel by focusing attention on the formal elements of the French novel. Wittig cites as influential models Sarraute, Beckett, Butor, Pinget, Ollier, Robbe-Grillet, and Simon.[39] These writers were reacting against two tendencies present in earlier French literature—Balzacian realist novels and the politically committed novel called for by Sartre (the *littérature engagée*), which put the novel in service of a specific ideology. As she notes, if one writes out of ideological commitment to a group, "What would happen to the writer if the group which one represents or speaks for stopped being oppressed? Would the writer then have nothing more to say? Or what would happen if the writer's work were banned by the group?" (*SM*, 69). The theme of the work is but one among many of the formal elements of the literary work and cannot, according to Wittig, be separated from them without doing violence to the works' literary status.

Yet, as Wittig observes, a writer's task is fundamentally different from that of other artists because the medium of the writer is language, which is also used in nonliterary ways. There are two kinds of language, then. Ordinary language, that of politics, history, and ideology, uses words in their abstract form—meaning is everything. For a writer, however, "Words are everything" (*SM*, 70–71). Moreover, a writer must deal with the materiality of the language and strip words of conventional meaning, treating them as raw material in order to create the shock that makes a war machine of literature (*SM*, 72). Other uses of language, like those of history, politics, and ideology, make it appear that one can split content and form—just as Marxism splits the material/economic realities from the languages and ideologies that express them. It is here that Wittig makes it clear she is not an idealist in the classic philosophical or Marxist sense. For her, one cannot split form and content, body and soul, abstract and concrete. Rather, language must be reintegrated so that "words come back to us whole again" (*SM*, 73). The meaning of a literary text is derived not only from the ordinary sense of words but also by their disposition and arrangement. A writer's task, then, is to deal with literary forms and through them create new meaning.

Wittig does not mean that the literary text is therefore divorced from social and political life. Rather, it operates "indirectly" by altering the nature of language and giving back its full power. Wittig insists several times on the material and physical operations of language on people. The "symbolic order," which includes all kinds of discourses, is directly linked to the exercise of power. She sees a continuum between the symbolic order and political/economic structures, which impose abstraction on matter "and can shape the body as well as the mind of those it oppresses" (*SM*, 58). No sign, nothing that signifies, can escape the political, and Wittig stresses the "material oppression of individuals by discourses" (*SM*, 25). Current debates about hate speech, particularly the U.S. military's "don't ask, don't tell" policy that equates speech with action, illuminate the ways in which language constitutes a potentially oppressive action.[40]

The work of a writer is therefore to renew language by manipulating its forms, which then create new meanings. But intervening in the history of forms raises another problem: Women, especially lesbians, have been excluded from the process of making meaning. In all domains, men have appropriated the position of the universal subject who is entitled to speak. Wittig expands on Beauvoir's insight that men are the universal, women the other. "The abstract form, the general, the universal, this is what the so-called masculine gender means, for the class of men have appropriated the universal for themselves. One must understand that men are not born with a faculty for the universal and that women are not reduced at birth to the particular. The universal has been, and is continually, at every moment, appropriated by men. . . . It is an act, a criminal act, perpetrated by one class against another" (*SM*, 80).

In speaking, women must constantly mark themselves as women, using forms peculiar to them. This marking particularizes and sets them apart from the general or universal forms that men use. To alter this linguistic subordination women must alter the basic structures of the language, and Wittig has taken on this task in her fiction.

Thus, it is the unique task of any writer to alter the forms of language and of the literary work, to intervene in the ongoing history of those forms. But by doing so in a round-about way, a writer also acts on political and social history. "Language," Wittig notes, "does not allow itself to be worked upon, without parallel work in philosophy and politics, as well as economics, because, as women are marked in language by gender, they are marked in society as sex" (*SM*, 82). Here Wittig shows herself to be opposed to the Lacanian notion that the symbolic order is by its very nature phallocentric, forever excluding the "feminine." There is nothing in the nature of language and discourses per se that excludes women—it is the act of appropriation by men that does so. The solution is therefore for women to retake the power to shape discourses, and Wittig has clearly explained her strategies for doing so.[41]

It becomes clear in this context why Wittig's work is so strongly intertextual. She realizes that inventing an entirely new idiolect would not intervene in the ongoing struggle over language and literary form. Literature, like society, has a concrete and material history that a writer ignores at her peril. One of the most striking strategies she uses is to reappropriate and recreate anew the classic (male) texts of Western civilization. Parody and irony are powerful tools with which to particularize the (formerly) universal masculine, thus revealing its false claims to represent all of humankind and universalize the formerly particular feminine in order to reveal what has been silenced throughout history. This is the source of much of Wittig's humor. Throughout her work she often cites such figures as Baudelaire, Scève, Lévi-Strauss, Freud, and other canonical male writers without attribution, stripping them of their authoritative status and putting their words into a context that reshapes their meaning. In other instances, such as *Virgile, non* and *Le voyage sans fin,* Wittig takes as her pre-text canonical works like *The Divine Comedy* and *Don Quixote.*[42] By making the characters lesbians, she simultaneously claims for lesbians the right to canonical status and forces readers to reexamine the older works. Similarly, in *Brouillon pour un dictionnaire des amantes,* Wittig and Zeig claim for themselves the right to remake language and at the same time write a history of the world in which lesbians are the only actors, illuminating the fact that standard history is written as if men alone were creating it.[43] At the same time, Wittig elevates the figure of the great poet Sappho, the only canonical lesbian writer, whose body of work was almost entirely destroyed by the heterosexual regime. The important image of the lacuna or gap, so vital to the structure of *Les guérillères*, is revealed not as a failure of women and lesbians to speak in the past but the willful silencing/destruction of their words and work.

Whereas the masculine and the heterosexual are universal by the weight of this long history of appropriating language and literary forms, the feminine and the nonstraight are immediately "minoritized" and seen as particular. Wittig is acutely aware of the problem a minority writer faces—readers will focus on her difference and see the lesbian theme as the only element of her work worthy of discussion. Wittig, however, strenuously opposes such a reading. Writing of Djuna Barnes, she says Barnes dreaded being adopted by lesbians as their writer, which would reduce her work's impact as a literary "war machine." When a text is read only for the theme of homosexuality it is not seen with regard to equivalent texts, as a formal innovation, but reduced to the symbol of a political group.[44] Wittig does not want her works to be read as manifestos. Separating the theme from the other elements ignores the fictionality—the literariness—of the work.

Neither does Wittig intend that one go so far as to ignore or downplay the theme around which her work is centered. Rather, literary work by a minority writer "is effective only if it succeeds in making the minority point of view universal, only if it is an important literary work" (*SM*, 64). Proust in French and Barnes in English were forced to create their own homosexual contexts word by word, and in the process they exploded the entire form of the novel. Wittig explains the relationship between the formal linguistic and literary impact of such works and the social reality within which they are produced and read:

> On the one hand the work of these two writers has transformed, as should all important work, the textual reality of our time. But as the work of members of a minority, their texts have changed the angle of categorization as far as the sociological reality of their group goes, at least in affirming its existence. Before Barnes and Proust how many times had homosexual and lesbian characters been chosen as the theme of literature in general? What had there been in literature between Sappho and Barnes's *Ladies Almanack* and *Nightwood*? Nothing. (*SM*, 64)

A minority writer must therefore attempt, like a straight writer, to universalize her or his particular, historically determined point of view. Both must struggle to reactivate language, which has a tendency to revert always to its abstract, everyday usage. A minority writer has the additional task of battling against the "that-goes-without-saying of the straight mind" (*SM*, 65). Moreover, a minority writer must assert the validity of the minority viewpoint without having that become the single meaning of the work. For Wittig, the successful literary work is polysemic, not univocal. It alters forever the textual and the social reality of its day. She insists repeatedly that the consciousness of a writer is not transferred directly to the work but is transformed through attention to the language and the formal elements through which that viewpoint is universalized. A minority writer must pay particular attention to elements "that can be open to history, such as themes, subjects of narratives, as well as the global form of the work" (*SM*, 75).

If the work succeeds, then, it will cause readers to inhabit a new point of view, to see the work and the world afresh, and both are thus transformed. It is not, as Ostrovsky asserts, the fact that straight readers can see her work as potentially heterosexual that makes it universal. Rather, it is that all readers, of all sexualities, come to inhabit a new space in which the perspective of the lesbian writer becomes their perspective, at least for the duration of the textual journey itself. Wittig, like Barnes and Proust before her, has truly created war machines that explode in the face of the straight mind that divides humanity into masters and slaves.

NOTES

1. Monique Wittig, *The Straight Mind and Other Essays* (Boston: Beacon Press, 1992), 68–69. Hereafter cited as *SM*.

2. Diana Fuss, *Essentially Speaking: Feminism, Nature and Difference* (New York: Routledge, 1989), 2.

3. Fuss, *Essentially Speaking*, 2–3. See also chapter 3 for Fuss's discussion of Wittig, which imputes to Wittig a lesbian essentialism and misses the critical point that Wittig's materialist viewpoint, whatever other differences there may be among lesbians (making it therefore difficult to impute any given stance to "the lesbian," as Fuss correctly notes), has allowed her to home in on the one thing all lesbians have in common—rejection of the institution(s) of heterosexuality on at least some level. Rejection of the material services that heterosexual women perform for men within those institutions is a political rather than an essentialist position.

4. Naomi Schor, "French Feminism Is a Universalism," *differences: A Journal of Feminist Cultural Studies* 7, no. 1 (1995): 19.

5. Fuss, *Essentially Speaking*, 40.

6. See Nicole-Claude Mathieu, "Quand céder n'est pas consentir" in *L'arraisonnement des femmes: Essais en anthropologie des sexes*, ed. Mathieu (Paris: Éditions de l'Ecole des Hautes Etudes en Sciences Sociales, 1985), 169–245, for a brilliant analysis of how material conditions of exploitation create mental constructs which then seem to be "natural" and even "desirable" both to oppressed and oppressors. The example of the basic differences between social constructionism as usually used in American feminism and materialist feminism was given to me by Colette Guillaumin in a personal conversation on March 13, 1992.

7. Fuss, *Essentially Speaking*, 6.

8. Colette Guillaumin, "The Constructed Body," in *Reading the Social Body*, ed. Catherine Burroughs and Jeffrey Ehrenreich (Iowa City: University of Iowa Press, 1993), 40–60.

9. The beginnings of these ideas are evident in Monique Wittig, *Les guérillères* (Paris: Éditions Minuit, 1969), trans. as *Les Guérillères* (New York: Avon Books, 1973), in fictional form, but "The Category of Sex" is the first theoretical article to present them in nonfiction.

10. In an early manifesto which Wittig coauthored, the authors developed at some length the analogy of women and serfs under feudalism. The term *serf,* whose feminine form in French is "serve," admirably played upon the relation between slave/serf and service, because women's unpaid labor in the family is generally conceived of as a service rendered out of love and not as "travail" or work in the paid sense. Monique Wittig, Gille Wittig, Marcia Rothenberg, and Margaret Stephenson (Namascar Shaktini), "Combat pour la libération de la femme," *L'Idiot International* 6 (May 1970): 13–16. The original title of the manifesto was "Pour un mouvement de libération des femmes." Personal communication with Monique Wittig, Feb. 19, 1998.

11. Numerous critiques of sex-difference research have been published in recent years. See, for example, the work of Ruth Bleier and Anne Fausto-Sterling.

12. Judith Butler, *Gender Trouble: Feminism and the Subversion of Identity* (New York: Routledge, 1990), 108–9.

13. Cheryl Chase, "Hermaphrodites with Attitude: Mapping the Emergence of Intersex Political Activism," *GLQ* 4, no. 2 (1998), 189–93.

14. Another good example of her tendency to assert, rather than demonstrate, male dominance: "If one judges by the expressions of 'desire' that men use toward women (rape, pornography, murder, violence, and systematic humiliation), there is no desire there but rather an exercise in domination." Monique Wittig, "Paradigm," in *Homosexualities and French Literature,* ed. Elaine Marks and George Stambolian (Ithaca: Cornell University Press, 1979), 120. The insertion of the "proofs" of her point into a parenthetical list is characteristic of her assumption that readers do not need lengthy elaboration of how men oppress women.

15. Wittig, *Les guérillères;* Monique Wittig, *Virgile, non* (Paris: Éditions Minuit, 1985), trans. as *Across the Acheron* by David Le Vay and Margaret Crosland (London: Peter Owen, 1987). Hereafter cited as *VN.* The short stories are reprinted in *Paris-la-politique et autres histoires* (Paris: P.O.L., 1999). "Le jardin" was formerly entitled "Un jour mon prince viendra."

16. It is surprising to see her referred to as reworking a "Lacanian presumption" by Judith Butler in *Bodies That Matter* (New York: Routledge, 1993), 259, and even as a Freudian/Lacanian by Catherine Nelson-McDermott in "Postmodernism Meets the Great Beyond: *Les guérillères* and *Le corps lesbien," Canadian Review of Comparative Literature/Revue Canadienne de Littérature Comparée* 21 (Sept. 1994): 326, 328. Wittig adamantly rejects all forms of psychoanalysis in "The Straight Mind," as well as in the entry for "Inconscient" in Monique Wittig and Sande Zeig, *Brouillon pour un dictionnaire des amantes* (Paris: Grasset, 1976), trans. as *Lesbian Peoples: Material for a Dictionary* (New York: Avon Books, 1975).

17. The many studies of Wittig's techniques and stylistic innovations are too numerous to list here. See especially Dianne Crowder, "Amazons and Mothers? Monique Wittig, Hélène Cixous, and Theories of Women's Writing," *Contemporary Literature* 24, no. 2 (1983): 117–44; Erika Ostrovsky, *A Constant Journey: The Fiction of Monique Wittig* (Carbondale: Southern Illinois University Press, 1991); and the work by Namascar Shaktini and Marthe Rosenfeld listed in the bibliography in this volume.

18. Butler, *Gender Trouble,* 118, 120.

19. Butler, *Gender Trouble,* 119, 125.

20. Nelson-McDermott, "Postmodernism," 326; Annemarie Jagose, *Lesbian Utopics* (New York: Routledge, 1994), 3.

21. Judith Roof, "Lesbians and Lyotard: Legitimation and the Politics of the Name," in *The Lesbian Postmodern,* ed. Laura Doan (New York: Columbia University Press, 1994), 55.

22. Ostrovsky is the principle although not the only critic in this line. Mary McCarthy's influential review of *L'opoponax* began this line of reasoning as she argued that the book is not just about lesbians but represents "Everybody's Childhood," the title of her review in *The New Statesman* 72, no. 15 (1966): 90, 92–94. It is true that most critics in the 1970s and 1980s treat Wittig as a "lesbian" writer, especially in reference to *Le corps lesbien* (Paris: Éditions Minuit, 1973).

23. Monique Wittig, *L'opoponax* (Paris: Éditions Minuit, 1964), trans. Helen Weaver (New York: Simon and Schuster, 1966); Ostrovsky, *Constant Journey,* 29–30. Ostrovsky also goes to great lengths to avoid using the word *lesbian* to describe Wittig's characters and themes and criticizes as limited or narrow any interpretation centered on lesbianism.

24. Wittig and Zeig, *Brouillon,* 94.

25. Wittig, "Paradigm," 115. Hereafter cited as "P." This essay was not included in the English version of *The Straight Mind* but is included in the French version, *La pensée straight.*

26. Wittig, *Les guérillères,* 86 (Fr. ed.), 61 (Eng. ed.).

27. Catherine Nelson-McDermott views the (male) converts as proof that this is a "totalitarian Utopian society" in which "men must become women or be destroyed" and the lesbian, as a marginalized figure, reinforces the system of power/dominance/violence ("Postmodernism," 326–27). The elles and ils in this novel, however, are not women and men, and the war is clearly one in which male dominance (and those who would perpetuate it) are under attack rather than male individuals themselves. Wittig has explained that the elles are intended to situate readers in a space where categories of sex do not exist, and that this is the utopian aspect of the text. The elles exist only at the level of the fiction for the duration of the reading. Monique Wittig, "Quelques remarques sur *Les guérillères,*" *L'Esprit Créateur* 34, no. 4 (1994): 119.

28. Wittig, *Le corps lesbien,* 86–87 (Fr. ed.), 78–79 (Eng. ed.). Wittig uses / and // to split first-person pronouns, indicating the alienation of the the lesbian lover from literary traditions.

29. Namascar Shaktini, "Monique Wittig's New Language," *Pacific Coast Philology* 24, nos. 1–2 (1989): 88–89.

30. Wittig prefers the English translation, "lost souls," rather than the more literal "condemned souls" because the former implies no moral judgment. They do not deserve to be in hell. Personal communication with Monique Wittig, Feb. 19, 1998.

31. In the novel, Wittig uses parentheses in place of quotation marks, as evidenced in this passage.

32. All English translations from *Virgile, non* are my own.

33. The intertextual reference is to Berthold Brecht and John Gay.

34. The word *sexe* refers more specifically to genitalia than does its English counterpart. I am grateful to the anonymous reviewer who suggested that I point out this difference.

35. Ostrovsky, *Constant Journey,* 157, notes that "Wittig" moves from monolog to dialogue to enchanted silence contemplating paradise and finally to music (the angels' opera) as the character moves from narcissism to compassion or "passion active" and finally to musical celebration.

36. Wittig emphatically intends hell to be understood as heterosexuality. A segment origi-

nally written for the novel became a separate text depicting lesbian hell: "Paris-la-politique." Personal communication with Monique Wittig, April 12, 1996.

37. Butler, *Gender Trouble,* 127.

38. For an excellent discussion of the problems the notion of "universalization" poses within current feminist theory, see Schor, "French Feminism."

39. Wittig, "Quelques remarques," 117.

40. For extended treatment of the complex relation between speech and political actions see Judith Butler, *Excitable Speech: A Politics of the Performative* (New York: Routledge, 1997).

41. Monique Wittig, "The Mark of Gender," in *The Poetics of Gender,* ed. Nancy K. Miller (New York: Columbia University Press, 1986), 63–73; Wittig, "Quelques remarques."

42. Monique Wittig, *Le voyage sans fin,* published as a special issue of the journal *Vlasta* 4 (1985) on Monique Wittig.

43. An exploration of how this work uses the genre of the dictionary appears in Kristine Anderson, "Encyclopedic Dictionary as Utopian Genre: Two Feminist Ventures," *Utopian Studies* 2, nos. 1–2 (1991): 124–30.

44. In discussing Wittig's ideas about language and what happens when she and Zeig translated *Brouillon* into English, Kristine Anderson notes that reviewers almost ignored the English version, and *Library Journal* recommended it only to libraries that had a strong interest in lesbian literature—a marginalization she attributes to the English title *Lesbian Peoples.* See "Lesbianizing English: Wittig and Zeig Translate Utopia," *L'Esprit Créateur* 34, no. 4 (1994): 99.

7

A New Grammar of Difference: Monique Wittig's Poetic Revolution

Linda M. G. Zerilli

Elles disent qu'elles partent de zéro.
Elles disent que c'est un monde nouveau qui commence.

(They say they are starting from zero.
They say that it's a new world that's beginning.)
    —Monique Wittig, *Les guérillères*

How does one start from zero? How does a new world begin? These questions arise rereading Monique Wittig's 1969 text within the time-space of fin de siècle American feminism, a feminism which, notwithstanding its constitutive diversity, seems unable to conceive of radical novelty, spontaneous beginning. Beginning means not utopia—feminism is clearly characterized by a utopic dimension—but an event that would be something other than what Kant called "the continuation of a preceding series."[1] Indeed, the idea of something without precedent must seem either naive or foreign to feminists, for whom the question of agency and social change has entailed the "resignification" of gender norms rather than emergence of the new. Therein lies the outrageous wager of Wittig's revolutionary text, *Les guérillères:* to break the series, to create the unprecedented—a new grammar of difference.

Feminist receptions of *Les guérillères* in terms of preexisting categories—"science fiction," "lesbian literature," or "committed literature"—are testimony to the general ambivalence that feminism has toward the idea of spontaneous beginning.[2] But such ambivalence is hardly unique to feminism. As Hannah Arendt argues, the "problem of the new" haunts the entire spectrum of Western philosophy as well as political theory and praxis. At bottom, she claims, the new confronts us with the problem of freedom, with radical contingency—the "abyss of nothingness that opens up before any deed that cannot be accounted for by a reliable chain of cause and effect and is inexplicable in Aristotelian categories of potentiality and actuality" (*LMW,* 208). Although thinkers like Kant knew that "an act can only be called free if it is not affected or caused by anything preceding it," writes Arendt, they could not explain it within what they saw as the "unbreakable sequence of the time continuum," within which every act appears as the continuation of a series (*LMW,* 210).[3] So unable have philosophers been "to conceive of radical novelty and unpredictability," says Arendt (citing Henri Bergson) that "even those very few who believed in the *liberum arbitrium* have reduced it to a simple 'choice' between two or several options, as though these options were 'possibilities . . . and the Will was restricted to realizing one of them. Hence they still admitted . . . that everything is given."[4]

According to Arendt, the problem of the new has confounded not only "professional thinkers" but "men of action, who ought to be committed to freedom because of the very nature of their activity, which consists in 'changing the world,' and not in interpreting or knowing it." They, too, have covered over "the abyss of pure spontaneity" with "the device, typical of the Occidental tradition . . . of understanding the *new* as an improved re-statement of the old" (*LMW,* 198, 208, 216). This device is at work in the paradigmatic act of freedom: the founding of a new body politic. Thus it was that the Romans turned to Virgil to explain the founding of their republic as a revival of Troy. Thus it was that America's founding fathers turned to the Romans when they, too, faced the "abyss of freedom." Desperate to anchor their free act in tradition and thereby legitimate it, they tried to solve the "riddle of foundation—how to re-start time within an inexorable time continuum" (*LMW,* 214)—in effect by denying that the sequence of temporality had been broken at all.

In light of these remarks on the ambivalence that philosophers and political actors have had toward radical novelty, one might be tempted to make an exception of Wittig's account of the new and call it fantasy or just literature. Who would not grant fiction's right to creation, whose instrument is radical imagination? But that concession is a restriction that repeats the denial of the new and thus of freedom. Is not that why philosophers and "men of action," otherwise busy denying both, have been quite willing to recognize the creative imagination of the artistic genius?[5]

Indeed, fiction's right to creation appears suspect once we recognize that the restriction of the radical imagination to the domain of art is deeply connected to the trivial status accorded to the fictive in philosophy, political theory, and other social discourses. According to Ernesto Grassi, the fictive is at best associated with rhetorical figures that function as an aid to reason, human beings being what they are—namely, passionate creatures in need of images. As

Cornelius Castoriadis puts it: "The fictive has no status in ontology or in the preontology implicit in one's native tongue; it is only an inconsistent, enfeebled variant of what is not," that is, the positive expression of what every rational person knows is unreal. Moreover, "a full recognition of the radical imagination [in art] is possible only if it goes hand in hand with the discovery of the other dimension of the radical imaginary, the social-historical imaginary."[6] Until we recognize the capacity for radical imagination as a fundamental human one rooted not in the subject but in praxis, and which animates the social, historical, and political domains, creative imagination will remain an empty concept limited to the uniqueness of the individual genius and to (supposedly) politically irrelevant domains like art.

Radical imagination creates "phenomena," as Wittig puts it, "which as yet have no name, either in science or philosophy." This unmotivated positing of new forms is what Grassi, following the Italian humanist tradition, calls *ingenium* ("the viewing of unexpected relationships between sensory appearances"). Like Castoriadis, Grassi sees this ingenious activity not as the privilege of the artist but as an ordinary human practice that "enables us to surpass what lies before us in sensory awareness."[7] In contrast to reproductive imagination, the act of surpassing what is given in sensibility does not represent that which is absent in intuition or recombine already existing elements. It "finds the distinction of like and unalike within and from itself." In other words, says Grassi, "only through this comparison [i.e., analogical, metaphorical activity] do sensory phenomena acquire their meaning."[8] Ingenium is not the other of reason, language, and cognition. Providing the minimal order or logic necessary for the concept, ingenious activity, as Grassi writes, "outlines the basis or framework of rational argument; it comes 'before' and provides that which deduction can never discover." Imagination is the condition for thought, knowledge, and judgment.[9]

When Wittig writes of the radical creation of phenomena that have no name in existing social discourses, then we should think of that process as one which, by transferring [*metapherein*] meanings to sensory appearances (i.e., metaphorically) builds the minimal structure of a world. If it is the case that rational language—and activities we associate with it, judging, thinking, and knowing—are parasitic upon this archaic language, as both Grassi and Castoriadis argue, then the archaic language of images and metaphors generated by radical imagination is of critical importance for understanding what does and can appear as part of our world. The fact that this language is able only to manifest (show by leading before the eyes) and not demonstrate (show something upon the basis of reasons) in no way alters its importance for feminists like Wittig or anyone else concerned with generating frameworks in which it would be possible to create phenomena that have no name in our current system of reference and to affirm freedom, contingency, or the new. If "fantasy is defined as the activity of letting appear [*phainesthai*]," specifically, letting something unreal (nonphenomenal) appear by way of discovering similitudes among unrelated things, as Grassi argues, then *Les guérillères* is indeed a work of fantasy. It "leads before the eyes [*phainestha*]" that which is not cognizable (i.e., does not show itself in the concept).[10]

That which does not show itself in the concept, that which Wittig's fantasy text lets appear, is a space and form of human association that has no reality under the "category of sex" and no voice in the "social contract" based on heterosexuality, the "it-goes-without-saying." Discovering that she can no more define what "the social contract is" than she can say "what heterosexuality is," Wittig observes, "I confront [in both cases] a nonexistent object, a fetish, an ideological form which cannot be grasped in reality, except through its effects, whose existence lies in the mind of people, but in the way that affects their whole life, the way they act, the way they move, the way they think." Within the frame of this "heterosexual social contract," she writes, "homosexuality appears like a ghost only dimly and sometimes not at all."[11] Rather than denounce the social contract as a fraud, Wittig's surprising answer to the unreality of nonheterosexual practices in the social contract is to call for its creation anew as a genuine practice of freedom and voluntary association. The amazing achievement of *Les guérillères* is not to demonstrate (with concepts or arguments) but to lead before the eyes (with images and metaphors) the radical reformulation of the heterosexual social contract.[12]

What interests me about *Les guérillères* as a work of fantasy, then, is not the appearance of the new as a radical act of artistic genius but the textual elaboration of freedom (understood as the human power of beginning) and the new social contract.[13] The question of what Kant called "the faculty of beginning spontaneously a series in time" concerns not the imaginative power of the artist (Monique Wittig) to begin anew but the potential space of freedom that her texts at once inaugurate and celebrate: a space in which to "reformulate the social contract as a new one," as she puts it, a space in which what is presently a mere "ghost" can appear and become part of our sense of the real.[14]

Reading Wittig in terms of the question of freedom, I want both to interrupt the tendency of second- and third-wave feminism to conceive freedom as a property of individual will, which entails questions of identity or its failure, and relocate freedom in the public space as a practice of human association. For Wittig, freedom is a political phenomenon—a property of the I-can, not the I-will—that is inconceivable outside the realm of action and speech. Wittig's political essays sometimes voice the wish to retreat to the stoic position of the solitary subject and its putative inner freedom—"If ultimately we are denied a new social order, which therefore can exist only in words, I will find it in myself."[15] That wish, however, is more the expression of frustration at the anticipated defeat of the struggle for a very different kind of freedom.[16]

The freedom that concerns Wittig has an abyssal structure. It is not given in advance in the form of potentiality, it is not made necessary by something in the relations of oppression, and it is not legitimated by anything outside itself. It is a beginning that is completely arbitrary, contingent, and, thus, in Arendt's words, "could just as well have been left undone" (*LMW*, 207). To appreciate Wittig's dramatization of this abyss we need to loosen the hold of past receptions of her work, most of which fail to take seriously—or even see—the question of political freedom in it. This failure is testimony not only to the general ambivalence that feminism has toward freedom but also to the way in which questions of identity and its failure have come to define our approach to some of the most important texts of second- and third-wave feminism.

Judith Butler's well-known critique of Wittig as a humanist, for example, focused exclusively on the question of identity and neglected the problem of freedom (or, at best, redefined it in terms of identity) in Wittig's texts.[17] Butler's reading served for many American feminists as the definitive verdict on Wittig's work, which is stunningly absent from 1990s' feminist debates.[18] This dismissal of Wittig is not reducible to Butler's critique, let alone caused by it, but symptomatic of the dominant problematic of feminism at the time, namely, identity. Not surprisingly, then, to the extent that Wittig's work was not dismissed, it was assimilated to the feminist practice of radical doubt, which characterized the dominant strand of the category of "women" debates. This assimilation distorts the real promise of Wittig's work, which is not to put sex into doubt but to dramatize the space and practice of freedom, the power of beginning and new modes of human association.

The Limits of Doubt

Let us approach Wittig's texts afresh, then, as texts that concern political prac-tices of freedom and human association, collective attempts to begin spontane-ously a new series in time. The series that Wittig would break goes under the name *normative heterosexuality.* Breaking this series amounts to restarting time for Wittig because "heterosexuality is always already there in all our mental categories." It is always already there in our founding myths "as something that *has* not changed, *will* not change." It is there in our language: *"fathers, mothers, brothers, sisters,* etc., whose relations can be studied as though they had to go on forever." Both a system of reference "we cannot think outside of" and a political relationship that originally had nothing ontological about it, heterosexuality is a "social contract" to which no one formally consented but to which we say yes every time "we talk a common language, as we do now."[19]

We should not be deceived by Wittig's straightforward account of sex as a politically constructed category.[20] What she calls the "'already there' of the sexes" is an exceedingly complex problem, one inadequately addressed by the feminist commonplace "sex/gender is constructed."[21] Once a radical response to the idea of sex/gender as natural, this commonplace, over the course of time, has led to the mistaken view that sex/gender, being constructed, can be seen as just that and revealed as contingent, usually through an incredible act of intellection and skeptical doubt. This act turns on the mistaken idea that we could obtain an external standpoint from which to see cultural artifacts and practices like sex and gender as wholly constructed. In addition to highly problematic assumptions about the practice of doubting (e.g., that we could doubt all gender all at once), the basic fallacy of this approach is to confuse truth with meaning. For feminism, sexual difference concerns meaning, not merely truth or cognition. What is cognizable under rules in a (determinative) judgment is called "sex difference," and it is the proper (and, in principle, knowable) object of the social and biological sciences. The criteria that support judgments of binary sex difference are not grounded in putatively apodictic first principles but rooted in relatively stable modes of human praxis. They are what Wittgenstein calls a prior agreement in judgments, in our forms of life. These criteria are not beyond question and, in fact, have been questioned by feminists. What persists once binary sex difference as an object of knowledge is destabilized (e.g., once we "know" there are at least five sexes not two, as Anne Fausto-Sterling reminds us) is sexual difference as both a question and condition of meaning, understanding, and action.[22] It is a question we do not stop thinking about and a condition we do not eliminate once we know that binary sex difference is a contingent social and historical construct.[23]

To engage sexual difference as a question and condition of meaning, understanding, and action rather than truth or knowledge, then, is to engage not one's cognitive abilities but one's capacity for imagination. If Ernesto Grassi is correct to argue that an imaginative, archaic language of metaphors and images—what he calls rhetoric—is the basis of all rational speech, then the cognition that produces (and contests) knowledge of binary sex differences is itself rooted in the faculties of phantasia and ingenium.[24] This archaic language is the necessary condition for proof of sex differences, the question of a true or a false. What is more, it is a language that "entirely escapes the determination of the true-or-false." That is because, as Castoriadis reminds us, "The 'true' itself is thought starting from and by means of the presentation of its contradictory: the indeterminate from the determinate, the discontinuous with the continuous, the outside-time with time. What sense would there be in saying that the temporal figure furnished by the imagination, upon whose basis the outside-time is thought, is 'false' (or, moreover, 'true'), when, without this figure, there would be no thought of the outside-time?"[25] As Wittgenstein puts the same point, "If the true is what is grounded, then the ground is not *true*, nor yet false." Not subject to the determinations of the true-or-false, the system of reference formed by that figure/phantasm, within which our arguments about or proofs of binary sex difference have their life, is "the inherited background against which I distinguish between true and false."[26] Here we are dealing with questions of meaning, not with truth.

On the face of it, Wittig's political essays would seem to be at odds with this question of meaning, if not wholly defined by the practice of doubt. Her point appears to be that the "category of sex" is a social and political construct that poses as a universal, necessary truth, one she sets out to debunk through the assertion of counter truths (e.g., "sex is contingent"). Against this dominant reception of her work, I will show that Wittig's writing, both fiction and nonfiction, is a beautiful example of the tenacity of the category of sex and the limits of doubt. The category of sex, Wittig recognizes, poses questions of meaning that cannot be addressed through the cognitive practices of knowing and doubting. On the one hand, the problem with sex is precisely its status as truth, for "truth," as Arendt writes, "compels with the force of necessity" (*LMW*, 60). In Wittig's words: "[T]he category of sex is a totalitarian one. . . . It grips our minds in such a way that we cannot think outside of it. This is why we must destroy it and start thinking beyond it if we want to start thinking at all."[27] Thus sex as truth and necessity or destiny is at odds with freedom. On the other hand, to counter the totalitarian category of sex with a counter-truth like "there is no sex" does not touch the framework within which the truth of sex is rooted, the figure/phantasm that gives every proof within that framework its life. This recognition of the limits of doubt shapes the parameters of Wittig's revolutionary poetics: the free act that eschews truth in search of meaning and a new grammar of difference.

Understanding the limits of doubt when it comes to "the already-there of the sexes" can be deepened if we return to Arendt's account of the flight from radical contingency. The tendency to account for the new in terms of the old, Arendt argues, is accompanied by various forms of necessity, fatalism, and determinism. Following Bergson, she observes:

[Difficulty in acknowledging human freedom is related to] the equally valid experience of the mind and of common sense telling us that actually we live in a factual world of *necessity*. A thing may have happened quite at random, but, once it has come into existence and assumed reality, it loses its aspect of contingency and presents itself to us in the guise of necessity. And even if the event is of our own making, or at least one of its contributing causes—as in contracting marriage or committing a crime—the simple existential fact that it now is as it has become (for whatever reasons) is likely to withstand all reflections on its original randomness. Once the contingent has happened, we can no longer unravel the strands that entangled it until it became an *event*—as though it could still be or not be. (*LMW*, 31)[28]

The difficulty we experience reflecting on this original randomness does not amount to a failure on our part, which could be corrected by better knowledge of contingency. As Arendt explains, "The impact of reality is overwhelming to the point where we are unable to 'think it away'; the act appears to us now in the guise of necessity, a necessity that is by no means a mere delusion of consciousness or due only to our limited ability to imagine possible alternatives." This difficulty lies "at the root of many of the paradoxes of freedom" (*LMW*, 30). On the one hand, Arendt suggests, to assume that "everything real must be preceded by a potentiality as one of its causes implicitly denies the future as an authentic tense" (*LMW*, 15). On the other hand, that assumption and denial seem to be part of the fabric of human reality itself. Even if we *know* that truth claims are out of place when it comes to causality—a point Arendt never tires of repeating—that does not mean we will stop making them or thinking of human affairs in terms of causality.[29]

According to Arendt, every story—not just fiction, but every account of what is—eliminates as the condition of its telling the "accidental elements." It is not that no one storyteller could possibly enumerate all elements that composed an event but that "without an a priori assumption of some unilinear sequence of events having been caused necessarily and not contingently, no explanation of any coherence would be possible" (*LMW*, 140). The question would be, Could one tell a story that recognizes contingency, which shows not just what has been—*factum est*—but that "it could have been otherwise"? If Arendt is right we cannot eliminate causality from the telling of a story, but perhaps we can give an account of what has happened which, although touched, framed, and animated by causality, shows causality itself to be contingent.[30]

Sustaining the tension between causality and contingency, Arendt suggests that the problem for feminists like Wittig who would contest something (sex) that has "the quality of already-there," the *factum est,* and affirm that freedom is far more complicated than recent feminist affirmations of the contingency of sex would make it seem. Like Wittgenstein, Arendt helps us understand why we are mistaken to think we could obtain an external standpoint from which sex would be seen as "socially constructed," as contingent.

If we frame the problem of the new in a way that accounts for the genuine difficulty we have acknowledging contingency, while holding out the possibility that we might affirm something like contingent causality, we can begin to see that we need an alternative to the idea that sex is available to radical skeptical doubt. As already there, as part of what is given, as past, sex has *become* the necessary condition for my existence. To think of myself and my actions as outside sex is the equivalent of jumping over my own shadow.[31]

The Trojan Horse in the Ordinary

What Wittig calls "the already-there of the sexes" is an (albeit, irreverent) example of Arendt's account of how contingency is transformed into necessity. Sex seems to exist as universal form in nature, "a priori, before all society."[32] "There remains within . . . culture a core of nature which resists examination." This core, which presents itself in, among other things, the "primitive concepts" and universalist pretensions of anthropology, sociology, and linguistics, says Wittig, "I will call the straight mind."[33] Organized around the ancient conception of form as the ultimate root or cause of the being of entities, the straight mind, as Wittig elaborates it, sets out sex as the necessary predetermination or boundary of the form of a possible cognition: "you-will-be-straight-or-you-will-not-be."[34] In phenomenal terms this means that what can appear is what is sexed and that what is sexed is what is.

Wittig recognizes, more explicitly than Arendt did, that what is, and has therefore become, the necessary condition of my existence is less a phenomenal than a political fact that arises, to borrow Miguel Vatter's description of necessity according to Machiavelli, "from a certain employment of symbolic and political violence on the part of orders that in this way prevent the contingent and revocable character of their origins to appear in the light of day."[35] Political and social orders, in Wittig's view, conceal, in the necessity of nature, the contingency of the category of sex and with it their own origins, thereby denying both freedom and historicity.

The origin of society and the nature of our "consent," in Wittig's telling, is not like the pact or agreement that Hobbes and Locke talked about. It is more like the social contract as it was elaborated by Rousseau, according to whom, she writes, "The social contract is the sum of fundamental conventions which 'even though they might never have been formally enunciated are nevertheless implied by living in society.'" This de facto social contract is everywhere and nowhere, for it defines our existence as speaking beings. "The first, the permanent, and the final social contract is language," Wittig declares. Language is not something each of us agreed to but a prior agreement in judgments we were born into. One can try to speak outside our language games, but then one would have nothing to say that others could understand and with which they could agree or not. *"Outlaw* and *mad* are the names for those who refuse to go by the rules and conventions, as well as for those who refuse to or cannot speak the common language."[36]

Accordingly, the mode of critique for Wittig cannot be to posit a homosexuality that would be radically outside heterosexuality, as some readers interpret her project, for she sees that there is no outside to language and the heterosexual social contract. But perhaps there is a way to inhabit and disrupt the inside (the ordinary) without succumbing to the illusion of getting outside (the external standpoint). This possibility is suggested in Wittig's image of radical writing as akin to a "war machine," a "Trojan Horse":

> At first it looks strange to the Trojans, the wooden horse, off color, outsized, barbaric. Like a mountain, it reaches up to the sky. Then, little by little, they discover the familiar forms which coincide with those of a horse. Already for them, the Trojans, there have been many forms, various ones, sometimes contradictory, that were put together and worked into creating a horse, for they have an old culture. The horse built by the Greeks is doubtless also one for the Trojans, while they still consider it with uneasiness. . . . But later on they become fond of the apparent simplicity, within which they see sophistication. . . . They want to make it theirs, to adopt it as a monument and shelter it within their walls, a gratuitous object whose only purpose is to be found in itself. But what if it were a war machine?[37]

"Any important literary work is like the Trojan Horse at the time it is produced. Any work with a new form operates as a war machine, because its design and its goal is to pulverize the old forms and formal conventions," writes Wittig. A literary war machine is not "committed literature," that is, literature "with a social theme . . . [which] attracts attention to a social problem" and becomes "a symbol, a manifesto." Committed literature is doomed to reproduce the reality it questions, she claims, it can never bring forth something new. That is because it operates at the level of meaning, of the concept, rather than at the level of letter or form.[38] "What I am saying is that the shock of words in literature does not come out of the ideas they are supposed to promote," she explains. "And to come back to our horse, if one wants to build a perfect war machine, one must spare oneself the delusion that facts, actions, ideas can dictate directly to words their form. There is a detour, and the shock of words is produced by their association, their disposition, their arrangement, and also by each one of them used separately" ("POV," 72). If one avoids this detour, says Wittig, one will produce a work populated with recognizable figures like "the homosexual," which is "only interesting to homosexuals" and fails to transform the system of reference in which that very identity appears "as a ghost or not at all" ("POV," 63).

The two insights that shape Wittig's approach to changing the heterosexual contract, then, are, first, a radical work must remain recognizable in the ordinary language it would disrupt; and, second, the work must do more than represent, with recognizable concepts, arguments, and the like, the minority point of view. If the Trojan Horse is not recognizable as a horse, it will not be taken into the city. If it is too recognizable—not too strange, that is—it will not function as a war machine. Without in any way denying the importance of the strange in the disruption of the ordinary, Wittig shows that the ordinary is what allows us to recognize the strange in a way that is potentially subversive of those aspects of the ordinary that belong to our heteronormative system of reference. "At first it looks strange to the Trojans, the wooden horse, off color, outsized, barbaric. . . . Then, little by little, they discover the familiar forms which coincide with those of a horse" ("POV," 68). Recognition of the ordinary (the familiar forms of the horse) is what allows the strange to do its subversive work. Otherwise it remains strange (an off-color, outsized, barbaric mass of wood to which no one would lay claim), nothing more.

As for the second feature of Wittig's approach, because heterosexuality as a system of reference is beyond questions of the true-or-the-false, the subversive potential of committed literature, which makes arguments and claims, is limited. This does not mean that the social ideas of committed literature do not matter but rather that how they matter will depend on that system of reference, on whose basis we decide what is true, what false, and what counts as a good argument in the first place. "A text by a minority writer is effective," writes Wittig, "only if it succeeds in making the minority point of view universal," which is to say only if it alters our system of reference. If a writer does not alter our point of view, minority characters like homosexuals will be absorbed as exceptions that prove the rule: "the that-goes-without-saying of the straight mind" ("POV," 64, 65).

Wittig's literary war machine is outside the scope of the skeptical problematic that characterizes an important strand of feminist theory. The point here is not simply to question appropriations of her work as an example of radical doubt but to reconsider what it means to say, as she does, that sex is a political category. Emphatically stressing the *political* character of the category of sex, Wittig would have us recall both that a social contract requires consent and that the heterosexual social contract is contingent. What makes sex political, however, is not the mere fact of its contingency. Everything empirical is contingent, but not everything empirical is political. Eschewing arguments put in the mouths of minority characters, the war machine of *Les guérillères* will shift our point of view with a shock of words, both recognizable and strange. It will show that the whole question of what is necessary and what is contingent cannot be decided outside the space of action itself. If the social contract will yield to our actions, to our words, as Wittig declares, it is because, in her account, action (words and deeds) and not radical doubt alters the configuration of the necessary and the contingent. There is no point at which we can say: everything is contingent, nothing is necessary; or, conversely, everything is necessary, nothing is contingent. What Miguel Vatter says of Machiavelli's political theory could be said of Wittig's work: "Everything that is 'necessary' is endowed with an event-like character: things become necessary in and through the encounter of practices and times, not outside of them, and therefore can cease to be necessary in time."[39] With that in mind let us turn to Wittig's famous war machine, *Les guérillères.*

Necessity and Narrative

"TOUT GESTE EST RENVERSEMENT" (EVERY GESTURE/ACT/DEED IS OVER-THROW/REVERSAL). This phrase opens Wittig's *Les guérillères* and is repeated in a slightly modified form at its end: *SANS RELÂCHE/GESTE RENVERSEMENT* (WITHOUT RESPITE/ACTION OVERTHROW).

Critics have rightly emphasized the importance of the phrase as a statement of the revolutionary character of Wittig's poetics.[40] The amazing achievement of action/overthrow, what Wittig calls *renversement,* however, is lost if one approaches the text, as some readers have, in terms of the description found on the back cover of the English edition: "Depicting the overthrow of the old order by a tribe of warrior women, this epic celebration proclaims the destruction of patriarchal institutions and language and the birth of a new feminist order." This description implies that renversement is a stage in a linear movement from female slavery to freedom, which accords with temporal categories—past, present, and future—of narrative form. It reduces renversement to the destruction of the old order and the founding of the new and thereby distorts the fundamental achievement of Wittig's text, which lies not in the substitution of one (feminist) order for another (patriarchal) one but in the creation of the open structure of freedom.[41] What is radical in Wittig's text, in other words, is not the overthrow of patriarchy, as most commentators seem to assume, but the refusal to install another (albeit feminist) political form in its place, one that would "found" freedom. Identical with action, as I've observed, freedom cannot be founded.[42]

Laurence Porter has argued in a short but important essay that Wittig breaks with the closed structure of traditional utopian literature and its tendency to promote a new orthodoxy, a new set of fixed values. "In her [Wittig's] fictional world, the women's oral and literary traditions form no fixed canons. The women become aware of unending semiosis: no symbol is an absolute; . . . And they refuse to worship their origins. In short, the women [in Wittig's own words] 'cultivate disorder in every form.'"[43] There is no founder and no founding text. We have "feminaries," texts whose author(s) is unknown and whose status is uncertain—"[They] are either multiple copies of the same original or else there are several kinds." Once necessary to an earlier generation of *guérillères*, the feminaries are read aloud for sheer amusement by a later generation. Composed of playful retellings of the dominant myths of the heterosexual order from a minority point of view, feminaries remain caught in the system of reference they would contest. Revaluing what has been devalued (the feminine), they fail to universalize the point of view. The rhapsodies on female genitals, for example, provoke laughter among the new generation for they represent an inverted and outdated symbolic practice. "All one can do to avoid being encumbered with useless knowledge is to heap them [the feminaries] up in the squares and set fire to them. That would be an excuse for celebrations."[44]

Although Wittig's tale "begins with a clear hypothesis: What if women governed themselves?" as Porter writes, it does not end with anything like a stable political form such as a government (of women or any other recognizable political subject). That raises the question of whether *Les guérillères* can be considered a text about the founding of a new social contract or whether it is not more properly read as a poetic account of liberation from the old, heterosexual one. That all depends on how you define the practice and the object of founding. It is true that Wittig's *guérillères* do not found a new order in the form of a government with a constitution, laws, and political bodies. What they do found is a mode of interacting with others in a wide array of settings whose sole principle is freedom.[45]

If freedom is unfoundable, present only as action, the problem for Wittig's tale would be how to sustain action, how to stall the solidification of the political event (revolution) into the political form (rule of law/government). I've argued that the persistent and irreverent questioning of origins is one way in which Wittig's warriors remain poised to unsettle established truths or, better, to keep opinions from becoming truths in the first place. But the problem of the new, with which I began this essay, runs deeper. How can Wittig forestall the conclusion that the event (revolution) is the mere effect of a preceding cause and thus the continuation of a preceding series? How can she sustain contingency and save freedom?

Consider in this context the narrative structure of Wittig's text. As I said earlier, the back cover of the English edition of *Les guérillères* leads readers to expect a story told in conformance with a rectilinear notion of time: past (there was oppression), present (there is the struggle for liberation), and future (liberation will yield a new feminist order). This leads to the sense that the end is already contained in the beginning—the actuality (reality) of the new is already present as a potentiality (possibility) in the state of female servitude—and that the sole purpose of political action is to produce something that could be foreseen or strategically planned in advance. In that case, to cite Bergson, "the possible would have been there from all time, a phantom awaiting its [political] hour."[46] If Wittig's tale is one of spontaneous beginning, how can it be squared with the "unbreakable sequence of the time continuum," especially as it is mapped by classic narrative form? If it is true that without the assumption of necessity, the story would lack all coherence, as Arendt argued, how could one tell stories of freedom?

We might approach these questions by observing, first, that Wittig's story of a new social contract is unlike traditional tales of that kind. In contrast to social contract theory's solitary subject, whose move into political society is characterized by varying degrees of necessity (fear of death, protection of property), *Les guérillères* opens with scenes of collective association. The first fragment reads, "When it rains, they [*elles*] stay in the pavillion" (*G*, 9/9). There is no pact to be signed, which would then authorize someone or some agency to act on its signers' (or their posterity's) behalf—only horizontally structured practices of social interaction.

That is why, as Erika Ostrovsky observes, "The verbs in *Les guérillères* [with the exception of the last sequence] are all in the present, are mostly transitive, and in the active voice."[47] That is also why Wittig's warriors, always out-of-doors, are continually telling stories, both monumental and everyday, of their journey to freedom. "In Hélène Fourcade's story, Trieu has deployed her troops at daybreak"; "They persuade Shu Ji to tell them the story of Nü Wa"; "One of the women relates the death of Adèle Donge and how the embalming of her body was carried out"; and "Sophie Ménade's tale has to do with an orchard planted with trees of every colour" (*G*, 92/80, 69/52). And so on. Indeed, *Les guérillères* is a motley collection of stories told by a variety of speakers about the struggle for freedom and about every imaginable event or object. The storytelling is a form of virtuosity. It is also—critically in fact—the primary mode of interacting with others, which enables a relationship to the past that is not defined by necessity.

The sheer multiplicity of the stories puts into question the necessity that obtains in every single version of a story. The same goes for the story of stories, the collective tale of freedom, in which are recorded the deeds and words of those who fought:

> The great register is laid open on the table. Every now and again one of them [l'une d'entre elles] approaches and writes something therein. It is difficult to inspect it because it is rarely available. Even then it is useless to open it at the first page and search for any sequence. One may take it at random and find something one is interested in. This may be very little. Diverse as the writings are they have a common feature. Not a moment passes without one of them [l'une d'elles] approaching to write something therein. Or else a reading aloud of some passage takes place. It may also happen that the reading occurs without any audience, save for a fly that bothers the reader by settling on her temple. (G, 53–54/74–75)

The "common feature" of these "diverse" writings is freedom. Although accessible, this collective text is "rarely available." When it is read, there is no sequence to be discerned, and in any case any possible sequence is disrupted by the random insertions of readers. Accordingly, there is little chance that the great register will turn into the kind of founding text that constrains future action on the basis of what an earlier generation found worthy of remembrance in the past.

The nonsequential character of the great register raises the larger issue of narrative structure as it bears on the question of freedom. Insofar as classic narrative form is a great contributor to the illusion of necessity, it seems significant that, as Wittig explains, "the chronological beginning of the narrative—that is, total war—found itself in the third part of the book, and the textual beginning was in fact the end of the narrative. From there comes the circular form of the book, its *gesta,* which the geometrical circle indicates as a modus operandi."[48] Indeed the phrase, *TOUT GESTE EST RENVERSEMENT,* which closes the first page of *Les guérillères,* is immediately followed by the symbol O. This symbol recalls the zero or the circle and thus the continual return to beginnings that characterizes the strategy of renversement. It takes up an entire page and appears three times in the text. It can likewise be read as creating "a tri-partite structure" and an effort to negotiate the difficulties associated with rectilinear time.[49] If we consider that *gesta* is the Latin word for deeds, we can better appreciate how the circular form of the narrative responds to the problems posed by the time continuum (i.e., every act is a mere continuation of a series; the real follows the possible) and enables Wittig to foreground the novelty of action and thus freedom.[50]

The circular movement of *Les guérillères* is not a return to the pure origin or principle of beginning. The notion that later generations of warriors are bound in some way to preserve the origin of the new society would be inconsistent with the Wittigean practice of renversement. "They say [Elles disent] that references to [the goddesses] Amaterasu or Cihuacoatl are no longer in order. They say [Elles disent] they have no need of myths and symbols. They say [Elles disent] that the time when they started from zero is in the process of being erased from their memories. They say [Elles disent] they can barely relate to it. When they repeat, This order must be destroyed, they say [elles disent] they do not know what order is meant" (G, 30/38).

What must be destroyed and what is worthy of remembrance is not the same for every generation of guérillères, just as what is necessary changes with time. As a principle of beginning, renversement is at odds with any symbolic order that supports the sanctity of origins just as it demands the continual return to origins. This return is critical, for the free act that founds the new order is always in danger of taking on the appearance of necessity. The task of renversement is to reduce every order to its beginning and thereby reanimate the contingency of its emergence, its original randomness.[51]

No-More and Not-Yet

The radical understanding of the return to beginnings just described is what prevents Wittig's warriors from founding the new on the model of the old in the form of a return to a golden age before patriarchy. "Elsa Brauer says something like, There was a time when you were not a slave, remember that. You walked alone, full of laughter, you bathed bare-bellied. You say you have lost all recollection of it, remember. . . . You say there are no words to describe this time, you say it does not exist. But remember. Make an effort to remember. Or, failing that, invent" (G, 89/126, 127). The return to beginning, in other words, is itself an invention, a creation. There is, finally, no pure origin of primary female freedom to which one could return (in memory), not least because, retrospectively seen, a free act tends to take on the form of necessity. If one cannot remember a time when one was free, that is because, as Wittig claimed, woman and man are political forms that tend to present themselves to us as necessity and as the necessary condition of what can appear and what is. Thus freedom emerges not through the rememoration of the past but through invention: the act of beginning anew.

The idea of a golden age of female freedom to which one could return assumes further that *elles* (they) form a primal community of sorts, a "we" that is already given in time. The emergence and character of this "we" is a primary problem for feminist politics and for all human communities. As Arendt notes, "No matter how this 'we' is first articulated and experienced, it seems that it always needs a beginning, and nothing seems more shrouded in darkness and mystery as that 'In the beginning'" (*LMW,* 202). The question of the "we" is at bottom a question of meaning. It cannot be answered adequately with scientific (biological, archeological, and anthropological) evidence because the "we," writes Arendt, like "all that is real in the universe and in nature," was once "an infinite improbability" (ibid.).

For Wittig, the problem is how to articulate the emergence of the "we" as something constituted by a free act, that is, without naturalizing or predetermining its appearance in the possible, in the past. The idea that the new is the reestablishment of the old, a golden age when one was not a slave, amounts to denial of this free act. Not only is the "we" (the *elles* of *Les guérillères*) not the reemergence of a collective subject once unmarked by oppression, but it is also not reducible to or merely continuous with the subject that achieves liberation from oppression, for this liberation is not ever achieved once and for all. That is why the principle of renversment opens and closes the text of *Les guérillères.* Expressing both freedom and liberation but reducible to neither, renversment (action/overthrow) is an active principle without end (*sans relâche/geste reversement*).

The very title of Wittig's work, *Les guérillères,* indicates that the passage from liberation to freedom is marked by an abyss—a free act that brings about a new world. As Erika Ostrovsky observes:

> *Guérillères* is a poetic word in that it does not designate any existing thing. . . . While it is possible to interpret *guérillères* superficially as a term that merely indicates or accentuates women's bellicose role—that is, as a cross between *guerrières* or female warriors and the feminine plural of *guerilla*—thus reducing the subject of the book to a war between the sexes, on other levels of interpretation this title has far more complex meanings. The word itself can be compared to a "war machine" that destroys an existing order or a traditional view.[52]

Guérillères is irreducible to given significations.

Elles: A Fantastic Universal

If Wittig's masterpiece yields "new figures of the thinkable" (Castoriadis), it is not limited to the figure of the guérillères. Indeed, it is not quite right to say, as Ostrovsky does, that this word or figure functions as a war machine. What "destroys an existing order or point of view" is not the poetic word *guérillères*—which, in fact, does not appear in Wittig's text save in the title itself—but the ordinary pronoun *elles.* Deeply mistranslated as "the women" in the English edition of *Les Guérillères,* the pronoun *elles* lies at the heart of Wittig's radical project to transform the social contract. One can significantly

misunderstand the nature of that project if one does not appreciate the depth
of the mistranslation. To comprehend what is at stake, let us turn first to what
Wittig says in "The Mark of Gender" about her use of elles:

> As for *Les guérillères*, there is a personal pronoun used very little in French
> which does not exist in English—the collective plural *elles* (*they* in English)—
> while *ils* (*they*) often stands for the general: *they say*, meaning *people say*. This
> general *ils* does not include *elles*, no more, I suspect, that *they* includes any
> *she* in its assumption. . . . The rare times that it is [used], *elles* never stands
> for the general and is never the bearer of a universal point of view. An *elles*
> that would be able to support a universal point of view would be a novelty in
> literature or elsewhere. In *Les guérillères*, I try to universalize the point of
> view of the *elles*. The goal of this approach is not to feminize the world but to
> make the categories of sex obsolete in language. I, therefore, set up *elles* in
> the text as the absolute subject of the world. To succeed textually, I needed
> to adopt some very draconian measures, such as to eliminate, at least in the
> first two parts, *he* [*il*], or *they-he* [*ils*]. I wanted to produce a shock for the
> reader entering a text in which *elles* by its unique presence constitutes an as-
> sault, yes, even for female readers. . . . Word by word, *elles* establishes itself
> as a sovereign subject.[53]

Considering that the use of the pronoun *elles*, as Wittig states, "dictated
the form of the book," we can begin to appreciate what is lost in the English
translation. The translator lacked the lexical equivalent for elles, but his choice
of "the women"—rather than "they"—had dire consequences: "the process of
universalization is destroyed. All of a sudden, *elles* stopped being *mankind*.
When one says 'the women,' one connotes a number of individual women,
thus transforming the point of view entirely, by particularizing what I intended
as universal." What we have is the word *women*, which appears "obsessively
throughout the text." In addition, where there are women there are men, that
is, "the it-goes-without-saying" of the heterosexual social contract that was to
be put into question in the first place.[54]

Wittig proposes the pronoun *they* for a new translation of elles. "Only with
the use of *they* will the text [*Les guérillères*] regain its strength and strangeness."[55] That strength and strangeness belongs to what I call her "Trojan Horse
of universalism," whose primary vehicle in *Les guérillères* is the pronoun *elles*.[56]
The pronoun indicates not a subject whose freedom and relation to society
would assume the problems and aporias associated with that category, but
points of view from which it becomes possible to act and see something new.
More an image than a concept, elles inhabits and haunts Wittig's text. Should
we ask who belongs to the elles, the closest thing approaching an answer would
be the randomly inserted pages on which are lists of names such as:

DIONÉ INÈS HÉSIONE ELIZA
VICTORIA OTHYS DAMHURACI
ASHMOUNIGAL NEPHTYS CIRCÉ
DORA DENISE CAMILLA BELLA
CHRISTINA GERMANICA LAN-ZI
SIMONA HEGET ZONA DRAGA. (*G*, 67/95)

Nina Auerbach complains of Wittig's lists of names: "Though these names take on their own incantatory life, the empty resonance of their sound is also the death of the real people we used to read novels to meet."[57] Commenting on this remark, Toril Moi correctly observes that it is by no means clear that the names are spoken by anyone and that Auerbach's reading expresses the wish to attribute a subject or "unitary human voice" to Wittig's polysemous text.[58]

The names, international in character, I suggest, must be read in relation to Wittig's strange use of the pronoun *elles*. On the one hand, if the names *were* subject-centered, the translation of "elles" as "the women" would make sense. It might even make sense to describe *Les guérillères* as "a blue-print for women in the future."[59] On the other hand, if elles were a hegemonic, unitary subject, there would be no sense in continually disrupting the text with lists of names. Whereas "the women" connotes particulars with no claim to universality, a unitary "elles" would connote a universal with no relation to the particular. Clearly, both the first and the second alternative is at odds with the practice of freedom in *Les guérillères*, whose central principle is not a timeless universality of being but an active practice of becoming, renversement.

What makes *Les guérillères* a truly radical text is neither its daring account of the "destruction of patriarchal institutions and language" nor its coinage of the neologism *guérillères* but its strange use of an entirely ordinary pronoun, elles. That pronoun functions not at the level of reference and the concept but at that of an archaic language of metaphor, which brings things before our eyes, allowing us to see something not obvious or given as an object of cognition (which is what "the women" suggests although it, too, is based in that archaic language). Based in the human faculty of ingenium, Grassi, follow-ing Aristotle, writes that metaphor "is characterized by a unique strangeness because it reveals something unusual and unexpected."[60]

Whereas the already there character of the category of sex provided the basis for (a false) commonality among women, the similarities among elles are not given in sensory appearances but involve the creative act of transfer-ral (metapherein) and fantasy or letting appear (phainesthai). What Wittig shows by combining two existing concepts that are normally not related (e.g., the feminine gender and the universal voice) is not a new subject, let alone a hegemonic one, but a new enunciative position, a place from which to speak and act in concert (e.g., *elles disent, elles regardent,* and *elles portent*). Her text lets something currently unreal (free social and political relationships not defined by the category of sex) appear by way of ingenium—the discovery of not identity but similarities.

What *Les guérillères* achieves is an alteration in our sense of reality by means of the archaic language of images. Wittig's text disrupts the heterosexual social contract, whose synchronic or "always already there" picture of two groups, men and women, holds us captive, to paraphrase Wittgenstein. And she does so not with argument or skeptical doubt but with the strange use of an ordinary pronoun, elles. Inhabiting the enunciative position of the universal voice, the pronoun not only exposes the exclusion of women but also makes visible the fact that every locution on the order of what "everyone says," what goes unquestioned or without saying, is the product of people speaking, acting: elles disent. Without the melancholy or pathos of radical skeptical doubt, elles shifts our frame of reference in which certain doubts never arise.

The image elles, then, is a radical creation in the ordinary. It addresses itself as an image to questions of meaning not rational truth. The point here, once again, is not to set up a false opposition between meaning and truth, rhetoric and reason, or to deny the existence of logic and concepts in rhetorical texts but to reconceptualize their relationship and their source. As Grassi writes, "A logic that holds 'conveying meanings' and metaphor as the origin and basis of the interpretation of sensory phenomena is, in contrast to rational logic, a logic of images and metaphors. It will claim to be a logic of invention and not deduction. . . . Such a logic is 'fantastic' insofar as it shows a new world, that of humanity, and makes it open to view through metaphor."[61] Like rational logic, this rhetorical logic of images and metaphors also creates a universal, only it will be a "fantastic universal" not a logically deduced—that is, rational—one.

Elles is a "fantastic universal" that must be discovered in the practice of daily life, not an abstract rational universal that can be deduced from putatively timeless and apodictic first premises. As Grassi explains, "fantastic universals" have their source not in logical deduction but in ingenium "because concrete reality is revealed through them."[62] Accordingly, elles is nothing apart from the various modes of human praxis in which it is engaged. The new social contract or world Wittig builds through the innovative use of an ordinary pronoun is based in a rhetorical practice. I have suggested that this practice is not literary in the narrow sense traditionally given to that term and to rhetoric but rather social and political.

Wittig helps us think about feminism as a rhetorical rather than a skeptical practice, and that means rethinking the relationship of thought to action. Whereas a skeptical practice suggests that we first reveal that sex is contingent and then act to change it, a rhetorical practice suggests that it is not thought but action that recovers the contingency of sex (or for that matter the original randomness of any social and political order). It is through the ingenious practice of collective action that we alter—and become aware of the possibility of altering—the relationship of the necessary and the contingent.

NOTES

This essay appears as chapter 2 in my book *Feminism and the Abyss of Freedom* (Chicago: University of Chicago Press, in press). My literal translation of the epigraph avoids David Le Vay's unfortunate introduction of *the women,* a mistranslation of the French feminine form of "they" often criticized by Wittig. I wish to thank Samantha Frost, Gregor Gnädig, Bonnie Honig, and George Shulman for their comments. I also wish to thank Ella Myers and Torrey Shanks for their help with the research and preparation of the manuscript for this essay.

1. Immanuel Kant, *Critique of Pure Reason,* B478, quoted in Hannah Arendt, *The Life of the Mind,* vol. 2: *Willing,* one-volume ed. (New York: Harcourt Brace, 1978), 205. Hereafter cited as *LMW.*

2. See, for example, Hélèn Vivienne Wenzel, "The Text as Body/Politics: An Appreciation of Monique Wittig's Writings in Context," *Feminist Studies* 7 (Summer 1981): 264–87; Nina Auerbach, *Communities of Women: An Idea in Fiction* (Cambridge: Harvard University Press, 1978); and Namascar Shaktini, "Displacing the Phallic Subject: Wittig's Lesbian Writing," in *The Thinking Muse,* ed. Jeffner Allen and Iris Marion Young (Bloomington: Indiana University Press, 1989): 195–210. Wenzel observes that Wittig's novels "take the reader on a journey through time and space, self and other, language and culture, to arrive ultimately at a genesis of a new language, and its redefinition of woman" (216). An appreciative reader of Wittig, Wenzel is not wrong to see in this redefinition the creation of all "female worlds," but her analysis tends to reproduce the category of lesbian fiction that Wittig contests. As I will discuss, Nina Auerbach expresses her distress at the loss of the "female subject" in those all female worlds. Namascar Shaktini, in contrast, recognizes that Wittig's project goes way beyond the politics of inversion and the typical idea of "lesbian fiction." I have addressed some of the problems with the reception of Wittig in "The Trojan Horse of Universalism: Language as a 'War Machine' in the Writings of Monique Wittig," *Social Text: Theory/Culture/Ideology* 25–26 (1990): 146–70; and "Rememoration or War? French Feminist Narrative and the Politics of Self-Representation," *differences: A Journal of Feminist Cultural Studies* 3, no. 1 (1991): 1–19.

3. According to Kant, phenomena must be reproducible in successive moments, for a representation takes time to be completed in my consciousness. But "if I were always to drop out of the thought the preceding representations (the first part of a line, the antecedent parts of the time period, or the units in the order represented), and did not reproduce them while advancing to those that follow, a complete representation would never be obtained" (*Critique of Pure Reason* A102). Furthermore, the reproduced representation must belong to the same whole as the present representations to which it is added. "If we

were not conscious that what we think is the same as what we thought a moment before, all reproduction in the series of representations would be useless. For it would in its present state be a new representation which would not in any way belong *to the act whereby it was to be gradually generated.* The manifold of the representation would never, therefore, form a whole since it would lack that unity which only consciousness can impart to it" (*Critique of Pure Reason* B134, emphasis added).

4. Critically discussing the relationship of the possible to the real, Bergson writes: "The fault of those doctrines—rare indeed in the history of philosophy—which have succeeded in leaving room for indetermination and freedom in the world, is to have failed to see what their affirmation implied. When they spoke of indetermination, of freedom, they meant by indetermination a competition between possibles, by freedom a choice between possibles—as if possibility was not created by freedom itself! As if any other hypothesis, by affirming an ideal pre-existence of the possible to the real, did not reduce the new to a mere rearrangement of former elements! As if it were not thus to be led sooner or later to regard that rearrangement as calculable and foreseeable! By accepting the premise of the contrary theory one was letting the enemy in. We must resign ourselves to the inevitable: it is the real which makes itself possible, and not the possible which becomes real." Henri Bergson, *The Creative Mind: An Introduction to Metaphysics,* trans. Mabelle L. Andison (New York: Citadel Press, 1992), 104.

5. As Arendt explains, philosophers like Kant, among other thinkers, saw proof of spontaneity in artistic creation (*LMW* 183).

6. Cornelius Castoriadis, "The Discovery of the Imagination," in *World in Fragments: Writings on Politics, Society, Psychoanalysis, and the Imagination,* ed. and trans. David Ames Curtis (Stanford: Stanford University Press, 1997), 213–45, 223, 245. Castoriadis develops his idea of the first imagination by following a line of thought in Book 3 of Aristotle's *De Anima.*

7. Monique Wittig, "The Site of Action," in *The Straight Mind and Other Essays* (Boston: Beacon Press, 1992), 91; Ernesto Grassi, "The Roots of the Italian Humanistic Tradition" and "Rhetoric as the Ground of Society," both in *Rhetoric as Philosophy: The Humanist Tradition,* trans. John Michael Krois and Azizeh Azodi (Carbondale: Southern Illinois University Press, 2001), 1–17, 8 and 68–101, 97.

8. Grassi, "Rhetoric as the Ground of Society," 98.

9. Ibid., 97. Castoriadis calls upon Aristotle to make a similar point: "The imagination in general, and the first imagination in particular, can be defined as one of the potentialities (or powers) of the soul that permits the latter to know, to judge, to think" ("The Discovery of the Imagination," 243).

10. The reduction of fantasy and the act of ingenium to conventional understandings of artistic practices like literature confirms the privilege accorded rational language in the Western tradition. Within this tradition, as Grassi argues, fantasy, metaphor, and every form of figurative language is ascribed to the areas of rhetoric and literature. Ernesto Grassi, *Die Macht der Phantasie: Zur Geschichte abendländlischen Denkens* (Königstein: Athenäum Verlag, 1979), xvii; on fantasy as the activity of "letting appear," see 184–87. I argue elsewhere that figurative (rhetorical) language is the basis of rational (philosophical) language. The latter is founded on first principles, which, as such, cannot be demonstrated (proven) but only shown. The implications of this shift in perspective is to emphasize the importance of changing the images (tropes and figures) that sustain our ordinary practices, including those that fall under what Wittig calls the category of sex. Zerilli, *Feminism and the Abyss of Freedom.*

11. Monique Wittig, "On the Social Contract," in *The Straight Mind and Other Essays* (Boston: Beacon Press, 1992), 33–45.

12. In contrast to feminists such as Carole Pateman, for whom the very concept of the social contract is irredeemable, Wittig argues for the radical promise of contract theory. Pateman, *The Sexual Contract* (Stanford: Stanford University Press, 1988). In contrast to contemporary contract thinkers such as Jeremy Waldron, Wittig rejects the idea that the contract is rooted in a rational act of consent and that its creation anew would likewise entail a rational act. Waldron, "John Locke: Social Contract versus Political Anthropology," in *The Social Contract from Hobbes to Rawls,* ed. David Boucher and Paul Kelly (London: Routledge, 1994), 51–72. Instead, she pursues the insight that the contract, based in language, can be altered only through a change in the rhetorical figures that support rational speaking practices. And that change comes about through praxis, not radical doubt.

13. Like Arendt, I do not want to limit the notion of spontaneity to artistic creativity. Ontologically, I want to locate it in the faculty of ingenium, the ability to see associations in otherwise discrete phenomena (Grassi and Castoriadis). Politically, I want to locate it in the practice of freedom, associating with others in public (Arendt). Both conceptions are at odds with the philosophical tradition of Kant and most of his critics. Heidegger, for example, who was critical of Kant's "recoil" from the transcendental imagination in the second edition of the first *Critique,* was also hostile to the Italian humanist tradition from which we have the idea of ingenium. Ernesto Grassi, *Einführung in die humanistische Philosophie: Vorrang des Wortes* (Darmstadt: Wissenschaftliche Buchgesellschaft, 1986), 17.

14. Wittig, "On the Social Contract," 45.

15. Ibid., 11. This attempt to found the new order in oneself is part of the practice of literature and gives rise to a text like *Les guérillères.* That text, however, makes visible a space that is public not private in character and based on voluntary association with others.

16. Wittig sometimes refers to the universal subject of her writings as a "sovereign subject." Nevertheless, what she understands under "sovereignty" has nothing in common with the sovereign subject of the Western tradition that Arendt criticizes. On the contrary, her sovereign subject is only possible in the sphere of human plurality. Wittig articulates a distinction between the freedom of the I-will and that of the I-can when she proclaims, first, that feminists "can form 'voluntary associations' here and now, and here and now reformulate the social contract as a new one," only to conclude that "if ultimately we are denied a new social order, which therefore can exist only in words, I will find it in myself." Although Wittig seems to settle for the nonworldly freedom of an Epictetus, the bulk of her political essays as well as her fiction opposes the sovereign freedom of the I-will and insists, like Arendt, on the worldly, political freedom of the I-can. Wittig, "On the Social Contract," 45.

17. According to Butler, Wittig's work is situated "within the traditional discourse of the philosophical pursuit of presence, Being, radical and uninterrupted plenitude. In distinction from a Derridean position that would understand all signification to rely upon an operational *différance,* Wittig argues that speaking requires and invokes a seamless identity of things. This foundationalist fiction gives her a point of departure by which to criticize existing social institutions. The critical question remains, however, what contingent social relations does that presumption of being, authority, and universal subjecthood serve? Why value the usurpation of that authoritarian notion of the subject and its universalizing epistemic strategies?" Judith Butler, *Gender Trouble: Feminism and the Subversion of Identity* (New York: Routledge, 1990), 118. The charge of humanism misses the political project of Wittig's work, which is not to decenter the subject (although, in contrast to Butler, that, too, can be found in her texts) but to create the objective and discursive conditions for freedom.

18. I owe this point to conversations with Teresa de Lauretis and Namascar Shaktini. An examination of the "Selected Bibliography of Monique Wittig Criticism" (pages 203–222 of this volume) compiled by Shaktini in collaboration with Diane Griffin Crowder, for example, shows that only a handful of 301 entries were written after 1990. [*Editor's note:* A study of the distribution by year of 392 items published on Wittig between 1964 and 1999 shows a progressive increase, peaking at thirty-one items in 1990, the year when the influential critique of Wittig in *Gender Trouble* appeared. From 1991 to 1999 there were only 137 items, or 15.2 per year, a drop of 50 percent.]

19. Wittig, "On the Social Contract," 43, 40.

20. I disagree with Judith Butler's assessment of Wittig's essays as somehow less sophisticated than, and noncontiguous with, literary texts. The political essays set out precisely the nature of the problem that the literary texts engage: the tenacity of the two-sex system, a system that cannot be undone through the feminist practice of doubting.

21. Monique Wittig, "The Category of Sex," in *The Straight Mind and Other Essays* (Boston: Beacom Press, 1992), 1–8.

22. Anne Fausto-Sterling, "The Five Sexes: Why Male and Female Are Not Enough," *The Sciences* (March–April 1993): 20–24; Anne Fausto-Sterling, *Sexing the Body: Gender Politics and the Construction of Sexuality* (New York: Basic, 2000).

23. I am indebted to Arendt's idiosyncratic account of the Kantian distinction between reason (*Vernunft*) and intellect (*Verstand*). Whereas the faculty of reason is concerned with matters of meaning, which animate an unending process of thinking, the faculty of intellect turns on matters of truth, which demands testable criteria. For Arendt, this distinction (between reason and intellect, thinking and knowing, meaning and truth) is at the core of her critique of the philosophical tradition. "The basic fallacy, taking precedence over all specific metaphysical fallacies, is to interpret meaning on the model of truth" (*LMW*, 15). Failure to register the distinction between questions of meaning and questions of truth is one of the many reasons that someone like Luce Irigaray is read as an "essentialist" (her advocacy of sexual difference, that is, fails to question cognition of "sex difference"); why Monique Wittig is read as a "social constructionist" (her opposition to sexual difference does question the aforementioned cognition); and why it is practically impossible to establish a dialogue between them. The tendency to treat sexual difference as if it were only a matter of truth and practices of knowing characterizes not only science but also feminism in the age of science.

24. As Cornelius Castoriadis explains, the phantasm is the basis of the imagination's capacity to generate images rather than merely reproduce objects absent to intuition. The discovery of the phantasm and thus the imagination is in Book 3 of Aristotle's *De Anima,* where we are told that "for the thinking soul the phantasms are like sensations. . . . That is why the soul never thinks without phantasm" (3.7–8). Grassi makes a similar argument about the phantasm in *Die Macht der Phantasie* (184–86).

25. Castoriadis, "The Discovery of the Imagination," 242. "If the soul never thinks without phantasm [as Aristotle affirms], the idea that most of the products of the imagination are false becomes insignificant. The true-or-false is uninteresting when it is a question of those functions of the first imagination that are the presentation of the object, separation and composition, and, finally and above all, the Schematism" (Ibid., 241).

26. Ludwig Wittgenstein, *On Certainty* (New York: Harper and Row, 1969), sec. 205, sec. 94. "The proposition is either true or false only means that it must be possible to decide for or against it. But this does not say what the ground for such a decision is like" (sec. 200).

27. Wittig, "The Category of Sex," 8. In light of Wittig's account of an omniscient heterosexuality it is easy to see why she might be read as trying to jump over her own shadow and

construct a lesbian subjectivity that would be fully outside heterosexual norms. As Judith Butler critically interprets Wittig's project, "Lesbianism that defines itself in radical exclusion from heterosexuality deprives itself of the capacity to resignify the very heterosexual constructs by which it is partially and inevitably constituted." For Butler, the problem is attenuated in Wittig's literary texts, which use the strategy of "redeployment and transvaluation." Butler, *Gender Trouble*, 128, 124. Wittig does not try to get outside heterosexuality—there is no outside, as she recognizes—but to disrupt it from within (what I call her "Trojan Horse strategy"). The disruption cannot be understood properly in terms of the strategy of resignification as Butler understands it. Wittig's project is to create new imaginary significations, which, operating at an archaic or metaphorical level, would create the minimal conditions of visibility for that which is at best a "ghost" in heterosexual frames of reference. This approach also entails a continual destruction of concepts (*renversement*), including those created by the revolutionary subject of the text, because even these modified concepts tend to repeat the figures/phantasms that belong to the heterosexual social contract.

28. Arendt takes this point from Henri Bergson, who says, "For the possible is only the real with the addition of an act of mind which throws its image back into the past, once it has been enacted. But that is exactly what our intellectual habits prevent us from seeing" (*The Creative Mind*, 100). Although Arendt seems to be saying that the past presents itself to us in a certain way (e.g., as necessity), her view is different from empiricist accounts that put meaning in the object. Whether we see an object under multiple aspects depends not on something in the object but on the space in which the object is seen. Totalitarian societies and mass societies, for example, are those in which objects present themselves under only one aspect.

29. The tension between what we know and how we act, according to Arendt, reflects the deep tension between the faculties of willing and thinking. "That is what made John Stuart Mill say that 'our internal consciousness tells us that we have a power [freedom], which the whole outward experience of the human race tells us we never use'; for what does this 'outward experience of the human race' consist of but the record of historians, whose backward-directed glance looks toward what *has been—factum est*—and has therefore already become necessary?" (*LMW*, 139).

30. This possibility is suggested in Arendt's turn to the medieval philosopher Duns Scotus, who, in contradistinction to the entire philosophical tradition before him, affirms "the contingent character of processes": "The theory that all change occurs because a plurality of causes happens to coincide, and the coincidence engenders the texture of reality." This coincidence of causes, as Arendt explains, saves both freedom and necessity. To say something "is caused contingently," as Scotus does, is to affirm that "it is precisely the causative element in human affairs that condemns them to contingency and unpredictability" (*LMW*, 138).

31. The point here is not that so-called biological sex corresponds to gender, which is factually untrue, but that any combination of the two, as well as every effort to identify differently sexed bodies, remains within a two-sex system of reference. This system cannot be doubted, denied, or jumped over. It can only be reimagined. And this imaginative language is not the production of a solitary subject but of praxis, human beings talking with one another.

32. Wittig, "The Category of Sex," 5.

33. Monique Wittig, "The Straight Mind," in *The Straight Mind and Other Essays* (Boston: Beacon Press, 1992), 21–32, 27.

34. "The consequence of this tendency toward universality is that the straight mind cannot conceive of a culture, a society where heterosexuality would not order not only all human

relationships but also its very production of concepts and all the processes which escape consciousness as well" (Wittig, "The Straight Mind," 28). On Wittig's references to the ancient conception of Being, see Monique Wittig, "Homo Sum," *The Straight Mind and Other Essays* (Boston: Beacon Press, 1992), 46–58. I have discussed in greater detail the relation of form to universality in Linda M. G. Zerilli, "This Universalism Which Is Not One," *Diacritics* 28 (Summer 1998): 3–20.

35. Miguel Vatter, *Between Form and Event: Machiavelli's Theory of Political Freedom* (Dordrecht: Kluver Academic Publishers, 2000), 9.

36. Wittig, "On the Social Contract," 41, 38. For Wittig, the objection of someone like Hume to the idea of the social contract as a historical document or pact is beside the point. The issue for her is not that we search in vain for this document let alone affirm our obligations to each other in its absence, as David Hume would have us do. What Rousseau teaches, says Wittig, is that "each contractor has to reaffirm the contract in new terms for the contract to be in existence" (Ibid., 38). But isn't that what we do when we move, act, or speak? In a sense, yes, for the contract is nothing apart from these ordinary human relations. But the very idea of the social *contract,* she suggests, also allows one to ask, Is this consent to my advantage? "Only then does it become an instrumental notion in the sense that the contractors are reminded by the term itself that they should reexamine its conditions. Society was not made once and for all. The social contract will yield to our action, to our words" (Ibid.).

37. Monique Wittig, "The Trojan Horse," in *The Straight Mind and Other Essays* (Boston: Beacon Press, 1992), 68–75, 68.

38. Monique Wittig, "The Point of View," in *The Straight Mind and Other Essays* (Boston: Beacon Press, 1992), 67; hereafter cited as "POV." Language is not only meaning, argues Wittig, but also "letter." Wittig seems to have in mind the figurative power of language, or what Ernesto Grassi calls its "rhetorical aspect." The original presence of letter is lost in meaning, much as that of rhetorical speech is lost in rational speech. "Meaning hides language [letter] from site." Wittig substitutes "letter and meaning" (which "describe the sign solely in relation to language") for the traditional semiotic distinction between signifier and signified in order "to avoid the interference of the referent prematurely in the vocabulary of the sign. Meaning is not visible, and as such appears to be outside language [i.e., given in the nature of things]." When language takes form, she writes, "it is lost in the literal meaning. It can only reappear abstractly as language while redoubling itself, while forming a figurative meaning, a figure of speech. This, then, is writers' work—to concern themselves with the letter, the concrete, the visibility of language, that is, its material form." Wittig's literary practice turns in large part on the employment of tropes and figures to combat certain political formations and their entombment in the concept (e.g., "sex").

39. Vatter, *Between Form and Event,* 10. Describing the return to beginnings in Machiavelli, Vatter observes, "In these events, the necessity of a given legal and political order is revoked (reduced to its beginnings, as Machiavelli says) to the contingency of its emergence, and therefore lets itself be overthrown; while, conversely, the contingency of new orders are given the appearance of necessity. Without this possibility of 'repeating' the necessary as the contingent, and the contingent as the necessary, there would be no radical political change."

40. Erika Ostrovsky, *A Constant Journey: The Fiction of Monique Wittig* (Carbondale: Southern Illinois University Press, 1991), 3–9, 35; Laurence M. Porter, "Feminist Fantasy and Open Structure in Monique Wittig's *Les guérillères,"* in *The Celebration of the Fantastic: Selected Papers from the Tenth Anniversary International Conference on the Fantastic in*

the Arts, ed. Donald E. Morse, Marshall B. Tymn, and Csilla Bertha (Westport: Greenwood Press, 1992), 261–69, 267.

41. As Laurence Porter correctly notes, "Even fine feminist critics like Toril Moi and Nina Auerbach have read *Les guérillères* as a closed structure, in which women win the war and institute a new equilibrium of women ruling men" ("Feminist Fantasy and Open Structure," 261). See also Zerilli, "The Trojan Horse of Universalism."

42. Recall Arendt's claim, which is why she concludes, "Men *are* free . . . as long as they act, neither before nor after; for to *be* free and to act are the same." Hannah Arendt, "What Is Freedom?" in *Between Past and Future: Eight Exercises in Political Thought* (New York: Penguin, 1993), 153.

43. Porter, "Feminist Fantasy and Open Structure," 267. I have addressed similar issues in Zerilli, "Rememoration or War?" Porter's essay is virtually alone in its attempt to thematize freedom as an open-structure in Wittig's work rather than as something that follows from the overthrow of patriarchy and that is founded in the creation of a new political form.

44. Monique Wittig, *Les guérillères* (Paris: Éditions Minuit, 1969), 14, 49/17. Hereafter cited as *G;* the first number refers to the English translation, and the second number refers to the French original. Erika Ostrovsky argues that the feminaries "represent traditional notions of a particular kind that must be annihilated and reformulated," and that "their authors, judging from the contents, are obviously male" (*A Constant Journey,* 56). I agree that the feminaries are texts that must be contested and eventually annihilated, but it is not clear to me that they were written by men. They contain stories that appear to be rewritings of the central myths of Western culture and a wealth of sexual symbolism that could very well be associated with a *female*-centered culture and must therefore be rejected. The feminaries seem somewhat like the books found in New Age sections of feminist bookstores.

45. Porter, "Feminist Fantasy and Open Structure," 267. This mode of interaction is akin to what James Tully describes as "governance." In its less restrictive sense governance involves "relations of intersubjective recognition, power, modes of conduct and strategies of freedom." This older meaning has been lost to an equation of government with formal institutions of political power. The recovery and reimagining of this older notion of governance, he argues, animates the work of Foucault and Arendt. The distinction is crucial for those feminists who refuse to reduce the sphere of the political to the official public sphere or democratic practices to the institutions of representative democracy. James Tully, "The Agonic Freedom of Citizens," *Economy and Society* 28 (May 1999): 161–82, 177.

46. Bergson, *The Creative Mind,* 101.

47. Ostrovsky, *A Constant Journey,* 61.

48. Monique Wittig, "The Mark of Gender," in *The Straight Mind and Other Essays* (Boston: Beacon Press, 1992), 76–89, 85–86.

49. Ostrovsky, *A Constant Journey,* 43.

50. Just as Wittig's tale does not locate an originary freedom in the past, neither does it invoke the idea of a historical process and its outcome-victory for the elles: to give meaning to the particular event. This tendency to justify the particular, the event, in terms of its place in an overall process is distinctly modern. As Arendt puts it, "The process, which alone makes meaningful whatever it happens to carry along. . . . bestow[s] upon mere time sequence an importance and dignity it never had." For we moderns, that which is worthy of remembrance is that which the 'objective' judgment of history has revealed to us in accordance with the criteria of victory or defeat. Hannah Arendt, "The Concept of History," in *Between Past and Future: Eight Exercises in Political Thought* (New York: Penguin, 1993): 41–90, 65. *Les guérillères* does not celebrate the deeds of the vanquished (men),

but it does disrupt the rectilinear time-concept, bestowing on the particular event a value that it would not otherwise have.

51. In his original reading of the return to beginnings in Machiavelli, Miguel Vatter (drawing on the work of Derrida, Lacoue-Labarthe, and Deleuze) asks, "How can something like repetition or return coincide with something like innovation or beginning?" The problem is that "if history amounts strictly to repetition of the same events, then there exists no innovation, and as a consequence it is possible to remain, forever, at the beginning (of history)." Arguing that Machiavelli's account of the return to beginnings "rejects the belief that repetition is itself 'secondary,' dependent on the 'firstness' or 'priority' of the form (archetype)," Vatter shows that "there is no beginning to return to because what begins is this very return" (*Between Form and Event*, 239).

52. Ostrovsky, *A Constant Journey*, 34, 33.

53. Wittig, "The Mark of Gender," 85.

54. Ibid., 86.

55. Ibid., 87. This translation works, however, only if one changes the last section of the book in which the men share the pronoun *they*. "In a new version [English translation] the masculine gender must be more systematically particularized than it is in the actual form of the book. The masculine must not appear under *they* but only under *man, he, his* in analogy with what has been done for so long to the feminine gender (*woman, she, her*)."

56. Similar literary strategies characterize two of Wittig's other novels, *The Opoponax* and *The Lesbian Body*. In *The Opoponax*, she works with the pronoun *on* (one), which is neuter and can represent a certain number of people all at once while remaining singular. With this pronoun, she builds a universal perspective around the central character of the text, a little girl. In *The Lesbian Body*, Wittig works creatively with the pronoun *j/e*, which she describes in "The Mark of Gender" (87) as "a sign of excess." See Zerilli, "The Trojan Horse of Universalism."

57. Auerbach, *Communities of Women*, 190–91.

58. Toril Moi, *Sexual/Textual Politics* (New York: Methuen, 1985), 80. Moi contends that Auerbach longs for an end to the war and for a time when, in Auerbach's words, "it would be possible to return to the individuality of Meg, Jo, and Amy," characters in another text, *Little Women*, that Auerbach examines (*Communities of Women*, 191).

59. This description, found on the back cover of the English translation, is from the *New York Times*. It is followed by a wise comment from Edna O'Brien: "Ms. Wittig is a dazzling writer. Her words are lucid and gleaming like moonlight."

60. Grassi, "Rhetoric as the Ground of Society," 95.

61. Ibid., 99.

62. Ibid.

8 Transformation of Gender and Genre Paradigms in the Fiction of Monique Wittig

Erika Ostrovsky

Nothing . . . that doth fade,
But doth suffer a sea-change
Into something rich and strange.
    —*The Tempest,* I, 2

Time is not the adversary of great works of art. Instead, each new encounter reveals further meanings, deeper insights, and increasing complexity. Thus, in the 1990s it seemed certain that *renversement* (upheaval, reversal, subversion) could be considered the key to Monique Wittig's writing.[1] A rereading now, however, suggests that rather than the overthrow or annihilation of existing literary canons in order to allow new growth to occur, her major accomplishment consists of an action far more subtle yet also more demanding. Transformation, transmutation, and transfiguration all indicate various degrees of change and an ascending order of magnitude.

Transformation demands great imagination and skill for it alters existing canons and creates forms that were previously nonexistent. Transmutation, however, implies more than a mere change in form and involves movement to a higher level. Transfiguration, the most complete type of alteration, suggests an exalting, glorifying metamorphosis. In all three instances, even more so than in the case of renversement, the process requires unusual artistry and originality.

Reconsideration of Wittig's fiction shows that every area of her writing, once this new key is accepted, gains in depth and brilliance. Although it could be shown in its workings from the broadest to the most detailed aspects of that writing, it is probably the most striking and significant when it comes to a transformation of gender and genre paradigms. Both are such deeply ingrained concepts that any change seems almost inconceivable; as time-honored traditions they are only rarely questioned. If a few literary genres have been subject to questioning during the twentieth century, and boundaries between them have at times been obliterated, no fundamental alteration has affected the majority. As for the paradigm of gender, notions concerning it are so firmly established as to appear to be universal laws and eternal truths. To suggest a possible transformation of either appears unimaginable. And yet Wittig has succeeded in effecting that seemingly impossible feat.

Genre transformation is already apparent in her first work, *L'opoponax* (1964). Although Marguerite Duras called it "un chef-d'oeuvre [car] c'est l'exécution capitale de quatre-vingt-dix pourcent des livres qui ont été faits sur l'enfance" (a masterpiece because it deals a death-blow to 90 percent of the books written about childhood), its most meaningful action is not Wittig's execution of the autobiographical novel of childhood but the changes she wrought in it.[2] This genre is common for first novels, and its parameters are well established by tradition. In achieving complete transformation, she immediately shows the creativity as well as the subtlety of her inventions. The title of the work is proof. It deviates from the usual one that refers to an author's self and experience, the most frequent being "My Childhood" or a variation thereof.

The title of the novel is a term that is both enigmatic and evocative. Thus, it provides an opening for conjectures and leads readers on by means of curiosity. Yet it remains mysterious. The dictionary definition—a medicinal plant of the Mediterranean region that produces a gumlike substance that can be used as perfume—does not apply to the novel. The definite article that precedes the term (in the original French)—*L'opoponax*—suggests that it refers to a particular opoponax and thus further precludes the use of the dictionary definition. In the work itself the term has multiple meanings. It is a force that propels the text; the love that dares not speak its name; a cryptonym (i.e., a name that hides and, by hiding, shows that it hides); and, finally, a word that has poetic resonance.[3] By the word's complexity and subtlety Wittig achieves transformation before the book is ever opened.

Yet this is only the beginning of the process. First-person singular narration and a subjective point of view, traditional for the genre, are radically altered to an impersonal narration and a neutral relation between the narrator and her material. Immediately noticeable also are the multiple protagonists of the work, a variation from the paradigmatic *I* as hero or heroine. Furthermore, characters tend to merge, move in unison, and create a continuous flow. That is achieved in an original manner by presenting their names in long lists and omitting the commas in enumerations such as "Marielle Balland Nicole Marre Laurence Bouniol Julienne Pont Marie Démone Anne Gerlier Denise Causse Anne-Marie Brunet Marguerite-Marie Le Monial Marie-José Broux Sophie Rieux."[4] This invention also enlarges perspective by effacing boundaries and distinctions, produces an incantatory effect through the sound chain of the names, and emphasizes the notion of naming as a form of creation.

An additional transformation of the traditional elements of the auto-biographical novel of childhood is Wittig's treatment of fictional time. In *L'opoponax* there is an absence of temporal segmentation or fragmentation and emphasis on duration, fluidity, and endlessness. That emphasis is rendered simply but effectively by the exclusive use of present-tense verbs (except for the final phrase), which creates a sense of the present as well as of presence. Moreover, it alters the genre's traditional notion of time, which emphasizes the past and loss of that which once was.

Treatment of space, moreover, parallels that of time. Scenes shift, blend, and refuse all demarcations or separations rather than have distinct settings. Distances are not measured in miles, and movement is accomplished with ease. Sometimes the shift takes place so swiftly as to pass almost unnoticed because nothing in the text (neither spacing nor punctuation) indicates displacement. Scenes that would take place months and miles apart (e.g., *O*, 86, 95, 187, 223) appear without separation. Such transformation creates an unusual time/space continuum that echoes the notions of flux and unity to enlarge the perspective and thus move beyond the confines of the genre paradigm.

This is even more striking when it is a question of gender. Instead of establishing a definite identity, the voice that narrates the text remains impersonal, represented by the pronoun *on*, a word extremely difficult to translate into English. The closest approximation would be "you," which still cannot render all the qualities of the French *on*, which implies being neutral, neuter, collective, or generalized. It is thus impossible to decide on the speaker's gender and determine whether the voice is singular or plural. True, the vast majority of the work's protagonists are clearly young girls, and from their midst two figures emerge as central: Catherine Legrand and Valérie Borge. Yet the attributes of all the young girls, especially these two, do not fit the gender paradigm. Its transformation is evident throughout the novel. They are neither submissive, ignorant about sex, nor timid (as young girls are traditionally described) but defiant, sexually aware, and tough. They enjoy (play) battles and hunting. Catherine Legrand carries a knife, and Valérie Borge is skilled in the use of a rifle and considers the offering of three bullets a token of her love for Catherine Legrand (*O*, 267). It is a most unusual gift for one young girl to make to another, the cliché being of far more tender and sentimental gestures.

The evolution of their feelings for each other occupies a large part of the work, and the term *l'opoponax*, which gives the book its title, is linked to intense, often violent, desire, all the more powerfully present because it is never directly named. Moreover, Legrand invents the term, which is linked to fictional creation (*O*, 179) and the text of the novel itself, allying her to the writer and writing. *L'opoponax* is also a fluid, protean force that constantly changes (*O*, 180–81), accentuating the notion of transformation.

Of course, the nature of their desire also alters the gender paradigm that limits the awakening of love in adolescent girls to dreams of a prince charming and fantasies of a heterosexual nature. Although tender attachments and delicate feelings for members of the same sex during adolescence are not considered unusual, the violent and secret desire that occurs here is a quite different matter. It is described not only via the action of the "opoponax" but also through appropriation and inclusion of several well-known love poems written by men, among them Charles Baudelaire and Maurice Scève.[5] Large parts of the first poem (*O*, 254, 268, 270, 281) and some lines from the second (*O*, 239, 281) are so closely interwoven with the primary text as to seem pronounced by the speaker (especially because no quotation marks or other forms of punctuation separate the two). What results is confusion or fusion of male and female voices, a further departure from the gender paradigm.

Perhaps most striking, however, is the transformation of one of the best-known Greek myths, that of Orpheus and Eurydice. The famous lovers, a male and a female, here are described as seen in a bas-relief that illustrates a passage in the *Georgics* by Virgil, but their image has been altered to suggest that both are female (*O*, 251). The transformation of the mythical couple, unchanged since ancient times and therefore considered immutable, is noteworthy. Although it might be interpreted as prefiguring the changes of well-known myths that will occur in Wittig's later works (e.g., *Les guérillères* and *Le corps lesbien*), it is striking in *L'opoponax*.

The genre Wittig chose for her second work, *Les guérillères*, is that of the epic. It is an especially audacious transmutation because the epic is a literary form traditionally considered to be the exclusive property of males as authors, protagonists, and audience. So well established is this tradition that in the best-known epics in French literature (e.g., *La chanson de Roland*) women have almost no part. For example, Aude, the betrothed of Roland, plays a far lesser role than his horse. From the title of the work, *Les guérillères*, it is evident that Wittig is altering established notions of the genre. The term announces that this epic will have, as its protagonists, not *guérrièrs* (warriors) but fictional characters designated by the neologism that combines the word *guérrière* (the feminine form of *guérrièr*) with *guerilla*. The fact that it is a neologism is of the highest importance. It is a vehicle for taking and re-creating forms that have become petrified or, as Wittig has stated elsewhere, "incapable of transformation."[6]

Whereas epics are traditionally written in poetry, *Les guérillères* transmutes the conventions of the genre by combining a poem with a central text that consists of numerous short prose passages. Moreover, the structure and typography of the work also change established notions regarding epics. It is divided into three parts, each introduced by a large circle on a right-hand page; a long list of women's names (in large capital letters) interrupts the narrative on every sixth page. The names come from all parts of the globe and every period. They are drawn from a variety of mythologies, literatures, and historical events and enlarge the perspective of the genre, which is traditionally limited to a particular culture and specific moment.

Further transmutations include multiple protagonists. That in itself would not change the conventions of the epic genre, but in this work they are all female. Moreover, the fact that they are designated by the pronoun *elles,* the plural of *elle* (she), has a variety of repercussions. It affects both the genre and the gender paradigm. The tradition according to which the masculine pronoun (*il*, he, singular, and *ils*, plural) bears the universal point of view is changed by employing the feminine pronoun. Moreover, the long list of women's names, also characterized by the elimination of spatial and temporal limitations, also clarifies the term *elles* and renders it more powerful. Although elles suggests a collectivity that is quasi-universal (or at least representative of half the world's population) yet impersonal, the names provide powerful identity to the collectivity. Furthermore, although a canon of the epic genre is the appearance of outstanding hero figures, Wittig transmutes that by introducing a vast number of heroines, all of whom are equally important and valiant.

If one examines the individual components of the list of names beginning with the first, Osée, it becomes clear that Wittig has achieved complex ends by a relatively simple means. The name has numerous meanings, among them "she who dares"; it also refers to the Old Testament prophet Osée (or Osea in English). The ending of the word in French is ambiguous, which suggests that it could be of a woman's name. Thus the prophet is turned into a prophetess, and a gender transformation has been accomplished. That is farther carried out by giving female attributes to such well-known male mythological figures as Dionysus, Prometheus, and Hermes or depicting Eve alone in Paradise, without Adam and accompanied only by her favorite serpent, Orphée.[7] In the last instance the gender paradigm is variously transmuted. Because the ending of "Orphée" is also ambiguous, the name might be that of a female, which makes the serpent's gender uncertain. Moreover, by the linkage with Orpheus, known for the powers of his artistry, the serpent companion of Eve confers similar powers upon her and eliminates distinctions between two mythologies (Greek and Judaic). Finally, as in *L'opoponax,* the couple of Orpheus-Eurydice appears to consist of two female figures, suggesting yet again a transmutation of the traditional notion of lovers being of opposite sexes.

Wittig further alters the gender paradigm by the action to which she sub-jects common nouns that habitually appear in the masculine form in French and are given in the dictionary solely in that form (e.g., *maçon* [mason], *soldat* [soldier], and *parleur* [speaker]). She "feminizes" them in her text and uses them in the plural (*maçonnes, soldates, parleuses*). Although it is impossible to render them in English, the effects of that change are extremely striking in French. The words also point to an alteration in the social roles assigned to men and women by portraying the latter in positions or professions tradi-tionally occupied by men. *Parleuses,* for example, transmutes the image of women as silent and/or silenced into speakers or speaking subjects, further emphasized by a phrase that appears throughout the book: *elles disent* (they say, they speak [f.]).

Even more arresting is a change of the gender paradigm that concerns armies, present in almost every epic but traditionally consisting of male sol-diers. In *Les guérillères,* however, the armies are composed exclusively of soldates or guérillères, forming a coalition that unites various tribes or nations of women, all of whose names are neologisms (*G,* 149) and thus constitute a transmutation in themselves.

If the gender change of human figures is surprising, that of superhuman ones is truly astonishing. Certainly, the most important transmutation concerns an *ur*-concept. From time immemorial and in almost every culture woman has been linked with the moon, as have female divinities. Wittig, however, creates a pantheon of sun goddesses drawn from a wide variety of mythologies (*G,* 31, 34–35, 37, 92). Although it is traditional for male divinities to be associ-ated with the sun and, by extension, with light, autonomy, and life, choosing female ones to represent those attributes transmutes the gender paradigm, which in the case of lunar associations links women with darkness, passivity, and death.

Sometimes Wittig goes so far as to change not only the attributes but also the name of a mythological figure. The Egyptian goddess Hathor, for example, is described as carrying the solar disc (instead of the lunar one) on her head and is called Othar (*G,* 183), an anagram of her original name. In all these instances and by such various means Wittig achieves a fundamental and com-plex transmutation of genre and gender paradigms. It was in her next book, *Le corps lesbien,* that she accomplished the total transfiguration of both.

In order to appreciate the creativity of Wittig's enterprise and the subtle means she used to achieve it, it is not sufficient to consider the title or list of bodily functions that figures prominently on the dust jacket of the first edition. The latter begins with the term *la cyprine,* the secretion that marks erotic pleasure in females. Although the transgression of several taboos is thus made evident, it is even more significant that the gender paradigm of woman as heterosexually inclined and supposedly not meant to enjoy the sexual act is totally altered. The details of this undertaking are only visible when the text is examined in entirety.

Changes in the conventions of the genre, however, are almost immediately noticeable. In *Le corps lesbien,* Wittig has chosen to transform the time-honored (or time-worn) concepts that rule over love poetry. *Le corps lesbien* is undoubtedly one of the greatest love poems ever written, and it re-creates every aspect of that literary genre. A comparison with *The Song of Songs,* for example, or "Etroits sont les vaisseaux" in Saint-John Perse's *Amers* (both written by male authors and addressed to female love objects) or those composed by women (e.g., the poems of Sappho or the "Sonnets" of Louise Labé), makes it evident that they cannot equal the violent passion characterizing *Le corps lesbien,* an emotion maintained throughout with almost unbearable intensity. The book is the most complete exploration of every possible aspect and imaginable facet of the emotional and physical experiences that constitute love.

The prevalent tone that distinguishes *Le corps lesbian* from stereotypical love poetry is one of extreme ferocity and just as extreme tenderness. However (and this also changes the conventions of the genre), the emotionally charged sequences that compose the central portion of the text are contrasted with a list of anatomical terms that winds its way through the work. The tone of the latter is objective (another change in the paradigm). Yet it also has the effect of a recitation, a litany, or an incantation. That can be interpreted as a form celebrating the bodies of the lover and the beloved and even, by extension, the relationship between the writer and the work. The most passionate *corps à corps* that takes place in *Le corps lesbien* involves writing itself. The pleasure of the text finally outstrips all others. It is an orgasmic experience of the most intense kind. And the various types of actions performed as described on the body of the beloved can be considered symbolic of the writer's acts on the body of language.

The genre paradigm is also altered by humor. Laughter, only very rarely found in love poetry, is almost constantly present in this work. The verb and the noun *rire* appear in dozens of instances in the text, almost always in a context of joy, fulfillment, and plenitude. Often as well, painful emotions are dissolved or resolved by laughter. The final sequence of *Le corps lesbien,* for example, closes on a joyous note among jugglers and acrobats, festive sounds, happy shouts, and bursts of laughter.[8] Most of all, however, laughter in this work seems a visceral form of expression that arises from the body's core and, as a result, is central to the text.

Although the genre paradigm has undergone numerous changes at the hands of Wittig, gender is the most completely transfigured. The change is evident in the direct reference at the beginning of *Le corps lesbien* to sexuality that is exclusively between women, to the female sexual organ, and to the secretion that marks erotic pleasure in the female. Totally frontal in approach and a form of celebration, the words on the cover of the book alter the conventional gender concept of Western culture—indeed, the majority of cultures—which tend to glorify the phallus and male sexuality.

Further into the body of the text there occur repeated examples of the transmutation of concepts concerning the female gender. Whereas women, stereotypically, are seen as timid, gentle, and passive objects of desire, in *Le corps lesbien* the *amantes* (lovers [f.]) are active, audacious, and often violent. The notion of the subject and object in the domain of desire is completely changed through alternate sequences in which lover and beloved exchange roles. Perhaps an even more complete departure from the paradigm is that the lovers are transfigured into superhuman beings (*CL*, 45–46, 58, 95, 113–14, 134–35, 158–59) or mythological figures (16, 30, 39, 45, 73–74, 87, 102, 103, 118, 124, 138–39). Chief among the last of these are two couples—Orpheus and Eurydice and Isis and Osiris—whose traditionally male partners have been changed into females. In both instances the alteration relates not only to their gender but also to the great mysteries of transformation, from life to death and death to life. In the sequences devoted to the latter (*CL*, 86–87, 127, 130) the transformation itself is transformed. Isis reconstitutes the dispersed parts of the body of her beloved (Osiris [f.]), but instead of the phallus, which in the original myth occupies a central place, various parts of the female genital organ are emphasized (*CL*, 127). Moreover, instead of the son who comes from the union of the lovers Isis and Osiris, little girls will be born (*CL*, 87). Christ—here, "Christa" (*CL*, 30)—also undergoes death and resurrection, and his last words are "feminized" to read (*CL*, 138–39) "Mère, mère, pourquoi m//as-tu abandonnée?" (Mother, mother, why have you forsaken me?), thus transforming the final seven words of Jesus on the cross.

Among other mythological figures who have been treated in this fashion are Achilles, Atreus, Ganymede, Icarus, and Zeus. Not only have their names been altered but their well-known actions have undergone a change as well (*CL*, 12–13, 185–86). In *Les guérillères* Wittig created an entire pantheon of female solar divinities, but an even larger assembly appears in *Le corps lesbien*. It is one which originates in a great variety of mythologies: Aphrodite, Astarte, Artemis, Persephone, Ishtar, Albina, Epona, Leucippa, Isis, Hecate, Pomona and Flora, Andromeda, Cybele, Io, Niobe and Latona, Sappho, Gurinno, Ceres, Leucothea, Rhamnusia, Minerva, and Demeter (*CL,* 73–74).

In this group Sappho is elevated to the position of a divinity, as she is throughout the central text (*CL,* 58, 107, 108, 130, 143, 165), and she appears to be even greater than Isis. Although Isis is part of an established mythology and habitually associated with a male lover, Sappho's lovers are reputed to have been female. Moreover, her glory as a poet has endured throughout the centuries, although some of her writing was destroyed by the male establishment. Thus Wittig makes her a divinity as a form of affirmation and transfiguration.

Another arresting phenomenon in *Le corps lesbien* that unfortunately cannot be perceived by English-speaking readers (and is impossible to translate) is the transformation of the gender of all nouns and their accompanying adjectives. The resulting "feminization" is startling, even shocking, to a francophone. Examples are too numerous to cite, but some are so unusual as to invite quoting: *bourreleuse* (f. of *bourreau* [executioner]); *inquisitrice* (f. of *inquisiteur* [inquisitor]); *sphyngesse* (a doubly feminized form of "sphynx"); *ravisseuse* (f. of *ravisseur* [ravisher]); *voyeuse* (f. of "voyeur"); and *agnelles nouvelles-nées* (f. of *agneaux nouveaux-nés* [newborn lambs, archaic]). In some instances it is more than a feminization, it is the creation of a true neologism (e.g., *"enfourrurée"* [*CL,* 88]). In many cases these transformed words contain an echo of those that were originally of masculine gender but—through a "sex-change operation"—emerge in a re-created (and feminine) form.

At times the transmutation not only concerns gender but also constitutes a change of genus. The beloved, for example, is depicted in various forms ranging from a great variety of animals—from she-wolf (*CL,* 14–15), protozoa (42–43), whale (101–2), and kangaroo to female cat (136)—to fabulous creatures such as might be found in a medieval bestiary. One has a multitude of eyes everywhere on her body (*CL,* 151–52); another has a proboscis and enormous ears that can serve as wings (155–56); yet another is a kind of porcupine that has metal quills (166–67).

An even greater major transformation in *Le corps lesbien* encompasses its entire fictional world, one totally void of males. Boys are found (although not as protagonists) in *L'opoponax*, and young men are reconciled with the guérillères after the latter have won the war. In *Le corps lesbien,* however, males are nonexistent, whether in nature, where sea and islands (*la mer* and *l'île* both being feminine nouns) predominate, or the animal kingdom. Moreover, all humans are female, as are the fabulous creatures and figures from world mythology.

Among the islands most frequently mentioned in the text are Lesbos and Cyprus, the former associated with Sappho and the latter, birthplace of Aphrodite, also called "Cypris" and linked to the term *cyprine,* making both symbols of art and desire. In addition, the story of Aphrodite being born from the sea reinforces the association with *la mer* as well as with *eau* (water, [f.]) and its homonym, *O,* which carried complex meanings in *Les guérillères.* "O" was, for example, the song of a siren as well as the vulval ring or female sexual orifice (*G,* 16). The latter two are age-old, quasi-universal symbolic representations of the female as a means of procreation. Here, the vulva is valued over the womb, the site of pleasure over that of reproduction. "O" also links art (the song of the siren) and sexual desire in the female, that is, creation unrelated to reproduction.

Wittig goes so far in *Le corps lesbien* as to transmute a universally accepted scientific fact by having two pairs of female chromosomes unite in order to form a female embryo: "XX + XX = XX" (*CL,* 144). That phenomenon is physically impossible, yet it is included in a list of scientific physiological terms and thus stands out. Moreover, the equation suggests a miraculous birth and elevates the joining of two female chromosomes to the level of divine union.

All of these transformations are important, but it is perhaps the one that concerns language that is central not only to the fictional enterprise but also to redefining the gender paradigm that sees woman as silent, mute, excluded in a number of ways from verbal expression, and the object of male discourse. True, there had already been sequences in *Les guérillères* in which elles not only destroyed the *féminaires* that contained stereotypical descriptions of women (*G,* 68, 102) but also jointly created new texts (*G,* 106) and affirmed the search for a new language (*G,* 189). But it is in *Le corps lesbien* that the most striking transmutation takes place. Woman is now the one who becomes a speaking subject and, moreover, invents a new language (*CL,* 116–17). Such power is paramount to creation, even Creation. It constitutes a transposed version of Genesis ("In the beginning was the Word"). In this version, however, it is not pronounced by a male god but by thousands of female voices.

In her next work, *Brouillon pour un dictonnaire des amantes,* written in collaboration with Sande Zeig, Wittig once again transforms a well-known genre—a dictionary—and thus creates certain expectations. Yet these are modified in unexpected fashion by the addition of the words *des amantes.* Because they could mean either "by lovers" or "for lovers" (f.) the conventions of the genre, by which both the authors and readers of dictionaries are male, have been transposed. *This* dictionary implies that its authorship is female, and, moreover, there appears to be a much closer relationship between contributors and readers than is traditionally the case. It also becomes almost immediately evident that this text only superficially resembles a dictionary (with listings arranged alphabetically, cross-references, and definitions). In actuality, it is a prose poem. Neither genre is a fixed form but subject to redefinition and metamorphosis.

Another change in the conventions of the genre involves redefinition. Traditionally, dictionaries are characterized by a serious, authorative, perhaps even tyrannical approach to language, but *Brouillon pour un dictionnaire des amantes* is a blend of the lusory, the lyrical, and the ironic. In addition, the factual and the invented merge to the point where they are, at times, difficult to distinguish. A bibliography at the end of the work (again, a change from the usual dictionary) contains names of real and imaginary authors as well as invented places and/or dates of publication (see, for example, *DA*, 249, 250). The treatment of these entries can be playful, ironic, or malicious (*DA*, 249, 252)—anything but the traditional mode of scholarly seriousness and unquestioned authority.

Definitions themselves transmute more than the genre of the dictionary—a text so important to the Judeo-Christian world as to constitute something like genre by itself: the Bible. The first of these (*Age*) re-creates the portion of Genesis dealing with Paradise and the Fall (*DA*, 49), as does the entry *Vie* (*DA*, 128). Finally, words that have, in a traditional dictionary, a fixed or firmly established meaning are often redefined in *Brouillon pour un dictionnaire des amantes*; yet others are totally re-created and appear as neologisms (e.g., *DA*, 79, 121, 226).

Probably the most important redefinition concerns *amantes*, a word that is part of the title. Amantes are described in a manner that suggests still another literary genre—the fable. Their origins are in what resembles a miraculous birth or parthenogenesis, and they are also said to have created themselves. Their attributes and activities are equally fabulous. They can speak the language of animals, modify their body secretions and odors at will, change color, live on smoke, reproduce by way of the ear, fly, and create new sounds. Even more important, they are described as specialists in the art of transformation.

Their most significant function however is their active role in gathering, preserving, and transmitting literary texts, "l'ensemble de livres et de fragments du passé sauvés par les amantes pendant la dernière période du chaos" (the collection of books and fragments from the past saved by the lovers during the last period of chaos [*DA*, 22, 69, 101]). They are thus identified not only as lovers "éprouvant un violent désir les unes pour les autres" (filled with intense desire for each other [*DA,* 15]) but also as those who perform a labor of love—indeed, an act of love—in keeping with Wittig's fundamental approach to literature. This enlarges and transfigures the meaning of the term *amantes* and, once more, alters the traditional notion of the dictionary as a work in which love and/or desire plays no part.

In her final work of fiction, *Virgile, non,* Wittig undertakes the most complete transformation of genre (and genres). Although the title contains the name of Virgil and the works created by him (as was the case in *L'opoponax*), both are negated (and thus in a sense altered) by the addition of the word *non.* The title evokes more than Virgil's name, however. It is a reminder of his presence in Dante's *Divine Comedy.* And it is that work, one of the literary masterpieces of Western culture and so famous as to constitute a genre in itself, that Wittig transforms.

Instantly noticeable, too, is the metamorphosis of the protagonists. The gender, as well as the names, of Dante and his male guide, Virgil, have been changed. They have become, respectively, "Wittig" and Manastabal. In addition, the work depicts a profane rather than a sacred journey and its setting is twentieth-century San Francisco, as various place names indicate.[9] And while *Virgile, non* is divided into three zones that echo those of *The Divine Comedy,* Dante's topography is transformed by altering the religious content of the settings to profane ones. Moreover, the strict order so important in Dante's poem (implying the perfect order of God's universe) is entirely altered. The voyage that "Wittig" and Manastabal undertake occurs in disorderly, random, and even chaotic fashion (*VN,* 20).

The most important transformation of the genre paradigm, however, is the hybrid nature of *Virgile, non,* which combines a variety of forms of literature (including *Alice in Wonderland*) with the cinema, theater, and music. That results in what Manastabal describes as a "confusion des genres . . . [qui] a véritablement quelque chose de barbare" (*VN,* 63). This "barbaric confusion of genres" is actually a fusion that produces an altered, composite creation echoed in the text's temporal "confusions" or fusions. The traditional, linear, chronological progression is abandoned in favor of frequent anachronisms, many of which are extremely amusing. The same mixture is apparent in spatial matters. Wittig combines "real" sites with religious and/or literary inventions. Thus, a laundromat is also one of the circles of hell, a billiard parlor is also limbo, and a picnic ground is also Paradise.

Further transformations concern the area of language that would be expected to be lofty, noble, and poetic. *Virgile, non,* however, combines various registers, including slang (of a very up-to-date and low-down variety), mock-oratorial speech, and imitations of excessively lyrical pronouncements. There are even phrases in English (for the first time in Wittig's writing). What is perhaps most striking is the opposition of various tones that is achieved by different types of language. Moreover, a new tone emerges in *Virgile, non,* fierce irony. It, too, is unexpected given the high seriousness characteristic of the genre and the tragic nature of a large part of this descent into hell. Irony is most apparent in sequences that deal with outrages perpetrated on the victims (e.g., "Parade 1," 53–57, or "Les cartes à jouer," 58–59).

Yet another new tone, the opposite of irony, appears: compassion or, better still, *passion active,* an intense form of empathy and love that demands a different register of language. It should be not strident and harsh but sober and somber, muted in sound and slow in rhythm (e.g., "Le lac," 97) to accompany mourning rather than ferocious mockery. That tone, in turn, gives way to exuberant descriptions of pleasurable sensory experiences and joyful emotions, indicating the conquest of misfortune and the vision of a more felicitous state that might be called paradise.

Although various transmutations of the genre paradigm in *Virgile, non* result in a striking creation, the treatment of traditional notions of gender in the work is equally interesting. It tends to be harsh sarcasm, consisting of ferocious caricatures (something not present in Wittig's former works); compassionate portrayals that show the plight of victims; and celebration of the transformation that results in an active, powerful, and triumphant image. In the first instance women are shown in stereotypical fashion as submissive, self-effacing, and accepting of their role as sexual objects or masochisic slaves (*VN,* 53–57, 58–59). In the second, descriptions are somber and emphasize the tragic condition of women that leads to despair and suicide (*VN,* 76–82, 92–97). The third category is the most interesting because it provides portrayals of the protagonists, the beloved, figures who appear in paradise. It includes the figures of "Wittig" and her guide, Manastabal, who are so far removed from the gender paradigm that they defy all stereotypical description. They are hybrid creatures that echo various figures from myth, literature, and even cinema. They combine characteristics of both genders or move beyond any categories of gender, and their actions include those traditionally the sole prerogative of males (heroic deeds, epic adventures, cowboy exploits, and mystical journeys such as that in *The Divine Comedy*).

The Manastabal-"Wittig" couple might best be described by a term that appeared in *Brouillon pour un dictionnaire des amantes: héraïnes,* a neologism that indicates transmutation in language as well as function. Departure from the gender paradigm is also evident in their refusal of such traditional roles as those of *femme* or *mère* (very much as did the *amazones* and amantes in *Brouillon*). In a lighter vein they look and act in a manner that shows further departure from stereotypical images. They ride motorcycles, carry rifles, play billiards, and speak street slang. Most important, however, is their ability to spend a season in hell and emerge not only victorious but also able to aid, empathize, act, and speak out. Instead of despair, which seems the lot of hopeless victims, they are able to achieve life-affirming domains. These are depicted in the last portion of *Virgile, non,* which portrays the ultimate festivities in paradise: the encounter of "Wittig" with her beloved (*VN,* 89) and the presence of angels (f.) who resemble jazz musicians and are joined by a chorus of birds and angelic motorcyclists (who sing a song from *Alice in Wonderland*).

The final sequence in the book, "La cuisine des anges" (the kitchen of the angels) is dominated by an activity that could be part of the gender stereotype—cooking—but is here transformed to become a free and joyous act rather than a type of enslavement for women. It involves a series of sensual delights (tastes, odors, and colors) and, most important, is an act of transformation and creation.

In *Virgile, non* just as in *Le corps lesbien,* the fictional world is entirely transformed in that it contains no male characters. The protagonists, although their voyage resembles that of Dante and Virgil, are héraïnes rather than heros; the angels are not "sons of God," nor are any archangels named Michael or Gabriel; and even the damned souls (*âmes damnées*) do not include males. Victims, opponents, detractors, and celebrants, the victorious (both human and superhuman) exist in a world completely devoid of males other than the unseen but hideous presence of tormentors and executioners. Even the song that accompanies the feast in paradise comes from a work that celebrates the adventures of a little girl, *Alice in Wonderland.*

In an overview of Wittig's entire corpus of fiction, from *L'opoponax* to *Virgile, non,* it becomes apparent that she has admirably succeeded in transforming both gender and genre paradigms in a number of highly innovative and imaginative ways that change from one work to the next, proof of the seemingly inexhaustible creative possibilities at her disposal. Never is either of the two paradigms altered in the same fashion, and often a previous invention is abandoned or even apparently rejected.

While various literary conventions are changed and a number of genres (from the autobiographical novel of childhood to the epic to love poetry to the dictionary) are entirely transmuted, Wittig transfigures the gender paradigm in the most radical and original fashion. Although it is true that all of her fiction shows such artistry, it is most certainly in *Le corps lesbien* where she achieves the greatest diversity and depth, making it a masterpiece that outdistances Duras's evaluation of *L'opoponax.*

NOTES

All translations from the original French in the text are by the author; translations from Monique Wittig's writing are by special agreement with Wittig.

1. This is the key concept developed in Erika Ostrovsky's *A Constant Journey: The Fiction of Monique Wittig* (Carbondale: Southern Illinois University Press, 1991).

2. Marguerite Duras, "Une oeuvre éclatante," *Le Nouvel Observateur,* Nov. 5, 1964, 18–19.

3. Suzanna Stamponini, "Un nom pour tout le monde: 'L'Opoponax de Monique Wittig," *Vlasta* 4 (1985): 93, a special issue on Monique Wittig; Mary McCarthy, "Everybody's Childhood," *New Statesman,* July 15, 1966, 94.

4. Monique Wittig, *L'opoponax* (Paris: Éditions Minuit, 1964), 269. Hereafter cited as *O.*

5. Charles Baudelaire, *Les fleurs du mal,* in *Oeuvres complète de Baudelaire* (Paris: Editions de la Pléiäde, 1954); Maurice Scève, *Délie* (Paris: Hachette & Cie, 1916).

6. Monique Wittig, "The Trojan Horse," *Feminist Issues,* no. 4 (1984): 45.

7. Monique Wittig, *Les guérillères* (Paris: Éditions Minuit, 1969), 30, 62, 204, 72–73. Hereafter cited as *G.*

8. Monique Wittig, *Les corps lesbien* (Paris: Éditions Minuit, 1973), 188. Hereafter cited as *CL.*

9. Monique Wittig, *Virgile, non* (Paris: Éditions Minuit, 1985), 7. Hereafter cited as *VN.*

PART 4

THEORETICAL APPLICATIONS

Quixote's Journey: How to Change the World and Degenderize the Stage

Jeannelle Laillou Savona

Le voyage sans fin (The Constant Journey), Monique Wittig's only published play, is not easily accessible to English-speaking readers and its stage production has never been studied.[1] Because I propose to read it as one of the first "lesbian" plays performed on the French stage I shall begin by situating it in the context of its French historic background of the late 1970s and early 1980s.

In 1979, when Wittig wrote *The Constant Journey*, women playwrights and directors had just begun to be heard and respected, but the subject of lesbianism remained rare and suppressed despite the atmosphere of experimentation created by feminism.[2] Even in the women's movement many women were embarrassed by lesbians, whom they tended to ignore or even silence. The clash between straight and lesbian feminists turned into a spectacular crisis in 1980, when *Questions Feministes,* a leading French feminist journal, ceased publication because of the resignation of radical lesbians from its editorial board.

One of the claims of those lesbians—and Wittig was among them—was that the principal source of women's oppression was heterosexuality, which they perceived as a political class system similar in its functioning to a capitalist regime. According to their reasoning, greatly inspired by Marxism, living with a man amounted to a sort of collaboration with the dominating class.

Although their denunciation of heterosexuality appeared shocking to many women who were emotionally involved with men, their theoretical contention also seemed short-sighted to many other feminists, who, influenced by psychoanalysis, considered homosexuality as part of a psychological continuum and refused to see a dialectical opposition between homosexuality and heterosexuality. That was the case with Hélène Cixous, who, in her pioneering play on the subject, *Portrait of Dora* (1976), refuted Freud's theories while partially integrating them into her stage representation of Dora's passion for Madame K. Her play was undoubtedly the first and most explicit stage representation of female homosexuality in the 1970s.

One should also mention the importance of Simone Benmussa as a predecessor to Wittig. Although she had been the director of *Portrait of Dora* and thus put her talent at the service of a psychoanalytical concept of theater and female homosexuality, Benmussa had also written and mounted *La vie singulière d'Albert Nobbs* (The Singular Life of Albert Nobbs, 1977), which Sue-Ellen Case later classified as a "materialist feminist" play.[3] Indeed, Benmussa's play is remarkable in its awareness of gender class differences. Set

Sande Zeig as Quixote in "The Burning of the Books" scene of Wittig and Zeig's Paris production of *The Constant Journey* (1985) at the Petit Théâtre du Rond-Pont. (Copyright © 1985 by Colette Geoffrey, all rights of reproduction reserved)

Sande Zeig in "The Windmill Scene" (scene 5) of *The Constant Journey*. (Copyright © 1985 by Colette Geoffrey, all rights of reproduction reserved)

in Ireland at the end of the nineteenth century, it stages two English women who must pass as men in order to make an adequate living. The play stresses gender labor inequalities and how they relate to heterosexual relationships. After Herbert and Albert have "come out" to each other as women, Herbert confesses to Albert that she has married a woman and found happiness. Albert then starts dreaming of a similar marriage as both an economic and emotional solution to her difficult social situation.

Although Benmussa asserts in her introduction to the play that her only concern is that of gender and working conditions, which implies that her two main protagonists are in no way sexually involved with a woman, it is very tempting to see a lesbian subtext in *The Singular Life of Albert Nobbs*, considering the traditional misogyny and homophobia of French theater at that time.[4] In fact, Benmussa's play seems to anticipate *The Constant Journey* on an ideological level because it presents two human beings who, by escaping assigned gender roles and asserting freedom, have ceased to be "women" in the conventional sense of the word. Albert deplores that she has become "neither man nor woman, just a perhapser."[5] She has lost her gender by violating the triple obligation of Victorian females: marriage, motherhood, and either economic dependence or acceptance of inferior working conditions. On a political level, Herbert and Albert could be considered politically "lesbian" according to Wittig's definition: "Lesbian is the only concept I know of which is beyond the categories of sex (woman and man), because the designated subject (lesbian) is not a woman, either economically, or politically, or ideologically. For what makes a woman is a specific relation to a man, a relation that we have previously called servitude, . . . a relation which lesbians escape by refusing to become or to stay heterosexual. We are escapees from our class in the same way as American runaway slaves were when escaping slavery and becoming free."[6]

The Singular Life of Albert Nobbs's counterideology, as I read it, is therefore very close to the radical thinking of the lesbians whose work appeared in *Questions Feministes* between 1977 and 1980. They denied the notion of natural sexual difference and complementarity between the sexes and underlined the political clash dividing men and women into two social classes of unequal economic, social, and sexual status.[7] These writers were the first to approach heterosexuality as an underlying, unexpressed, "social contract" or "political regime" (Wittig) dividing humans into oppressors and oppressed to the advantage of heterosexual men. The text of *The Singular Life of Albert Nobbs* suggests a "radical feminist" position.[8] Benmussa's staging, however, which was rather dreamlike and poetic, never used any of the self-conscious, distancing techniques usually associated with a materialist or political concept of theater.

While Wittig was writing *The Constant Journey* in 1979, Sande Zeig, who had been trained as a mime by Étienne Decroux in Paris, was devising her own original body technique as an actor and performer. Both her stage improvisations on the theme of Quixote and Wittig's theatrical rewriting of *The Adventures of Don Quixote* (1604) by Miguel de Cervantes Saavedra were simultaneous and interrelated. Wittig was inspired by Zeig's work on gestures and movements, and Zeig, who had previously coauthored with Wittig *Brouillon pour un dictionnaire des amantes* (1976) and *Lesbian Peoples: Material for a Dictionary* (1979), became greatly enthused by Wittig's text.[9]

In 1980 Zeig started to translate Wittig's work into English, and it was first produced in 1984 in the United States at the Haybarn Theater of Goddard College under the direction of both Syn Guerin and Wittig with the help of John Towsen for physical comedy. Zeig was Quixote, and Pam Christian was Panza.[10] The play was mounted again in its French version in Paris in 1985 and ran for a month at the Petit Théâtre du Rond-Point under the direction of both Wittig and Zeig, with Zeig again as Quixote and Paule Kingleur as Panza. The French mise-en-scène was more polished than the American because it benefited from major financial support from the Ministry of Culture, Cultural Section of the Ministry of Women's Rights (Ministère des Droits de la Femme) and the collaboration of the Renaud-Barrault Company, whose actors provided the voices on the sound track. Lena Vandrey, the painter, also contributed innovative properties and costumes.

The French text of *The Constant Journey* consists of a "montage" of fifteen short scenes featuring only female actors.[11] The montage, by opposition to a traditional composition, separates individual episodes in space and time, thus disrupting the continuity of a performance. Such a mode of presentation "in jumps," borrowed from the process of film editing (Eisenstein), had been highly recommended by Bertolt Brecht because it prevents the audience from becoming unconsciously carried away by the flow of the action.[12] In a way, this sort of theatrical montage is comparable to the formal presentation Wittig used in at least three of her works of fiction (*Les guérillères*, *The Lesbian Body*, and *Across the Acheron*). Distinct paragraphs are separated from one another and introduce totally different scenes or descriptive vignettes.

Another striking element of the play is the disjunction of its stage action, mainly focused on the presence and movements of the two protagonists from recorded dialogues that often involve other characters who remain invisible: Quixote's mother, aunt, and two sisters, the narrator in the puppet show, and five galley slaves (who are, however, onstage in the form of metal figures). Even when Quixote and Panza are both onstage their dialogue, which is recorded, does not necessarily correspond with their acting. That cinematic technique had already been used in such experimental plays as Jean Cocteau's *Les Mariés de la Tour Eiffel* or Marguerite Duras's *India Song.* As Wittig rightly remarks, such a dislocation of words and gestures, which creates two simultaneous, physically different narratives, obliges spectators to concentrate on the signs of what makes the essence of theater: the bodies of the actors and the human voice. "If one demands this kind of attention from spectators in the theatre," she observes, "if sound track and action operate separately and autonomously, then both words and gestures will regain power and effectiveness."[13]

In this case, because *The Constant Journey* contains a political message it constitutes another Brechtian cinematic self-conscious technique or method of "blocking," which Maarten Van Dijk has described as "vertical montage" or "montage within the scene" that "amounts to simultaneous story telling."[14] The technique, which entails the active mental participation of the audience, combines with several other original self-conscious stage strategies to make *The Constant Journey* an ambitious epic play whose aesthetic complexity demands attention and reflection.[15]

The Constant Journey borrows all successive episodes from *The Adventures of Don Quixote.* On a superficial level, Wittig's two protagonists can be perceived as similar to Cervantes's two antiheroes who embark on a succession of "crazy" adventures motivated by Quixote's chivalrous craving to live up to his ideal of knight-errantry. Like Cervantes's character, Wittig's Quixote sees monsters where there are only sheep (scene 3, sound track); attacks "giants" that turn out to be windmills (scene 5, image; scene 6, sound track); confuses puppets with real persons (scene 11); and worships Dulcinea, an imaginary perfect figure grafted onto the actual person of a peasant (scene 7).

Faithful to its Spanish source, the play depicts a Quixote who seems naive, dauntless, and ascetic in her determination to save the world and a Panza who is down-to-earth, fearful, and sensuous in her paid mission to serve Quixote. The contrast between the two characters generates similar comic effects in both works. At the same time, however, Wittig's protagonists are perceived onstage as two actors who have athletic ability and are able to jump and somersault in their casual contemporary outfits. Wearing red American football shoulder and kneepads (her "medieval armor") and carrying a black and red striped baton for a lance, Zeig/Quixote resembles a twentieth-century American football player or gymnast. We learn from the sound track that Quixote has left her disapproving conventional family, and Panza ran away from her husband and two children when she became "infatuated" (9, 8) with Quixote. Thus the play retains the theme of knight-errantry but both the stage imagery of *The Constant Journey* and the voices on the sound track introduce us to another, more contemporary, action: the adventures of two women, who, having escaped from their families and traditional gender roles, have joined their lives in order to fight injustice.

Another significant difference from Cervantes concerns the theme of reading, which is central to Wittig's play. Quixote is often seen holding a book (scenes 1, 2, 8), and in scene 2 she keeps watch over her own library, a large pile of bound volumes, while the voices of her family discuss the necessity of burning all her books. The scene ends with a symbolic magic effect. The book Quixote holds suddenly takes fire, which lights her face and threatens to burn her. Unlike Cervantes's hero, who fed his imagination exclusively on medieval tales of heroism, various books depicting the lives of amazons and female warriors such as Joan of Arc or Guibourc of Orange have "fired" the mind of Wittig's Quixote (41–42, 74–75).

Many historical figures who have inspired her to rebel seem to refer to two other sources: Wittig's *Les guérillères* and Wittig and Zeig's *Lesbian Peoples,* which both construct a legendary world of powerful amazonian heroism and cultures. This self-reflexive reference is partly confirmed by the sound track of scene 4, when the aunt suggests that she wrote such documents as "The Artemisiad" or "The Epic of the Amazons" that have inflamed Quixote's mind. Quixote's models are lesbian queens who lived and fought side by side with their companion lovers, "Oreithyia and Antiope, Cleite and Penthesilea, Myrine and Libya, Anna and Artemis, Larina and Tulla" (9, 7), exactly like those of *Lesbian Peoples.* The warriors in *Les guérillères* are all engaged in fighting men's oppression as well as cultural and intellectual values attached to patriarchal regimes. We may therefore assume that the giants and monsters Wittig's Quixote fights stand for the fierce, overpowering forces of (hetero)sexist institutions.

The double intertextuality of *The Constant Journey* creates a twofold vision of the two antiheroes who are not exactly sixteenth-century knights living in imaginary medieval times, although they often speak and act as if they might be. Nor do they seem to coincide entirely with the image of credible twentieth-century lesbian heroines attempting to construct a society where freedom and sexual justice would prevail. The two coexisting subtexts of the play seem to invite a bifocal vision that underlines contradictions spectators have to understand and resolve. The character of Panza, for example, is particularly ambiguous. On the one hand, as her master's "squire" she seems motivated by self-interest and is very keen on inheriting the island Quixote has promised her. On the other hand, she supports Quixote, considers her a role model, and appears to be extremely fond of her. Moreover, the self-reflexive references to former works of the two authors (Wittig and Zeig) as the origin of Quixote's "madness" complicate issues because one may wonder whether they may indicate a retrospective self-critical, humorous comment. But to understand the full impact of the whole play one must analyze its performance and visual strategies.

Wittig and Zeig's mise-en-scène was characterized by many fragmenting metatheatrical techniques that in the best of Brechtian tradition encouraged spectators to achieve an intellectual synthesis and understanding of the play.[16] The properties—a screen, a wooden horse and donkey, a table, and books and puppets—were few and beautifully crafted. Extremely stylized, they all had a practical stage function. Some were carried back and forth between scenes by three visible stagehands who wore ankle chains and bells. In the galley scene (scene 9), which featured the shadows of five metal human figures on sticks, the arms and hands of the figures' manipulators were visible behind a screen. All speech except that of the narrator in scene 11 was whispered, as if adding verbal interaction to the show (Quixote and Panza) or commenting on it (Quixote's family). The diction of both Quixote and Panza was extremely slow and almost unnaturally clear so as to remind spectators that they were listening to actors. The production made ample use of spotlights and partial blackouts, which like a camera helped the audience focus on the production's bright colors and impressively long shadows and often on the motions of the performers.

In thirteen scenes these striking, very beautiful visual effects were concentrated on Quixote's and/or Panza's bodies, which became the loci of visual action. The miming techniques that Zeig and Kingleur used sometimes borrowed from the burlesque tradition of the circus. In scene 4, for example, as Kingleur chased Zeig in an attempt to remove her helmet, both actors fought amicably, jumping and somersaulting around and on top of a table. The emphasis was on flexibility, dexterity, and skill.

Zeig also used Etienne Decroux's mechanical and balletic scales of movements, which insist that the human body function as a degenderized machine. In scene 7, paying homage to Dulcinea, she held a red heart in her lifted right hand and swung her head, shoulders, and left leg repeatedly while slowly walking in an elegant, automatic pattern that made fun of Quixote's romantic aspirations and idealization of love.

On the whole, the well-coordinated performance of the two mimes seemed to do away with the usual genderized mannerisms of all the Western acting traditions as they both worked to reach a neutral style of movement.[17] At the same time, both actors stressed the healthy sensuousness of their bodies without presenting themselves as female voyeuristic objects. In scene 6, for example, Panza/Kingleur, seated on her donkey and with a napkin around her neck, drank from a gourd and cut and ate a pear with "unfeminine," practical gestures and voracious appetite. Her pleasure, however, was gradually spoiled by Quixote's dangerous attack against the windmills on the sound track. In scene 10, entitled "The Chin Washing Ceremony" and performed in total silence, two "magic hands" came out of a table to wash Quixote/Zeig's chin. She seemed at first surprised and then proud, pride gradually giving way to total physical delight and bodily contentment.[18] This insistence on the material workings of the body recalls *The Lesbian Body*, where lists of organs and detailed descriptions of biological functions seem to deconstruct any romanticized notion of women's bodies as the basis for innate "feminine" psychological or social characteristics.

The interaction between Quixote and Panza, which entailed much physical contact, was often imbued with warmth, energy, and subtle eroticism. In scene 12, Quixote, who had been arrested, was encaged, and her body and face expressed discouragement, pain, and violent anger as the sound track presented a heated confrontation between her and Sister 2. Panza manifested her love and concern, supporting her mistress with her own body. While Quixote leaned heavily against her shoulder, the intimacy between the two was apparent.

In the sound track of the following scene Quixote, gaining the upper hand in the onstage argument with Sister 2, suddenly burst out of her cage. With Panza's help the bars of the cage (strips of canvas) were gradually turned into a regal costume and crown. In a sham coronation ceremony, Quixote, seated on her throne and holding a scepter, seemed to become a queen, at least for Panza, who could then be seen as her companion lover.

It was as if they had both succeeded in turning slavery into a triumph of freedom and combined strength. For the first time in the play Panza's acting *gestus* seemed to change. Rather than a mixture of pedestrian criticism or fear mixed with genuine concern for Quixote as in the windmill scene, she now appeared more willingly engaged in Quixote's political quest for freedom. Scene 13 exuded an extraordinary combination of joy, empowerment, physical energy, and bodily closeness that called to mind Audre Lorde's essay on the "erotic as power."[19]

In the next scene, Quixote gave Panza a lesson in how to handle her lance. With Quixote as her model, Panza was learning the skill of fighting, and sexual intimacy was suggested again (at least for lesbian spectators) as the two actors touched and looked at each other while handling the lance. But the lance was, in fact, a Peking Opera baton, which gave the drilling exercise a metatheatrical connotation. Spectators were also prompted to see a performer practice a theatrical technique with another during a rehearsal. By the scene's end Panza was as skilled as her teacher and stood out as her equal as she sat behind Quixote on the horse, holding Quixote tightly around the waist.

It is tempting to read these three visual scenes in linear sequence as a gradual demonstration of Wittig and Zeig's political notion of lesbianism in

which eroticism is inextricably linked with the energy of fighting side by side
against the slavery of gender and heterosexism. Panza, shown at the beginning of the play as Quixote's whining employee, gradually asserts herself as
a loyal companion and possibly a lover. What becomes evident in *The Constant Journey* is that lesbianism is not an essence but a long-range process of
change that entails belief in community, both past and future, and personal
transformation through erotic and political interaction with others.

One of the effects of the disjunction between images and sound in the
performance of the play is to provide a dialectical commentary on the adventures of the two main protagonists through the voices of Quixote's family
members, who form a sort of Brechtian chorus. Within this chorus the mother
and Sister 1 always side against Quixote, insisting on her madness and the
dangers of the rebellious adventures that have taken her away from marriage
and motherhood. The aunt, however, who has never married and admires
Quixote for her courage and love of freedom, defends her eloquently against
the others' verbal attacks. She saves Quixote's books from the fire, and at the
end of the play she offers shelter to Sister 2, who suddenly declares she does
not want to be pushed into marriage (48, 81).

Sister 2 is the only family member who converses directly with Quixote,
and at first she proves to be her most vehement critic, particularly when she
talks about Quixote's same-sex involvements (Panza and Dulcinea) (48, 81).
If we read the play as a process of lesbianization, the aunt, who is totally independent from heterosexual bonds, can be seen as a sort of nonpracticing
lesbian, like Herbert and Albert in Benmussa's *The Singular Life of Albert
Nobbs.* Sister 2 is an unusual case. She not only "protests too much" about
Quixote's emotional and political interest in women but also takes her first
step toward freedom (and possibly lesbianism) by agreeing to go and live with
her aunt.

The aunt's refusal to consider Quixote as "mad" is remarkable because
she is the only one in the play not to view Quixote's liberation of slaves or
destruction of puppets as insane acts. Indeed, the most political scene of *The
Constant Journey* is that of the galley slaves (scene 9). In the dialogue between
Quixote and the five "criminals," Quixote declares them innocent because their
alleged crimes—prostitution, abortion, murder, and robbery—were motivated
by imposed poverty, rape, physical violence, and forced marriage.

The most spectacular of the galley slaves is Gina de Passamonte, whom
Panza admires greatly. She is a sort of modern Molly Cutpurse who only robs
rich people in order to give to the poor out of a sense of justice. She is writing her memoirs with the help of young Vera de Mirador, whom, we assume,
is her lover because she has "followed [her] all the way on her own accord,

even when [Gina de Passamonte] exacted ransom from her family" (32, 37). The scene denounces both the oppression of women by men and the injustice of a legal system that favors the latter because they are powerful and rich. Gina de Passamonte is "laden with more irons than the others" because she constitutes a threat to property, and according to her, "nothing is more sacred than property" in our societies (32, 37). So the scene seems to condone and even celebrate rebels whom unfair sexist and capitalist laws have forced to take justice into their own hands and become outlaws.

But we know from the sound track of scene 5 that the freed galley slaves finally turn against Quixote and rob her, just as they do in Cervantes's novel. In scene 9 the audience is therefore left to decide whether to side with the aunt or all the other characters on the validity of Quixote's act of liberation. Wittig would probably stand on the side of the aunt because in *The Straight Mind* she declares, "*Outlaw* and *mad* are the names for those who refuse to go by the rules and conventions, as well as for those who refuse to or cannot speak the common language." It seems that the galley slaves have all broken the social contract, "which consists in living in heterosexuality," in order to free themselves from men's acts of cruelty that are left unpunished or accepted as normal.[20] Over the course of the play they do not develop a political conscience, nor do they learn from Quixote's social ethics.

The question of Quixote's madness is posed repeatedly and appears most acute in the puppet show scene (scene 11) in which the voice of a narrator recounts one of the most famous battles of the Thermodontine amazons against Theseus's Greek army, a battle mentioned in *Lesbian Peoples*.[21] It is illustrated onstage by illuminated and colorful metal figures representing Antiope, Hippolyte, and Theseus's ship and palace. After Theseus tricked Antiope, queen of the amazons, and imprisoned her in Athens, Hippolyte, her companion lover, attacked Athens and rescued her. Before the end of the story, when Quixote, who with Panza is an onstage spectator, hears about the dangers the two heroines encounter, she attacks the puppets (the Greeks) and destroys them. Despite the outcry of the innocent narrator who finds herself "ruined," Quixote exclaims, "Look at what would have happened to Antiope and Hippolyte if I had not been here!" (36, 72).

At this point it is difficult not to wonder at Quixote's sanity, especially because she is supposed to be a writer who should know the difference between signs and their referents. Even if the episode underlines the potential impact of theater on the imagination of its spectators, Quixote's destruction appears naive and self-defeating. Are spectators supposed to view Quixote as deranged, or are they expected to use the bifocal vision previously mentioned and therefore see Quixote as both Cervantes's hero, a comic character who destroys the puppets, and Wittig's protagonist, a twentieth-century radical lesbian carried away by political passion? Or should they consider Quixote as a twentieth-century lesbian performer impersonating Quixote and pointing to his foolish behavior?

Whatever interpretation one chooses to give to this scene, it seems that the audience, as in several other parts of the play, is prompted to perceive Quixote not as a static entity but as a succession of social comportments, heterogeneous and often surprising in variety. The social *gestus* of the main protagonist, which has to be constructed by both actors and spectators, seems to be that of someone whose rebellious intentions to change the world would be exemplary if her wild imagination and passion for heroism were not somewhat extreme.

The Constant Journey also addresses the question of social change. Although I have suggested that it revealed a process of "lesbianization" affecting the aunt, Panza, and Sister 2, the last scene casts doubt on Panza's change and on the play's opening onto a different future. Visually, the scene is very much like scene 1 except that the brief illuminated vignettes presenting Quixote and Panza on their horse and donkey are played in reverse. The first sequence is at the end and the last at the beginning. The final dialogue between Quixote and Panza reveals a Panza still skeptical about the meaning of Quixote's enterprise: "All of this will end badly, . . . you want to be right while disagreeing with everybody" (52, 5). Quixote's last words reassert the validity of her vision: "Even if the whole world thinks that I am mad, and not only those half-wits in the village who have not seen anything, I will say that the whole world is crazy and that I am right" (52, 5). The statement recalls Wittig's concluding words to her chapter on "The Social Contract" in *The Straight Mind:* "For if there is something real in the ideas of Rousseau, it is that we can form 'voluntary associations' here and now, and here and now reformulate the social contract as a new one, although we are not princes or legislators. Is this mere utopia? Then I will stay with Socrates's view and also Glaucon's: If ultimately we are denied a new social order, which therefore can exist only in words, I will find it in myself" (45).

In *The Constant Journey,* the "voluntary associations" reformulating the social contract are not easy to create, as the selfish behavior of the galley slaves and the resistance of Panza and Sister 2 demonstrate. The aunt's faithful support, however, shows that Quixote is not totally alone. Dulcinea, whom Quixote would like to enlist in her adventures as an equal partner, remains an ideal but absent figure throughout the play, perhaps underscoring Quixote's unrealistic faith in the perfection of women and the importance of romantic love.

The action of *The Constant Journey* may not lead to a total reversal of the world, as it did in the utopian narrative of *Les guérillères*, but it could be viewed as part of a slow, ongoing process of transformation. If so, the ending of the play, with its repeated but reversed visual pattern, would reaffirm the necessity of the almost protean and "mad" task of freeing women from slavery. The play, as a whole, could also seem paradigmatic of Western feminists' self-questioning and discouragement during the 1980s. It could be read as a parable expressing humorous distancing from lesbian feminists' past heroic battles on behalf of other women (mainly heterosexual), who often respond to lesbians with skepticism and even betrayal (like the galley slaves). That interpretation would make *The Constant Journey* very close to *Virgile, non* (Across the Acheron) in its disenchantment toward heterosexual women, a disenchantment Wittig shared with many radical lesbians.[22]

Wittig's play never uses the word *lesbian* and is not at all explicit in its representation of homosexual desire. In fact, one could read the play or watch its performance without being fully aware of its erotic lesbian hints; the only direct reference to lesbians appears in the mention of amazons. Such discretion may in part be due to the tacit rules of the French stage in 1985 that allowed no representations of sexuality between people of the same sex.[23] It can also be explained by the fact that the play focuses on an overall political construction of lesbianism through Quixote's multiple dealings with Panza, Dulcinea, past heroic figures, and present "gigantic" political forces. According to Wittig, lesbian is neither a psychological nor a narrowly sexual notion limited to desire. It does not imply identification with other women based on similarity of either biological or psychological experience but rather a political commitment born of a universal sense of justice and requiring destruction of the "category of sex" as the underlying basis of all ways of thinking or modes of existence. This cause is, therefore, open to all women and possibly men willing to denounce and free themselves from the enslavement of gender. Because the play features human beings who are social actors rather than psychological entities it attempts to ignore the usual notion of "difference" between the sexes through a bifocal vision of Quixote as both Cervantes's hero and as a contemporary "lesbian" amazon. A narrow definition of "lesbian" restricted to same-sex sexual desire would not fit the play because Wittig's epistemological revolution is meant to make such a binary category as "heterosexual" versus "homosexual" eventually as unimportant or obsolete as that of men versus women.

The Constant Journey did not receive the recognition it deserved, perhaps because its complexity, both formal and ideological, took its middle-class audience by surprise, the more so because both the Petit Théâtre du Rond-Point (on the Right Bank) and the Renaud-Barrault Company were mainstream institutions. At a time when, according to Bernard Dort, political themes and the Brechtian inspiration had become so unfashionable in France that critics chose to ignore the epic aspects of Ariane Mnouchkine's production of *L'Histoire terrible mais inachevée de Norodom Sihanouk roi du Cambodge* (1986) by Hélène Cixous, it is hardly surprising that they also overlooked the epic qualities of *The Constant Journey*.[24] Insofar as the play interpellates (a verb I use in its Althusserian sense) its audience on an ideological level, it is obviously addressed to feminists, lesbians, and gay men, who all have an interest in subverting the notion of gender. Its parable, however, that of Quixote, appears universal enough to appeal to open-minded, cultured spectators interested in a theatrical modernization of a classical theme through an original combination of Brechtian cinematic techniques and unusual body movements. Reviewers were either blind to the play's experimentation, insensitive to its beauty, or insultingly sexist in their mention of its feminist references. They all ignored its lesbian content. It seems that both the innovative forms and radical political ideas of *The Constant Journey* were lost on mainstream critics, for whom the play acted as a "Trojan Horse" or "War Machine" (*SM*, 68–69), an object so foreign that it caused them to overlook its importance.

Wittig's play represents a remarkable attempt to eradicate the heavily genderized traditions of the Western stage. It dares to impart to the classical narrative of Quixote a fresh feminist significance and an uncompromising lesbian vision that is meant to shake spectators by forcing them to question what they tend to consider their most "natural" human characteristic: gender. Such a "lesbianization" of the world can appear so unsettling that it may provoke a strong resistance manifesting itself through blind denials or shallow dismissals, as it does in the play itself through the voices of Quixote's mother and sisters. *The Constant Journey* requires a receptive audience, well aware of and sympathetic to feminist, lesbian, and gay issues. That audience did not exist in Paris in 1985 and is unlikely to exist even now. If the play were to be mounted again either in North America or in England for a feminist or lesbian and gay audience it would undoubtedly rouse a great deal of appreciation.

NOTES

Some passages in this essay, which was written in 1999, appeared in "Lesbians on the French Stage: From Homosexuality to Monique Wittig's Lesbianization of the Theatre," *Modern Drama* 39 (Spring 1996): 132–55. I would like to thank Patricia Skippon for editorial assistance and Monique Wittig, Sande Zeig, and Louise Turcotte for providing precious information and documents on the mise-en-scène of *The Constant Journey*.

1. Before *The Constant Journey* she had also written *L'amant vert* (1967), which was produced in Bolivia in 1969, and *Le grand-cric-Jules, Récréation,* and *Dialogue pour les deux frères et la soeur,* three short plays commissioned by Stuttgart Radio. *Le voyage sans fin* was published as a supplement to *Vlasta* 4 (1985), an issue entirely devoted to Wittig.

2. Judith Miller has underlined the antifeminist climate and discriminatory practices that French female playwrights, directors, and actors had to contend with, even in the 1990s. Miller deplores the lack of women's theatrical companies in France and never mentions the presence of lesbians in the theatrical world. Such a silence illustrates well the closeted atmosphere of the French stage. Judith G. Miller, "Les femmes et le théâtre, et la France d'aujourd'hui: Entretiens avec Simone Benmussa, Marie-Claire Pasquier et Brigitte Jaques," *Jeu* 71 (1994): 110–18.

3. Simone Benmussa, *The Singular Life of Albert Nobbs,* trans. Barbara Wright, in *Benmussa Directs* (London: John Calder, 1979), 75–121; Sue-Ellen Case, *Feminism and Theatre* (New York, Methuen, 1988), 89.

4. The situation was different in Quebec, where in 1976 the actor and director Pol Pelletier, in *La nef des sorcières,* was directing her feminist anger at men, mothers, and heterosexual sex while praising in explicit terms the ecstasy and rebellious nature of lesbian passion. Her totally shaved head, bodily eroticism, and violence on the stage of a mainstream theater (the Théâtre du Nouveau Monde) were much more openly revolutionary than any other francophone plays I have heard of or seen. Pol Pelletier, "Marcelle II," in Luce Guibeault et al., *La nef des sorcières* (Montreal: Éditions Quinze, 1976), 67–71.

5. Benmussa, *The Singular Life of Albert Nobbs,* 86.

6. Monique Wittig, "One Is Not Born a Woman," in *The Straight Mind and Other Essays* (Boston: Beacon Press, 1992), 20. The essay was first published in French as "On ne naît pas femme" in *Questions Feministes,* no. 8 (1980): 75–84.

7. Other than Wittig, the most famous of these women were Christine Delphy, Colette Guillaumin, and Monique Plaza, all sociologists, and Nicole-Claude Mathieu, an anthropologist. They all later wrote specialized books on gender.

8. This is how Christine Delphy, who did not belong to the radical lesbian group, described her own political standpoint, which insisted on the material exploitation of women as a class, especially through unpaid domestic work in the home.

9. Although *Lesbian Peoples* can be read as a translation of *Brouillon,* the two books are quite different. For a comparison, see Kristine J. Anderson, "Lesbianizing English: Wittig and Zeig Translate Utopia," *L'Esprit Créateur* 34, no. 4 (1994): 90–102. Together with Wittig, Zeig taught semiotics of gestures and body movements at New York University in 1984. Later on she wrote and performed *Behind the Heart* (1988), which is adapted from two short stories of Djuna Barnes, and *Impersonators* (1990). She also wrote and performed a boxing piece, *What Will Be,* all in New York City. She then turned to the cinema and directed *Central Park* (1994), a short lesbian film, and *The Girl* (2001), a feature-length film based on Wittig's short story and which they coauthored.

10. The production also toured the Midwest. For a description, see Harriet Ellenberger: "The Dream Is the Bridge: In Search of Lesbian Theatre," *Trivia* 5 (Fall 1984): 32–33, 46–47, 50–53. For a review of two scenes of the performance, see Jill Dolan, "Women's Theatre Program ATA: Creating a Feminist Forum," *Women and Performance: A Journal of Feminist Theory and Performance* 1, no. 2 (1984): 5–13.

11. In quotations I shall use Zeig's unpublished translation (in the Lincoln Center Library for the Performing Arts), but my description of the play will refer to the French text, which is that of the Paris production. After each quotation I shall give two page numbers, that of

the French text and that of Zeig's translation. Originally, the work was longer, with twenty-two scenes.

12. Bertolt Brecht, *Brecht on Theatre: The Development of an Aesthetic,* ed. and trans. John Willett (New York: Hill and Wang, 1964), 37.

13. Monique Wittig, *"The Constant Journey:* An Introduction and a Prefatory Note," trans. Barbara Godard, *Modern Drama* 39, no. 1 (1996): 158.

14. Maarten Van Dijk, "Blocking Brecht," in *Re-Interpreting Brecht: His Influence on Contemporary Drama and Film,* ed. Pia Kleber and Colin Visser (New York: Cambridge University Press, 1990), 125. Each scene of *The Constant Journey* has two titles, another Brechtian device that points out the double montage of the play.

15. It therefore belongs to a very strong aesthetic current in feminist materialist plays, English, American, and Québecois, which have appropriated Brechtian techniques. The appropriation has been studied by English-speaking feminist critics. See Janelle Reinelt, "Beyond Brecht: Britain's New Feminist Drama," *Theatre Journal* 38, no. 2 (1986): 154–63; Elin Diamond, "Brechtian Theory/Feminist Theory: Toward a Gestic Feminist Criticism," *Drama Review* 32 (1988): 82–94; Karen Laughlin, "Brechtian Theory and American Feminist Theatre," in *Re-interpreting Brecht: His Influence on Contemporary Drama and Film,* ed. Pia Kleber and Colin Visser (New York: Cambridge University Press, 1990), 147–60; and Jeannelle Laillou Savona, "Problematics of a Feminist Theatre: The Case of *A ma mère, à ma mère, à ma mère, à ma voisine,"* in *Theatre and Feminist Aesthetics,* ed. Karen Laughlin and Catherine Schuler (Teaneck: Fairleigh Dickinson University Press, 1995), 25–39.

16. My study of the Paris mise-en-scène is based on a videotape produced by Anne Faisandier (Company Renaud-Barrault, Centre Audiovisuel Simone de Beauvoir, Paris, June 1985). I also owe many complementary details to Louise Turcotte, who was in charge of the production (Régie), and to both Wittig and Zeig, whom I interviewed together by telephone in May 1995.

17. This mode of acting seemed to illustrate Zeig's ideas, as they are expounded in her article "The Actor as Activator: Deconstructing Gender," *Women and Performance: A Journal of Feminist Theories* 2, no. 2 (1985): 12–17.

18. Historically, such a ceremony is associated with bearded kings or emperors. Here it has ironic meaning. Quixote has no beard but can be seen as a queen on account of her great courage and imagination.

19. Audre Lorde, "Uses of the Erotic: The Erotic as Power," in *Sister Outsider: Essays and Speeches* (Freedom, Calif.: Crossing Press, 1984), 53–65.

20. Monique Wittig, *The Straight Mind and Other Essays* (Boston: Beacon Press, 1992), 40. Hereafter cited as *SM.*

21. See the entry "Hippolyte and Antiope," in Monique Wittig with Sande Zeig, *Lesbian Peoples: Material for a Dictionary* (New York: Avon Books, 1979), 73–74.

22. In 1981 French radical lesbians created the Front of Radical Lesbians, which dissociated itself completely from the Mouvement de Libération des Femmes: Women's Liberation Movement (MLF). According to them, "radical feminists" and "homosexual feminists" were all "hetero-feminists." They declared that they "no longer wanted to fight on behalf of 'the mass of women' as some had done for years at the price of their own self-denial" (my translation). See Front des Lesbiennes Radicales, "La scission du Front des Lesbiennes Radicales," *Nouvelles Questions Feministes* 1 (Oct. 1981): 125.

23. Theater has always been more timid than fiction in its representation of taboo subjects. Even in novels, however, lesbian writers and topics have remained marginal and are almost never mentioned in French canonical histories or anthologies of literature, whereas homosexual male writers such as Marcel Proust, André Gide, or Jean Cocteau have always

been part of the canon. The writings of Liane de Pougy, Renée Vivien, or Violette Leduc, and even Colette's homosexual texts, are still ignored by mainstream critics in France, so the title of Wittig's novel, *Le corps lesbien* (1973), exploded on the French literary scene as a bombshell. For the importance of this novel in its French context, see Elaine Marks, "Lesbian Intertextuality," in *Homosexualities and French Literature: Cultural Contexts, Critical Texts,* ed. George Stambolian and Elaine Marks (Ithaca: Cornell University Press, 1979), 353–77.

24. Bernard Dort, "Brecht in France in the Eighties," in *Re-interpreting Brecht: His Influence on Contemporary Drama and Film,* ed. Pia Kleber and Colin Visser (New York: Cambridge University Press, 1990), 99–102. Dort also relates (100) how Giorgio Strehler's *The Threepenny Opera* at the Théâtre du Chatelet was a failure, although his earlier productions of the play in Paris in 1956 and 1972 had been very successful.

10   *The Critical Mind and*
The Lesbian Body

Namascar Shaktini

Because Monique Wittig's most experimental work, *The Lesbian Body,* is not situated at the same level as realistic novels, it has met with mixed reaction. The decomposition of the body and the typographical slashing of the French subject pronoun *j/e* in that text have elicited strong positive and negative reactions among Wittig's North American critics. How should the textual violence be read? What is the author's strategy? Wittig's detractors and her defenders both raise such questions. Here, I will present a brief review and discussion of recent readings of *The Lesbian Body.* I will also offer analysis of Wittig's own reading of her work as "a reverie about the beautiful analysis of the pronouns *je* and *tu* by the linguist Emile Benveniste."[1]

One who strongly rejects Wittig's work is Penelope Englebrecht, who, in a 1990 *Feminist Studies* article "'Lifting Belly Is a Language': The Postmodern Lesbian Subject," criticized Wittig's violence and "postmodern strategy."

> The trouble with Wittig's "j/e" is twofold. Namascar Shaktini has claimed that by "appropriating from the most central cultural contexts phallogocentric, heterosexual metaphor, Wittig has lesbianized it. In *Le corps lesbien* the default, or unmarked, phallic subject has been displaced by the lesbian subject," . . . ostensibly as a result of "violence" to the language. But that violence is done more visibly to the lesbian Subject herself by splitting her very sign (her/self). I reject this violation of the lesbian Subject, textual or corporeal, as a theoretical principle because I think that it reinforces a phallic violation which objectifies.[2]

Englebrecht's problem with the textual violence to the "self" of the "Subject" lies in her conflation of subject as signified and subject as signifier ("her very sign [her/self].") Wittig's strategy is to radically separate the two. Indeed, she creates a signifier with no signified. Wittig's book is about writing the lesbian body, about the reconceptualization of the body. Nowhere in the 110 prose poems is it a question of the "self." As we see at the end of Poem 97, Wittig's focus is instead on the "figuration" of lesbian love:

> May you conceive yourself as Ⱦ at last see you over the greatest possible space, may your understanding embrace the complexity of the play of the stars and of the feminine agglomerations, may you yourself in this place strive in a frenzied confrontation whether in the shape of the angel or the shape of the demon, may the music of the spheres envelop your struggle, may you not lose your way in pursuing the stillborn, may the black star crown you finally, giving you to sit at m/y side at the apogee of the *figuration* of lesbian love m/y most unknown.[3]

Similarly, figuration is the focus in Poem 17, where we become aware at the very end that the subject being addressed is a disembodied signifier: "m/y mere surface m/y so flat one m/y depthless one m/y veil of Lesbos your face all flat painted on the linen of Veronica like the anguished features of Christa the much crucified" (*LB*, 35).

To continue with Englebrecht's objections, "The secondary problems I perceive are Wittig's implications: that j/e can 'enter' language—j/e is language; that writing, which is language, can do 'violence' to itself, language; that 'enter[ing] by force' is a valid lesbian tactic, rather than a characteristically phallic intention antithetical to lesbian[ism]"("'LBIL,'" 96).

Englebrecht fails to note that Wittig's discussion of a minority writer's point of view entering the language by force is extratextual and not part of the original text of *Le corps lesbien*. Wittig's comment appears only in the "Author's Note" appended to the English translation of the original text. There, she is no longer bound by the textual strategy of *Le corps lesbien,* no longer required to sustain through *j/e* the attack on the signifier. Outside the text Wittig speaks in the voice of a critic, albeit about her own text. She is as free as any other critic, as free as Englebrecht, to use the subject pronoun according to the Cartesian convention we all still use, to say "I think."

When Englebrecht argues that "j/e is language; that writing . . . is language," she conflates a system and an act, ignoring a distinction well known in French critical thought since Ferdinand de Saussure first theorized the two basic aspects of language: *langue* (a system of grammar, lexicon, and images that preexist the subject) and *parole* (enactment of that system by a subject who signifies, for example in the medium of writing). It was because Saussure identified parole as distinct from langue that Emile Benveniste was later able to theorize subjectivity in language as a phenomenon existing only in a specific instance of discourse. Subjectivity exists only in parole, it is nowhere to be found in langue. *The Lesbian Body,* as Wittig points out, is among other things an extended play with (and illustration of) Benveniste's insight: "I have considered this text a reverie about the beautiful analysis of the pronouns *je* and *tu* by the linguist Emile Benveniste."[4]

One is also reminded of the distinction for theater made by Bertolt Brecht between the actor and the character being enacted. The actor is similar to the linguistic subject constituted by the system of language that logically preexists him or her. Any actor is constituted as actor by enacting the preexisting character, but a Brechtian actor becomes a signifying subject to the extent that he or she "shows" or comments on instead of identifying perfectly with the character being portrayed. Brecht's estrangement effect, or *Verfremdungseffekt,* thus involves multiple levels of signification.

Similarly, *The Lesbian Body* "shows" the dilemma of the lesbian author trying to signify within phallogocentrism. In Poem 8, Wittig rewrites "Heureux qui comme Ulysse," the famous sonnet written by Joachim du Bellay, who, as a male author, was able to appropriate the image of the hero of an all-male voyage. I think of Wittig's *j/e* as a Brechtian actor trying but failing because of assigned gender roles to identify with the hero: "Happy if like Ulyssea ɫ might return from a long voyage. . . . But no ɫ am well aware that ɫ am not part of this voyage, ɫ am on land" (*LB*, 23).

Among Englebrecht's objections is a remarkable statement: "Nor do I think that the "appropriat[ion of] . . . heterosexual metaphor" can accurately or adequately enscribe lebian[ism]." She thus would argue against a claim that no one, as far as I know, has made: that it is now possible to "accurately or adequately enscribe lesbianism." Indeed, Wittig's whole point is the impossibility of doing so within phallogocentrism. Finally, having failed to provide convincing evidence, Englebrecht comes to what appears a gratuitous conclusion: "It seems to me that Wittig fails to escape the flaws of the phallogocentric Subject she 'displaces,' and I think that her concentration on essence limits her postmodern strategy" ("'LBIL,'" 96).

Unlike Engelbrecht, other critics see no "concentration on essence" and approach the difficulty of reading *The Lesbian Body* quite differently. For example, Clare Whatling, in "Wittig's Monsters: Stretching the Lesbian Reader," reads "Wittig's embracing of the grotesque as a profoundly anti-essentialist and anti-assimilationist gesture." In the extended citations that follow, I point to Whatling's more subtle and developed analysis of Wittig's violence and the unique demands placed on Wittig's readers:

> To the extent that Wittig appears to set up an absolute notion of identity as implied in the title of her text, so *The Lesbian Body* invokes an implicit promise to *tell* the secrets of its ontology, namely that there is some such thing as a lesbian and its nature will be described (inscribed) within the text. In fact, and

as I shall show, this is a promise which is always already foreclosed upon. For *The Lesbian Body* is a text which, rather than celebrating a unified notion of the lesbian, institutes separation, multiplicity, contradiction and the fracturing of lesbian identity into a thousand possible combinations.[5]

It is in this poststructuralist context that Whatling addresses the violence so troubling to many critics of Wittig:

> That Wittig's lesbian community is tormented by violence in social and individual relations can present a problem for mainstream feminism. Indeed, contrary to the ease with which the righteous vengeance of the oppressed in *Les guérillères* was celebrated, the violence at work in *The Lesbian Body* has presented far greater problems for readers. Diane Crowder, for instance, observes that "*The Lesbian Body* has provoked marked hostility in many readers who object most often to its perceived violence." Hélène Wenzel concurs in noting how "Feminists who were thrilled by the literal violence of the guérillères against the patriarchy, were appalled by its prevalence in *The Lesbian Body.*" When contrasted with the equally extreme but male-directed violence of *Across the Acheron,* however, it seems clear that readers' problems with *The Lesbian Body* lie with the self-directed woman-on-woman nature of the violence depicted. In that there is no obvious justification for its occurrence, the violence which informs the text seems at the very least questionable, if not wanton. ("WM," 239)

Whatling offers the following explanation of this violence in terms of the unique ambivalent author-reader relation Wittig sets up:

> Separating herself once and for all from the womanist community which only misperceives, condemns or denies her writings, Wittig then sets her sights on another kind of reader. This is the reader who *dares* to read on, to partake of the abjection in which the book is inscribed, simultaneously seduced and revolted. For Wittig recognizes only too clearly the mix of fascination and repulsion that characterizes the experience of reading *The Lesbian Body,* recognizing this while simultaneously demanding a response. If this be characterized by ambivalence then so much the better, since the nature of her grotesque is to address and confront the reader, daring her to read on, as it were *despite* herself. ("WM," 242)

Whatling finds the protagonist of *The Lesbian Body* to be a "monster lover" with a difference: "The monstrousness of the love protrayed within the text demands the appelation. Still, its repetition is also an inversion of the traditional situating of the monster as irrecuperably bad. For the monster of *The Lesbian Body* is the 'adored monster.' . . , variously: 'my vile one.' . . , or the 'abominable mistress.' . . . Her identity unfixed, above all she is an example of Ellen Moers' 'monster of ambivalence'" ("WM," 245).

What then is Wittig about that so puts off mainstream readers? Dianne
Chisholm suggests a political answer in her analysis of Wittig's rhetorical strat-
egy in "Lesbianizing Love's Body: Interventionist Imag(in)ings of Monique
Wittig." Wittig, Chisholm says:

> (re)writes the body physical and the body politic in the name of the lesbian
> body, calling into question the "ambiguity" of the signifier "feminism." . . . In
> Wittig's fiction as in her criticism "lesbian" signifies a counter-attack on the
> categorical thinking that she calls "heterosexuality," which, as she sees it, is
> the prime oppressor of women's self-conception and existence as a body. . . .
> Wittig employs a lesbian feminist perspective to re-imag(in)e the body (politic),
> but she does not champion "lesbian writing" or a lesbian *écriture féminine.*
> . . . Just as Wittig's "lesbian" is not a "woman," so her lesbian body is not a
> female body; instead, the lesbian body signifies a categorical resistance to the
> "myth of Woman" and withdraws support from any critical venture that would
> recuperate the sign of "woman": in short, the lesbian body is an anti-body.
> . . . It should now be clear that Wittig's "lesbian body" does not represent a
> real, physical, or political body; it does not imagine lesbian persons nor even
> lesbian erotic experience. Rather, it acts as a body-metaphor; a catachresis,
> a metaphor without a literal referent that serves to conceptualize a radically
> different body/body politic, to think beyond representations of the conven-
> tional, naturalized body.[6]

Another fine analysis of Wittig's strategy is that of Karin Cope. Her *Hypatia*
article "Plastic Actions: Linguistic Strategies and *Le corps lesbien*" bases its
title on Wittig's claim that "language has a plastic action upon the real." Cope
follows "Wittig's strategy of suspending the more or less ontological determination of what a 'lesbian body' is in favor of a discovery of how a Lesbian Body
can be written." Borrowing her term from the situationists, Cope identifies
Wittig's strategy as one of *"détournement,* an appropriation and redeployment
as 'lesbian' literature of the old war horses of Western culture."[7] Referring
to Wittig's identification of her strategy as a Trojan Horse (*SM*, 68–75), Cope
analyzes Wittig's strategy as a ruse:

> Manufacture of any "woman" (or "man," for that matter) is accomplished by
> some kind of ruse and can only be countered by another, different ruse. While
> the first (patriarchal) ruse operates in a deceptive fashion, the second (femi-
> nist) counter-ruse plays upon an older etymological sense—from the French
> *ruser,* to force out of place, to drive back or down, itself derived from the
> Latin *recusare,* to refuse. . . . This combative ruse which Wittig reintroduces
> by way of strict attention to language I will call "lesbianization," a practice of
> the *détournement* of the presumptions and language of heterosexuality used
> as a strategic weapon in the battle for the liberation of "women" from the
> oppressions and omissions of dyadic logic . . . Wittig has made the activity of

lesbianization into a literary war machine . . . Wittig's use of the figure of the Trojan horse is thus an act of and an argument for a combative strategy that exploits the phagocytic aspect of dominant culture. . . . By means of such classical figurative vehicles, Wittig aims "to change the textual reality," the cultural and political horizon within which her texts are inscribed.[8]

As part of this strategy Cope explains how Wittig's text constitutes a different subjectivity. It is not of the same nature as the default subject at the center. It is a kind of minority subjectivity:

Wittig sets out to make the speaking lesbian subject not only central to her work but ineluctable as well. All other subjectivity is swept up in its wake, so that in the novels of Monique Wittig, if there is a subject it is necessarily a lesbian subject. We must be careful how we think about this subject, however, . . . Wittig's lesbian subject, while universal, is not a seamless whole, the One of patriarchal male "major" subjectivity. . . . As Wittig writes, "[T]he minority subject is not self-centered as is the straight subject. . . . This [involves] a constant shifting which, when the text is read, produces an out-of-the-corner-of-the-eye perception; the text works through fracturing." The power of minority subjectivity comes from multiplying sites of difference—so that even a "major" subject is revealed to be different from itself, fragmentary and fractured, minoritized, as in the so-called death of the subject.[9]

Cope makes an important point that has been missed by much superficial criticism that conflates the absolute, generic Subject and those subjectivites relegated to the status of special or specific. She draws a distinction between "Subjectivity" and "subjectivities":

Contrary to an all-too-popular opinion, "the death of the subject" does not mean the disappearance of subjectivity altogether but the abandonment of the myth of the supreme, fully present, fully conscious, fully intentional, universal subject as the only figure of subjectivity. When *the* subject is dead, subjects, however fragmented and fragmentary, remain to write and be written. Or, as Wittig describes this scenario: . . . "there is room for so-called minority writers to enter the privileged (battle) field of literature, where attempts at the constitution of the subject confront each other."[10]

As this brief review of the critical literature shows, we are seeing more critics able to read *The Lesbian Body,* admittedly a difficult text. Although a literal reading such as Englebrecht's only leads to a feeling of violation, more subtle readings elucidate Wittig's project. Whatling focuses on Wittig's profoundly antiessentialist and antiassimilationist gesture; Chisholm, on Wittig's body metaphor; and Cope, on Wittig's strategy of suspending the ontological questions in favor of how a lesbian body can be written. What the more positive readings of Whatling, Chisholm, and Cope have in common is a focus not on the signified but on the signifier. It is significant that the word *lesbian* appears only once in the prose poems of *The Lesbian Body;* it occurs only in the phrase "the figuration of lesbian love" (146).

Let us turn now for a final reading of *The Lesbian Body* to one suggested by Monique Wittig herself. In a well-known essay published in 1985, "The Mark of Gender," she made clear that at least sometimes she reads *The Lesbian Body* as "a reverie about the beautiful analysis of the pronouns *je* and *tu* by the linguist Emile Benveniste" (*SM*, 87). U.S. readers of *The Lesbian Body* have paid little attention to Wittig's reading of her own work in relation to her reading of Benveniste. Because Benveniste never treated lesbianism and never focused on the body, his name does not appear in a keyword search for Wittig's topics. At the time Wittig was writing *The Lesbian Body,* however, Benveniste's theory of the speaking subject was widely discussed by Paris intellectuals.

So let us ask why Wittig would make such an important gesture of acknowledgment of Benveniste and examine which of his concepts might have informed her view of the *The Lesbian Body*? I have found two. First, there is the issue of ontology. The lesbian body, like Benveniste's subject "I," does not exist in the way a tree exists. "There is no concept 'I' that incorporates all the I's that are uttered at every moment in the mouths of all speakers, in the sense that there is a concept 'tree' to which all the individual uses of *tree* refer. The 'I,' then, does not denominate any lexical entity. . . . It is a term that cannot be identified except in . . . an instance of discourse and that has only a momentary reference. . . . The essential thing . . . is the relation between the indicator . . . and the present instance of discourse."[11] Similarly, it is the specific instance of lesbianism that defines for Wittig the lesbian body. In general, there is no lesbian body, just as, in general, there is no "I."

The second point follows from the first. The referent of the subject addressed in *The Lesbian Body,* like Benveniste's subject, may have a different identity in each instance of occurrence. Readers of the 110 prose poems of *The Lesbian Body* may encounter, from the subject addressed in one poem to that addressed in the next, a completely different referent. Thus, the referent of the beloved in Poem 25 is a protozoan; in Poem 51 the referent is Osiris. The identity of the lover and the beloved of Wittig's book is specific to the poem. For Benveniste, similarly, the identity is specific to the instance of discourse: "*I* and *you* . . . do not refer to 'reality' or to 'objective' positions in space or time but to the utterance, unique each time, that contains them. . . . [They are] 'empty' signs that are nonreferential with respect to 'reality.' These signs are always available and become 'full' as soon as a speaker introduces them into each instance of his discourse."[12] *I* and "you," empty signs, recur throughout Wittig's prose poems, to be "filled" for each specific instance of discourse.

Because the lesbian body is not a thing that occupies a place in the realm of ontology, it can in no sense precede the viewpoint. As Ferdinand de Saussure put it regarding linguistic objects of study, "Far from it being the object that antedates the viewpoint, it would seem that it is the viewpoint that creates the object."[13] *The Lesbian Body* illustrates a range of viewpoints on its subject and even the denial of its existence.

Although lesbianism as energy, desire, practice, or situation has no doubt always existed everywhere, it has only recently come into existence as a word/ concept. Only since Baudelaire popularized it has the word *lesbian* come into usage in the West. What is called *lesbianism* in the West in the twenty-first century is without a name in other times and places.

Wittig's lesbian lover is addressed as "unnamable, unnamed" (*LB,* 46), and this negative lexical situation is recurrently alluded to. In *The Lesbian Body* there are eight occurrences of the word *unnamable* and twenty-seven occurrences of *name:* "I am she who has the secret of your name" (*LB,* 130). Because the lesbian body is not an entity like a tree, it can be (and largely has been) denied.

When men have not completely denied lesbianism, they have monstrously distorted it. Baudelaire, following in the literary path of his predecessors Diderot and Balzac, continued the alien, male-identified view of the lesbian couple, portrayed as "monster" and "victim." That is the "given," initial portrait of lesbianism with which Wittig must deal and the one that opens *The Lesbian Body.* In Poem 1, "you" is identified as a monster: "Not one will be able to bear seeing you with eyes turned up lids cut off your yellow smoking intestines spread in the hollow of your hands your tongue spat from your mouth long green strings of your bile flowing over your breasts, not one will be able to bear your low frenetic insistent laughter" (*LB,* 15).

Another viewpoint, the positive one of the lesbian, constructs the beloved as "adored" (ten occurrences), "adorable" (ten occurrences), or even deified: "You are the tallest, Ishtar goddess of goddesses you are the powerful one, blessed be your name over centuries of centuries" (*LB,* 93).

The older I grow, the more I appreciate Monique Wittig's work not only as poetry but also as a radical analysis of point of view. Point of view cannot be seen by those who construct it, for they think the objects they see are natural. They think these objects precede their points of view. The heterosexist point of view that has dominated civilization (at least since Sappho) has created a class of human beings called "women." Monique Wittig was among the first to see "women" not as a natural group but as a class. She reacted politically in 1969, even before the first actions of the Mouvement de Libération des Femmes, by writing *Les guérillères*. In one of her early theoretical pieces, "Paradigm" (1979), she said: "The reality 'woman' must disappear just as the reality 'slave' after the abolition of slavery, just as the reality 'proletarian' after the abolition of classes and of forced labor."[14] That "woman" was a historical creation of the dominant phallogocentric point of view could only be clearly seen from the point of view most antithetical to it—that of lesbianism.

Lesbians, unlike women, do not exist for men. That is true in two senses. First, men do not provide the raison d'être for lesbian existence, and, second, men do not recognize lesbian existence. Thus the viewpoint of lesbianism provides the most radical position from which to mount a critique of phallogocentrism. The originality of Monique Wittig's work is to show—in a profoundly Brechtian sense—how civilization has been brought to read certain human beings as women. Wittig makes readers conscious of this as they become aware of the act of writing itself, which, for Wittig, is also an act of unwriting and rewriting. To write the lesbian body as a lesbian materialist is also to unwrite the heterosexist images, myths, grammar, lexicon, practices, and relationships that create the object "woman." Woman does not precede the viewpoint of heterosexism. Woman is nothing other than an object created by the so-called transcendental phallic signifier. By displacing this signifier, Monique Wittig has showed that "lesbians are not women" (SM, 32).

NOTES

1. Monique Wittig, *The Straight Mind and Other Essays* (Boston: Beacon, 1992), 87. Hereafter cited as *SM*.

2. Penelope J. Englebrecht, "'Lifting Belly Is a Language': The Postmodern Lesbian Subject," *Feminist Studies* 16, no. 1 (1990): 96. Hereafter cited as "'LBIL.'"

3. Monique Wittig, *The Lesbian Body*, trans. David Le Vay (Boston: Beacon Press, 1986), 145–46, emphasis added. Hereafter cited as *LB*.

4. Emile Benveniste, *Problems in General Linguistics* trans. Mary E. Meek (Coral Gables: University of Miami Press, 1971), 87.

5. Clare Whatling, "Wittig's Monsters: Stretching the Lesbian Reader," *Textual Practice* 11, no. 2 (1997): 239. Hereafter cited as "WM."

6. Dianne Chisholm, "Lesbianizing Love's Body: Interventionist Imag(in)ings of Monique Wittig," in *Reimagining Women: Representations of Women in Culture,* ed. Shirley Neuman and Glennis Stephenson (Toronto: University of Toronto Press, 1993), 196–97, 201–2, 204.

7. Karin Cope, "Plastic Actions: Linguistic Strategies and *Le corps lesbien*," *Hypatia: A Journal of Feminist Philosophy* 6, no. 3 (1991): 79, 75.

8. Cope, "Plastic Actions," 76–77.

9. Ibid., 78.

10. Ibid.

11. Benveniste, *Problems,* 226, 219.

12. Ibid., 219.

13. Ferdinand de Saussure, *Course in General Linguistics,* ed. Charles Bally and Albert Reid Unger, trans. Wade Baskin (New York: Philosophical Library, 1959), 8.

14. Monique Wittig, "Paradigm," in *Homosexualities and French Literature,* ed. Elaine Marks and George Stambolian (Ithaca: Cornell University Press, 1979), 116.

PART 5

A NEW GENERATION OF READERS

11 *Dialogic Subversion in Monique Wittig's Fiction*

Dominique Bourque

Translated by Harriet Ellenberger

> Any work with a new form operates as a war machine, because its design and its goal is to pulverize the old forms and formal conventions.
> —Monique Wittig

Monique Wittig's protagonists frequently quote, aloud and from memory, the words of others. They will echo liturgy, for example, or Mao Tse-tung, or Descartes.[1] For the most part in fiction, when a character quotes from others the words quoted articulate the character's own view of the world. Because of Mikhail Bakhtin's definitive study of dialogism in Dostoevsky's work, however, we know that when words are quoted in such a way that two distinct perspectives, two different linguistic awarenesses, are perceptible, we are in the presence of an utterance that is double-voiced or dialogic.[2] There is dialogism when we notice certain words in the speech of characters, a tone or manner of speaking not properly belonging to them—when their discourse becomes dissonant, cautious, or polemical. Utterances are dialogic, for example, when characters borrow a style or intentions that they seem to question or mock. By extension, a novel is double-voiced, or dialogic, when it sets heterogeneous utterances in dialog with each other such that a new point of view on the world can emerge.

In a dialogic novel it is the free interaction between diverse visions that undermines the fixed (ahistorical) and absolute (single-voiced) perspective characterizing an epoch. Monologic novels, in contrast, may reproduce fragments of other discourses, but they situate them firmly within their own interpretation of the world. Novelists, then, who simply introduce dissident discourse into the speech of their characters do not thereby create subversive works. In fact, insofar as they remain within the bounds of formal logic, they perpetuate the conceptual system that underlies the tradition, social organization, or ideology they denounce.[3]

Abandoning the single-minded approach, a dialogic novelist also leaves behind the old authoritarian narrative mode that encouraged readers to passively identify themselves with the one to whom a story was being told. Instead, the dialogic novelist frees up the relationship between reader and author by inventing a narrative mode that positions the reader as an "interpretive subject," one who actively decodes the text.[4] Addressing itself to a reader who is open to change, a dialogic work dislodges and diverts the discourse of power for the purpose of swaying that reader's point of view on the world.

Nerval, Baudelaire, Mallarmé, Flaubert, Dostoevsky, and Sarraute have each used dialogism to open new perspectives. Wittig, too, employs the device of dialogism but in a strikingly original manner. She extends its application in two directions. The first involves inscription of subjects in language through pronouns, and the second involves inscription of their relationships through the act of narrating.

Extending Dialogism to Pronouns

To subvert the discourse of power on the literary front, Monique Wittig transgresses not only literary genres but also gender in language and "the categories of sex in politics and in philosophy."[5] Her choice of protagonists who do not fit the social paradigm leads, at the grammatical level, to reevaluation of the personal pronouns *je/nous* (I/we) and *tu/vous* (you). In her first two books, *L'opoponax* and *Les guérillères*, the reevaluation begins by confining those pronoun forms within reported conversations and quotations from texts while the narrative voice identifies itself only by the indefinite pronoun *on*.[6] For example, "On dit que Catherine Legrand dit à Valerie Borge, tu ne m'aimes pas" (We/one say/s that Catherine Legrand says to Valerie Borge, you don't love me) (*O*, 267). The author, by this stratagem, clearly delimits two subjective universes: the speech of identifiable subjects and the speech of an unidentified subject (the narrative voice). In both books the identity of that narrative voice remains uncertain until the very end.

Wittig adds to the uncertainty by abolishing the typographical frontier between words of the narrative voice and words of various characters. In the following dialogue between the nun and the schoolchildren, for example, nothing but a comma separates one voice from another:

On dit à la soeur, il revient quand [du ciel ton mari], il ne revient pas, mais quand, jamais, alors il est mort, non il n'est pas mort, et où c'est qu'on met les gens qui sont morts, dans un trou, mais ils vont au ciel?

(We/one say/s to the sister, when is he [your husband] coming back [from heaven], he is not coming back, but when, never, then he's dead, no he is not dead, and where do they put dead people, in a hole, but they go to heaven?) (*O*, 14)

If lifting barriers between words that quote and words quoted obliges readers to redouble attention in order to decipher who is saying what, it also makes the text a place where narrator and protagonists can meet, enter into conflict, or become accomplices much more freely. The textual space becomes more democratic, allowing playfulness and dialogue to emerge.

In that space where the story and its telling overlap, Wittig exploits the referential suppleness of the indefinite pronoun *on* to the utmost degree. Neutral as to gender and number, the pronoun possesses universality that the other pronouns do not share and can, in effect, replace or combine all of them. In fact, Wittig uses it to represent not only the narrative voice and not only a single character or homogeneous group of characters (for instance, Catherine Legrand and the other children or one or more *guérillères*) but also a constantly varying array of characters or groups of characters who are potentially in conflict. The indefinite pronoun *on* thus comes to represent all different types of subjects (including the reader because "on" more often than not includes the interlocutor) as well as categories of individuals (children/adults or females/males) traditionally treated separately.

In Wittig's hands, the indefinite pronoun even crosses barriers of time and space, as shown in the following passage that quotes from Baudelaire's "Invitation to the Voyage":

Valerie Borge dit à Catherine Legrand que le train ne s'arrêtera plus. . . . On rit. . . . On dit, des meubles luisants polis par les ans décoreraient notre chambre les plus rares fleurs mêlant leurs odeurs.

(Valerie Borge says to Catherine Legrand that the train will no longer stop. . . . We/one laugh/s. . . . We/one say/s, gleaming furnishings burnished by the years should embellish our room, the rarest flowers mingling their fragrance.) (*O*, 269–70)

Here the indefinite pronoun *on* widens its scope to include Catherine and Valerie as children, the grown-up Catherine (who, we eventually discover, is the narrator), the lost beloved to whom she is speaking (Valerie as an adult), and even the vanished poet Baudelaire.

After this amplified usage of the pronoun *on* has been well established in *L'opoponax* and *Les guérillères* (where the *on* of the narrative voice adopts the perspective of one after another of the warriors, coming to represent them both individually and as a collectivity), Wittig next extends dialogism to the more codified first and second-person pronouns. In her third book, *Le corps lesbien,* narration is in the first-person singular but not at all the first-person singular we are used to, as the forward slash that severs its written form (*j/e*) shows: "j/e te suis tu m//es" (Ɨ you am you m/e are).[7]

We are never allowed to know which of the two lovers is the voice we hear; perhaps it is one, perhaps the other, perhaps they take turns speaking. What we are introduced to, however, is a lived subjectivity utterly unlike the idealist conception of self as a separate, defined, and knowable entity. For Wittig, the lesbian lovers—through all their fantastical metamorphoses, explorations, and literal absorptions of each other—defy simplistic representations of lesbians (and females) and inscribe the text with their complexity and wholeness as human beings. Neither sacrifices herself for the other, and neither becomes an object of the other; what happens between them is woven into the fabric of their being. They meet, and both the "I" and the "you" are empowered by that meeting.

Orchestrating the Voices: Dialogism Extended to Narrative Structures

In *L'opoponax* the central character, whose path we follow from her first day at school to the end of childhood, learns to join her voice with the voices of others. She sings along with other children "à ma main droite il y a un rosier qui fleurira au mois de mai et on montre la main droite" (on my right is a rosebush that will flower in the month of May and we/one show/s our right hand); repeats after the teacher "Liliane lave le linge" (Liliane washes clothes); and learns to pray and go to mass on Sundays (*O*, 8, 16). But all this recitation of the words of her culture does not stifle Catherine Legrand's rebellious individuality. She learns to speak as others speak and do as others do, but as if she were learning a game to be played only until she found it boring. This refusal to give up her own desires makes Catherine Legrand's cultural apprenticeship a kind of parody.

Still, some of the stories she hears exercise a certain fascination. Two older children fear being kidnapped by a devil; she does, too. A teacher fears a ghost in the forest; so does Catherine Legrand. Her mother quickly squelches Catherine Legrand's repeating of these tales, showing her it is possible to disagree with what others say. But it is only at the end of the novel that Catherine Legrand will be ready to confront the question of beliefs:

> On réfléchit. On ne sait pas. On dit qu'on a beau offrir son âme au diable le diable n'en veut pas quoi qu'on ait entendu raconter à ce sujet. On dit qu'il ne vient pas à minuit quand on l'invoque.

> (We/one think/s. We/one don't/doesn't know. We/one say/s we/one might as well offer our soul to the devil the devil wants no part of it no matter what the stories tell. We/one say/s that he doesn't come at midnight when we/one call/s him.) (*O*, 263)

In the meantime, Catherine Legrand will become aware of her separate existence. She will discover her presence in the world, as when her inability to make classmates laugh provokes a first reflection on self:

> C'est tout lourd au-dedans d'elle, c'est immobile à la hauteur des yeux, ça regarde dehors à travers les orbites, c'est pris, ça ne pourra jamais être autre chose que Catherine Legrand.

> (It's all heavy inside her, it's motionless up to her eyes, it looks outside through the sockets, it's stuck inside, it can never be anything other than Catherine Legrand.) (*O*, 95)

Bit by bit, the protagonist begins to memorize and quote from schoolbooks the words of poets—writers witnessing their presence in the world. This recitation of lines canonized by the institution allows the narrative voice to imply what is not stated directly: The profound aloneness of Catherine Legrand, not in another country (like the imprisoned poet Charles d'Orléans, whose lines she copies into her personal notebook) but in her own, and her growing love for another girl in her class are subjects rarely associated with child characters in novels and banished from the discursive space around them.

Catherine Legrand's twisting and rerouting of canonized speech marks an important stage in the construction of her subjectivity, signaled in the second part of the novel by the progressive narrowing of what the indefinite pronoun *on* represents. However, it is only with the introduction of a poet's ł, likened to the narrowed "on" in the text's final quotation—"On dit, tant je l'aimais qu'en elle encore je vis" (One says, I loved her so that in her I still live)—that the character Catherine Legrand and the narrative voice finally coincide (*O*, 281).[8] Like Proust's Marcel at the end of *A la recherche du temps perdu,* the narrator at last materializes as the apprentice writer, beginning the story we have just read. But in *L'opoponax* the narrative voice's use of *on* rather than *je* allows her to tell her own story as if she had become someone else, formally inscribing the gap that separates child from adult.

In effect, the use of the indefinite pronoun writes a subtext into the story, that of passage from a self little conscious of the discourses that form it to a self attentive to the resonance of other voices within its own. And, in opting for this neutral pronoun, Wittig removes all her characters from the philosophical category of the feminine that the French language has assimilated, thus raising them from the status of Other to the status of universal subjects.

A world order based on the notion of sexual difference is ironically evoked throughout *L'opoponax*, from a teacher's outright declaration—"[l'homme qui a vu le fantôme] a eu le temps de se sauver parce que c'est un homme et qu'il n'a pas perdu son sang froid" ([the man who saw the ghost] was able to escape because he is a man and didn't lose his head) (*O*, 19)—to fairy tales to history lessons to edifying films for Catholic youth. And though Catherine Legrand and several of her classmates remain audacious and combative under this repeated cultural barrage, the critique of the structures of power that regulate the universe of the story is made indirectly—not by the principal character herself, who has not yet acquired the consciousness of her social position.

The Selective Assimilation of Discourses

It is only in the following novel, *Les guérillères*, that protagonists collectively become aware of their situation. In this work they have assimilated many discourses (scientific, philosophical, psychoanalytic, political, and religious) on "Woman." The following passages illustrate their re/citation of these converging representations:[9]

> On leur a donné pour équivalents la terre la mer les larmes ce qui est humide ce qui est noir ce qui ne brûle pas ce qui est négatif celles qui se rendent sans combattre. (They have been given for equivalents earth sea tears that which is wet that which is black that which does not burn the negative those who surrender without fighting.) (*G*, 111)

> Esclave tu l'es vraiment si jamais il en fut. (Slave you are if ever there was one.) (*G*, 153)

> Vile vile créature dont la possession équivaut au bonheur. (Vile vile creature the possession of which equates to happiness.) (*G*, 166)

The protagonists have also assimilated dissenting discourses: revolutionary songs like "La carmagnole" and "L'internationale" as well as certain socialist, Marxist, and feminist analyses and mottos such as Flora Tristan's "les femmes et le peuple marchent la main dans la main" (women and the people walk hand in hand) (*G*, 189). By quoting these words the protagonists articulate their consciousness of belonging to a category of beings oppressed in a given history, culture, and time—that is, in a not-unchangeable order of things.

This consciousness materializes in polemic—"active dialogism," as Bakhtin would say—that engages with official discourse and transforms characters into combatants on the rhetorical level. Their declarations set a critical distance from the principal ideological unities ("ideologemes") of this discourse, as shown in their treatment of Freud's concepts (the feminine as "dark continent") and those of Lacan (the primacy of the phallus as universal signifier). "Elles ne disent pas que les vulves sont comme les soleils noirs dans la nuit éclatant" (they do not say that vulvas are like black suns bursting in the night), and "elles n'utilisent pas pour parler de leurs sexes des hyperboles des métaphores" (they do not use hyperboles or metaphors to speak of their sex) (*G*, 81, 93). In this way they burst open the hierarchical structure of binary terms that characterizes dominant discourse, thereby preventing the reproduction of "History" by a simple reversal of its terms.

Similarly, they denounce the passive and pacifist nature attributed to them as individual females, affirming that it is better to die than to live in servitude (*G*, 132). And, finally, they undermine the reifying comparisons to which their bodies are subjected by using humor: "Elles disent, n'est-ce pas magnifique en vérité? Les vases sont debout, les potiches ont attrapé des jambes. Les vases sacrés sont en marche" (They say, isn't this truly magnificent? The vessels are standing up, the ornamental vases have acquired legs. The sacred vessels are on the march) (*G*, 206). In doing so they reveal the constructed and ideological character of gender.

Beyond the transformation of received opinion, dialogism also manifests in the choice of protagonists to speak and listen to each other. In doing so they strategically position the reader in their place:

> [I]l a fait de toi celle qui n'est pas celle qui ne parle pas celle qui ne possède pas celle qui n'écrit pas, il a fait de toi une créature vile et déchue, il t'a bâillonnée abusée trompée. Usant de stratagèmes, il a fermé ton entendement, il a tissé autour de toi un long texte de défaites qu'il a baptisées nécessaires à ton bien-être, à ta nature.

> (He has made of you one who is not one who does not speak one who does not possess one who does not write, he has made of you a creature vile and fallen, he has gagged abused tricked you. Using stratagems, he has closed your mind, he has woven around you a long text of defeats that he has deemed necessary for your well-being, for your nature.) (*G*, 159)

On the one hand, this address underlines, by virtue of the powers that language confers on those who use it, their status as full subjects. On the other hand, it mocks the exclusion of half of humanity from the schema of communication.

The system of diffusing words that protagonists have given themselves reveals the narrative plan of the novel. This system functions by rotation so each character can attain the posture of speaker. Whether bearer of news, teller of fables, engineer, hunter, or archeologist, each *guérillère* can acquaint the others with what she knows or has discovered.

In the same way, each of them participates in the writing of the "great register," an assemblage of different kinds of writing in no particular order that can be opened at random and added to and which subsumes even the novel itself. Thus, the story we are reading is told by each protagonist, and no single voice dominates the others; even the narrative voice becomes one among many. Abolishing the traditional separation between teller and recipient, writer and reader, Wittig opts for a polyphonic structure in which each voice—underrated, unrecognized, or misunderstood though it may be—can express itself in turn. Only because each protagonist has first realized herself through speaking out can a "we" then emerge as the narrative voice in the final sentence of *Les guérillères:*

> Et lorsque [la guerre] fut fini[e] . . . quelqu'une au fond de la salle cria, camarades, souvenons-nous de celles qui sont mortes pour la liberté. Et nous entonnâmes alors la Marche funèbre, un air lent, mélancolique mais pourtant triomphant.
>
> (And when the war was finished . . . someone at the back of the room cried out, comrades, let us remember those who died for freedom. And then we began singing the Funeral March, a slow, melancholy, but triumphant air.) (*G*, 208)

This new "we" abolishes sexual difference because the French plural pronoun *elles* has successfully fought the false neutrality/universality of its masculine counterpart *ils.* In fact, by outnumbering the masculine "they" in the novel, the feminine "they" have reversed the "natural" order of things and become the parodic equivalent of the masculine. Similarly, the neologism *guérillères* contests the binary terms *guerriers/guerrières* that describe men warriors (historically synonymous with "winners") and women warriors (historically synonymous with "losers"), thus opening the way to neutral grammar.

Elaborating a De/citational Discourse

The narrative devices of *L'opoponax* and *Les guérillères* are characterized by a constant back-and-forth between a narrative voice distanced from received opinion (the adult Catherine Legrand and the ensemble of warriors) and the voice of characters grappling with that speech (the child Catherine Legrand and each warrior individually). These voices join to the extent, in the first instance, that the awareness of individual self emerges (*on* becomes *je*) and, in the second instance, that awareness of a collective self emerges (*on* becomes *elles/nous*). In other words, the narrative and individual voices join to the extent that there is a passage from mechanical recitation to re/citation, an ironic recontextualizing of the dominant discourse.

In the novels that follow, *Le corps lesbien* and *Virgile, non,* the narrative voice is no longer limited by personal consciousness or emerging collective consciousness. The design of these novels is no longer linked to authoritarian speech but is free to combat its power by not reproducing it. Rather than re/citing the surrounding clichés, the narrative voice skirts them and tries for a "total *exclusion* of dominant discourse."[10] In this way Wittig's last novels inherit from the prose poem that nineteenth-century *l'art pour l'art* writers created to free language from its normalized referential and instrumental functions within the dominant discourse.

Unlike Baudelaire or Mallarmé, however, Wittig does not intend to create a work that has no end other than itself and can, for lack of content, only illustrate the turning of subjects into objects that the dominant discourse effects: "The pure work," writes Mallarmé, "implies the elocutory disappearance of the poet."[11] Rather, she tries to articulate a perspective that would be emancipated from this discursive desubjectifying. To do so she turns to lesbian protagonists not as representatives of an essential category of subjects but because lesbians are—by their unaccounted for and thus subversive position—nearly absent from authoritarian discourse and thus less marked by it than other types of protagonists. The articulation of this new perspective is accomplished in two stages. In *Le corps lesbien,* the author reformulates the amorous subject in the poetic mode; in *Virgile, non,* she reformulates the political subject in the argumentative or rhetorical mode.

Reformulating the Amorous Subject

In *Le corps lesbien* narration is done in the first-person singular (*j/e*), but the narrator remains unknowable. No sign lets us know if this narrative voice represents one of the lovers or, in turn, each of them. In fact, the particular identity of the lovers is of no importance in this work. What counts is the point of view that gives meaning and form to being loved in and for itself.

The narrative structure of *Le corps lesbien* is constituted by *j/e* telling about interactions she has with *tu,* by her interiorizing the words and actions of *tu*. To the degree that these interactions reterritorialize mythic or historic moments they acquire universal dimension. We recognize, for instance, the return from hell of Orpheus and Eurydice:

> J/e m/e mets à hurler de désespoir . . . à te supplier de m/e laisser dans m/a tombe à te décrire avec brutalité m/a décomposition les purulences de m/es yeux de m/on nez de m/a vulve. . . . Tu m//interromps, tu chantes . . . ta certitude de triompher de m/a mort.

> (Ɨ begin howling from despair . . . begging you to leave m/e in my tomb brutally describing m/y decomposition the purulence of m/y eyes m/y nose m/y vulva. . . . You interrupt m/e, you sing . . . your certitude of triumphing over m/y death.) (*CL,* 12)

This representation of the emotion of love, unusual because stripped of particularities, allows Wittig to highlight the different registers of the discourse, from argument, seduction, blackmail, and questioning to supplication and even prayer: "Pourquoi folle exécrable m/a très chérie t'es-tu faite pierre alors que j/e t'aime si tendrement?" (Why m/y execrable fool m/y most cherished one do you turn to stone when Ɨ love you so tenderly?) (*CL,* 25). Similarly, she uses a great variety of stylistic devices, including enumeration, alliteration, paralipsis, comparison, and play on levels of meaning. That systematic representation of a passionate dialogue becomes a formal exploration of the complexity of the love emotion. In this sense it highlights the human condition of the protagonists, including their aggressiveness. In orthodox representations of lovers, aggressiveness is most often masked or associated with only the male lover, but in *Le corps lesbien* it manifests in both. Moreover, Wittig transposes onto the discursive level the violence of amorous desire to an extent that even Baudelaire did not dare:

> Si quelqu'une dit ton nom . . . j/e sens m/on sang devenir plus chaud dans m/es artères . . . j/e deviens brusquement le lieu des plus sombres mystères . . . j/e suis le couteau qui tranche la carotide des agnelles nouvelles-nées, j/e suis les balles des fusils-mitrailleurs qui perforent les intestins, j/e suis les tenailles rougies au feu qui tenaillent les chairs . . . Sappho m/on incomparable, donne-m/oi les doigts par milliers qui adoucissent les plaies.

> (If someone utters your name . . . Ɨ feel m/y blood become warmer in m/y arteries . . . Ɨ suddenly become the place of darkest mysteries . . . Ɨ am the knife that slits the carotid of new-born lambs, Ɨ am machine-gun bullets that perforate the intestins, Ɨ am red-hot pincers that torture flesh . . . m/y incomparable Sappho give m/e by the thousands of fingers that soothe the wounds.) (*CL,* 8)

If this complex direction of a love dialogue breaks radically with representations of love in ordinary conversation, popular songs, or literature, it also breaks with the rare representations of lesbian lovers, either as demonized in pornography or made insipidly sentimental by a majority of authors treating "particular friendships" (Verlaine, Pierre Loüys, Renée Vivien). *Le corps lesbien* troubles and shocks because its anatomical and scientific descriptions do not fit with any previous erotic discourse:

> L'éclat de tes dents ta joie ta douleur la vie secrète de tes viscères ton sang tes artères tes veines tes habitacles caves tes organes tes nerfs leur éclatement leur jaillissement.

> (The brightness of your teeth your joy your pain the secret life of your viscera your blood your arteries your veins your hollow dwelling places your organs your nerves their rupture their outpouring.) (*CL*, 7)

This choice of language brings about the difficult, rigorous, amorous rediscovery of the material body under the mass of pornographic or sentimental representations that dismember or erase it.

Le corps lesbien also enters into polemic by attacking two types of censorship characterizing dominant discourse over the centuries: silencing lesbian experience and perceiving of lesbians as monsters.[12] Repeatedly evoking Oscar Wilde's de/citational formula "the love that dare not speak its name," Wittig satirizes the long Christian injunction to silence: "Ce qui a cours ici . . . n'a pas de nom pour l'heure" (What takes place here . . . has no name for the time being) (*CL*, 7). In fact, the title of the book itself, which begins and ends with the lists of the bodily parts and humours that punctuate the text as well as twenty-four mentions of Sappho's name, definitively revokes this silence.

The second type of censorship, the association of lesbians with monstrous beings, intervenes before and after the reign of the Christian law of silence. Horace qualifies Sappho as "masculine."[13] Ovid speaks of "monstrous loves."[14] Baudelaire calls lesbians "demons" and compares them to wolves.[15] And the *Dictionnaire universel du XIXe siècle* describes lesbians as women who have an abnormally developed clitoris.[16] Taking unexpected advantage of this propaganda, Wittig suppresses the idea of shame attached to metamorphoses and makes the transformations of her lovers occasions of erotic encounter and signs of victory over violences suffered. She transforms them into fascinating monsters like Argos, guardian of Io, whose hundred eyes become ten million eyes that sparkle and make music with each movement. She also transforms lovers into insects and animals, giving value to the determination of the fly, the pride of the mare, and the sensuality of the she-wolf and thereby articulates a body of desire that is eminently inventive and playful:

Il vient un moment où tout enfiévrée tu m/e prends sur ton dos m/a louve m/es bras autour de ton cou m/es seins m/on ventre appuyés à ta fourrure . . . tu te mets à galoper.

(There comes a moment when, in a fever, you take m/e on your back m/y she-wolf m/y arms around your neck m/y breasts m/y belly pressed against your fur . . . you begin to run wild.) (*LC*, 14–15)

Parallel to her ironic de/citing of orthodox love discourse Wittig also attacks the embedding of dominant discourse in language. Her parodic universalization of the feminine, already present in *Les guérillères,* combined with an extensive use of the passive form that neutralizes the subject's domination over the "object" as well as intransitive verbs with a direct object, transgresses orthodox French syntax while facilitating "the expression of relations between the self, the other, and the world."[17] Moreover, in treating the theme of passion Wittig summons the force for change that desire itself can represent.

Reformulating the Political Subject

In Monique Wittig's following novel *Virgile, non,* the narrative voice embodies an author who searches for a way to describe the world not as it has been shown to her but as it appears to her. By orchestrating interactions between the character of this narrator-author and the other protagonists, Wittig gives herself opportunity to question the writer's authority in the body politic. That she chooses to give her own name, "Wittig," to the author-character signals a dialogic perspective opposed to that of monologic novels that traditionally have a transcendent author pretending to "Truth."

The strategy works even better in that the character "Wittig" to some degree resembles Monique Wittig, at least insofar as one can judge by reading her works. They possess the same cultural background, embracing mythology, ancient literature, the Bible, and tales of chivalry. They are also both partisans of political lesbianism, which aims to destroy the categories of sex as the foundation of thought and existence, in order to achieve a just society.[18] Both, in this sense, subscribe to the philosophical tradition of the humanists, who place the human being at the center of their preoccupations and seek to further human liberty. Lesbianism thus becomes for both author and character/author an ethical and political strategy aiming to break with the social contract that maintains half the human population in servitude, particularly on economic and political levels.

The personality traits of "Wittig"—her tendency to play the smooth-talking troubadour or propensity to trip over her own feet while playing the hero—may or may not resemble those of the book's author, but their primary function is to signal that the character belongs to the category of antiheroes exemplified by Cervantes's Don Quixote (even the oratorical style of "Wittig" resembles that of Quixote). It is the link to Cervantes's parody that gives *Virgile, non* its ironic tone and confirms that it belongs to the tradition of the polyphonic novel. By representing a creator who is fallible and exists in the same world with the other characters, open to their attempts at dialogue and their criticism, slander, and attacks, Wittig demystifies writing in general.

Indeed, criticism rains down on "Wittig." The most cynical emanates from an eagle that swoops down on her. Having succeeded in bringing down the raptor, "Wittig" discovers it is no more than a robot whose vocal mechanism has been jammed in the fighting and so repeats the same clichés over and over. The eagle's words are aimed at returning the rebel to "slavery," the condition assigned to the "lost souls" (*âmes damnées,* the name given to "women" in *Virgile, non*) by the various powers-that-be and their "gods" throughout history. After reading this essay, Monique Wittig suggested a translation for *les âmes damnées:* lost souls.

The second type of critique is of an entirely different order and comes from the character Manastabal. Both she and "Wittig" are lesbians (renamed in the novel *marronnes,* "runaway slaves"). Manastabal guides "Wittig" through the circles of hell, the dwelling places of the lost souls, while rebuking her lack of realism:

[Wittig] Comment se peut-il, Manastabal mon guide, que tu fasses tant crédit à l'intelligence des âmes damnées. . . . J'ai toujours tendance à penser, quant à moi, que seul un certain degré d'abêtissement peut expliquer qu'on reste en enfer.

(How can it be, Manastabal my guide, that you give so much credit to the intelligence of the lost souls. . . . I've always tended to think, myself, that only a certain degree of mindlessness could explain remaining in hell.)

[Manastabal] C'est que ton principe à toi c'est: ou bien . . . ou bien. Tu n'établis pas de nuances. Tu ne vois rien de complexe à ce sur quoi repose l'enfer. Tu déclares qu'il faut le détruire et tu t'imagines qu'il suffit de lui souffler dessus.

(And that's your principle: either . . . or. You don't establish nuances. You see nothing complex in what hell rests on. You declare that it must be destroyed and you imagine that you can blow it out like a candle.) (*VN,* 86–87)

Manastabal's reproaches highlight the social responsibility of the writer, one who uses language and concepts that still bear the imprint of the dominant ideology. For Manastabal, the world will not know how to change if those who compose it are not truly "in the world."

As an author in charge of dialogue, "Wittig" must learn to ask good questions. She must learn to clarify the latent ideas of others and, so doing, better know herself. "Wittig" will serve out this apprenticeship among the "lost souls" who accuse her of arrogance, lack of morals, and lack of pragmatism. The first such shower of invective takes place in a laundromat:

> Va-t'en retrouver les gouines répugnantes. . . . Vous n'en prétendez pas moins vouloir sortir tout notre sexe de sa servitude. Il y a de quoi mourir de rire, si ce n'est que ma bile m'étouffera avant, quand je songe que la seule chose qui vous intéresse, c'est de le corrompre tout entier, notre sexe.

> (Go back to your repulsive dykes. . . . You claim to want nothing less than to lead our entire sex out of servitude. That's enough to make me die laughing, if I didn't choke on my own bile first when I consider that your only interest is to corrupt our entire sex.) (*VN,* 13–14)

Faced with differing reactions to her aims, "Wittig" responds in different ways. She gives the eagle a dose of his own medicine: "Ferme ta gueule, vieux radoteur . . . le silence est d'or" (Shut up, driveling old fool . . . silence is golden) (*VN,* 12). But Manastabal's interventions provoke sincere protest and supplementary explanations, pushing "Wittig" to make her arguments more convincing to the lost souls. In fact, one of them becomes convinced: "Je t'en prie, laisse-moi venir avec toi car j'apprends vite" (I beg you, let me come with you for I learn quickly) (*VN,* 105).

The accusations of the lost souls also guide the evolution of the character "Wittig," obliging her to sharpen her reasoning and rhetorical skills and adopt attitudes conforming to her principles. Their testimony confirms the validity of her thesis that they are subject to systematic oppression: "Viens-tu évaluer les coups que j'ai reçus? Faut-il que tu dénombres mes marques . . . mes organes éclatés . . . mes os brisés? (Do you come to assess the blows I have received? Must you count the marks on me . . . my ruptured organs . . . my broken bones?) (*VN,* 119).

If the eagle's commonplaces serve as a foil and Manastabal's reproaches function as a springboard, the protests of the lost souls are a yardstick for the intentions and words of "Wittig." In this way Monique Wittig places the subversive discourse of her narrator at the center of *Virgile, non* and orchestrates the entire ensemble of voices around it. Just as the character "Wittig" tries to describe a new paradise with the words of the "angels" (independent and powerful lesbians) she meets between the two circles of hell, Monique

Wittig constructs a new perspective on the world by playfully remapping the discursive system surrounding *Virgile, non.*

To represent a dialogic relationship between an author-character and the other protagonists transgresses the authority straightaway conferred on writers by the power system that diffuses their words, thereby leaving readers as sole masters of their judgment. Moreover, in opting for parody, Monique Wittig does not seek to convince her readership but to seduce them. By giving her lesbian subject the endearing aura of a Quixote, she invites readers to reinvent, along with "Wittig," the world in which they live.

Counter-Text

Monique Wittig's novels belong to the lineage of dialogic works that subvert the dominant discourse structuring social life. They do not, however, so much systematically oppose this discourse or attempt to reform it from within as they represent its limits and bias in order to form a dissident point of view on the world.[19]

To develop this new point of view, the question of subjects and their relationship to reality becomes central. And it is in her concern not only with artistic form but also with what has habitually been made to pass for reality that Monique Wittig most closely resembles the initiator of the *nouveau roman,* Nathalie Sarraute.[20] But while Sarraute devoted herself to making visible the violence covered over by everyday conversation, Wittig specifically attempts to make heard the voice of beings (children, feminists, prostitutes, and political lesbians) who are not allowed to speak or whose speech can only be out of step or at odds with surrounding and dominant discourse.

Thus, after Sarraute has unveiled the *sous-conversation* (words beneath the words), the place where "a speech of one's own" might be elaborated, Wittig, for her part, turns her attention to articulating and orchestrating the forms of that speech in a "counter-text." If her revisioning of the subjects who speak leads Wittig to break with the surrounding discourse much more violently than did Sarraute, it also incites her to create new literary forms. Those new forms, in turn, favor emergence of dialogue between conscious beings—those aware of what is at stake in their relationship to consensus reality and aware also of their power to transform that reality.

NOTES

I would like to thank especially Harriet Ellenberger, who not only translated this article but also acted as a precious collaborator. A French version of this text was read in June 2001 at a convention on Monique Wittig's work at Columbia University in Paris and was published in that meeting's proceedings: *Parce que les lesbiennes ne sont pas des femmes: Autour de l'oeuvre politique, théoretique, et littéraire de Monique Wittig*, edited by Marie-Hélène Bourcier and Suzette Robichon (Paris: Éditions Gaies et Lesbiennes, 2002).

1. Monique Wittig, *L'opoponax* (Paris: Éditions Minuit, 1964), 188 (hereafter cited as *O*): "et introibo ad altare Dei, et j'irai à Dieu qui est ma joie" (and I will go to God, who is my joy); Wittig, *Les guérillères* (Paris: Éditions Minuit, 1969), 204 (hereafter cited as *G*): "le pouvoir est au bout du fusil" (power comes from the barrel of a gun); and Wittig, *Virgile, non* (Paris: Éditions Minuit, 1985), 24 (hereafter cited as *VN*): "on ne peut concevoir que ce qui existe" (we can conceive only that which exists). All translations here and throughout the essay are the author's and Harriet Ellenberger's.

2. Mikhail Bakhtin, *Problems of Dostoevsky's Poetics* (Minneapolis: University of Minnesota Press, 1984).

3. This logic is founded on the concepts of identity, substance, definition, and causality, unlike the dialogic approach, which, according to Julia Kristeva, is characterized by "a transfinite logic of distance, relation, analogy, non-exclusive opposition." Kristeva, *Recherches pour une sémanalyse* (Paris: Seuil, 1969), 107.

4. Ross Chambers, *Room for Maneuver: Reading (the) Oppositional (in) Narrative* (Chicago: University of Chicago Press, 1991), 26–35.

5. Monique Wittig, *The Straight Mind and Other Essays* (Boston: Beacon Press, 1992), 81.

6. The French *on* generally corresponds to the English "we" and/or "one," but it can also correspond to the other pronouns. In the translation here, which is not meant to be literary, I chose "we/one" to emphasize the range and unusualness of Wittig's use of the pronoun *on*. Until not so long ago teachers used to banish this pronoun from written French, especially when it meant "we."

7. Monique Wittig, *Le corps lesbien* (Paris: Éditions Minuit, 1973), 135. Hereafter cited as *CL*. In this passage Wittig disturbs French syntax, which is reflected in the translation. In the case of the "I," following Wittig, I have adopted a more violent approach by slashing the letter—*Ɨ*. Wittig also uses a slash in the case of the first-person pronoun forms ("moi," for example, becomes "m/oi"), and when there is an apostrophe, she replaces it by another slash ("m'" becomes "m//").

8. Catherine Legrand appropriates this verse of Maurice Scève's poem "La délie" by using the imperfect tense instead of the preterite tense to conjugate the verb *aimer* (to love).

9. Borrowing Richard Terdiman's typology of counter-discourses, I will call "re/citational" the narrative structure that Wittig uses in her first two novels and "de/citational" the structure she uses in her last two novels. "Re/citation" involves recontextualizing the dominant discourse through the use of irony and leads to emergence of a sophisticated and personal perspective on the world. Terdiman, *Discourse/Counter-Discourse: The Theory and Practice of Symbolic Resistance in Nineeenth-Century France* (Ithaca: Cornell University Press, 1985).

10. This is according to Terdiman's definition of the procedure of de/citation (*Discourse/Counter-Discourse*, 280).

11. The quotation from Mallarmé is translated by Terdiman.

12. See the account by historian Marie-Jo Bonnet, *Les relations amoureuses entres femmes* (Paris: Odile Jacob, 1995).

13. Cited in Bonnet, *Les relations amoureuses entre femmes*, 52.

14. Ovide, *Les Métamorphoses* (Paris: Gallimard, 1992), 325.

15. Baudelaire, "Femmes damnées" (1 and 2), in *Les fleurs du mal* (Paris: GF-Flammarion, 1991, 162, 195.

16. Cited in Bonnet, *Les relations amoureuses eutre femmes*, 57.

17. Marthe Rosenfeld, "Vers un langage de l'utopie amazonienne: *Le corps lesbien* de Monique Wittig," *Vlasta,* no. 4 (1985): 57.

18. For her articulation of political lesbianism, see Wittig, *The Straight Mind and Other Essays.*

19. Following Terdiman's definition of "counter-discourse" (*Discourse/Counter-Discourse,* 16); also following Chambers's definition of "oppositional text" (*Room for Maneuver,* xvii).

20. Françoise Armengaud, "La contestation des conventions du discours chez Nathalie Sarraute et chez Monique Wittig," *Nouvelles Questions Feministes* 19, no. 1 (1998): 35–64.

12 *Politics and Poetics of Travesty in Monique Wittig's Fiction*

Catherine Rognon Ecarnot

Translated by Eileen Powis, Arthur Tang, and Namascar Shaktini

The following essay was written at the suggestion of Christine Bard, who is perceptive about the narcissistic exhibition of the souls of limbo and the game of appearances that the *guérillères* enjoy in Monique Wittig's work. I wrote it when I was finishing my doctoral thesis on the poetic power of the fiction of Monique Wittig, poetic power that permits emergence of a lesbian point of view.

I have always wanted to show that if one pursued an approach appropriate for a lesbian who sees lucidly the heterosexed world to which she does not completely belong, one could no more speak of "lesbian writing" than of "feminine essence." Wittig's writing is so radically skeptical that she gives hope. It is skeptical not only in the sense of profound suspicion—of marking out every cliché, of Cartesian doubt, and the age of suspicion colliding—but also in the sense that citations and repetitions always undermine the illusion of personal utterance.[1]

Wittig is at once very far from and very near queer performance or travesty in general, which by passage from one sex to the other unmasks the illusion of sexed origin. Her field of battle is not that of appearance itself if by chance she touches it but that of utterance. One is already beyond sexual difference or finds herself displaced, for just as the drag king, like the butch, proves that masculinity is for those who seize it, all Wittig's writing tends to take over a general principle that is only masculine by usurpation.

Femininity Is a Travesty

> It is really a review, with just the right amount of glittering fabric and
> bare flesh: the women with tufts of feathers attached to their posteriors
> walk in front; those wearing rabbit ears and round white tails follow in
> succession.
>
> —Monique Wittig, *Across the Acheron*

Traveling like Dante through the circles of hell in *Across the Acheron,*
"Wittig" (the name Monique Wittig gives her character), guided not by Virgil
but by Manastabal, watches, impotent and with knots in her stomach, two
"parades." Long processions of lost souls display low-cut dresses and short
skirts, spike heels and wrists in chains, atrophied feet or lips, ablation of sexual
organs, and deformed bellies. Monique Wittig thus exhibits the stigmata of
a femininitude that, for her as for Beauvoir, has no reality other than social
definition.

The two processions take place in San Francisco—as attested to by the
evocation of its buildings, sea, and hills—and allude, as Khon has pointed out,
to the Halloween parade traditionally held in that city.[2] The parallel between
a carnival and two reviews of what constitutes woman both in France and
the United States reiterates, as Wittig has said elsewhere, that femininity is a
travesty, an atrocious travesty without desire or playful dimension.[3]

Like uniforms, the garments in heterosexual hell designate the role of
lost souls: "As soon as high heels, bare legs and thighs, as well as dress and
handbag are seen, the ensemble identifies the lost souls as open game."[4] Such
clothes guarantee "symbolic confinement" because they constrain gesture
and movement, imposing ridiculous postures.[5] "If they drop something, they
bend to one side, their thighs held tightly together, their arms close to their
bodies, forming a kind of accordion, but to no avail, for at a given moment
they end up showing their panties" (A, 47). The lost souls are dispossessed
of their deformed, weakened, and amputated bodies, remaining only as the
signs of subservience to serve the myth of woman. Strained in a constant effort
to conform to an image, like Wittig's "Tchiches," who work at losing weight,
they obliterate themselves.[6] They flatten themselves against a wall when an
"individual" goes by, thin (the feminine, we know, is small) up to the point of
losing the third dimension: "The world in which they live is two dimensional.
I compare it to the world of playing cards" (A, 50).

Surfaces difficult to tell apart, all relative to woman, "erected, constituted
in an essential difference, they are prisoners of the mirror" of phallic meaning,

their bodies are not perceptible or nameable other than as a univocal sign of sexual difference.[7] More Echo than Narcissus, "man's reflection" as Saint Paul said, they are invisible. Their body, a unique index of their individuation, is imperceptible; it is neither made up, disguised, nor masked but becomes the "monstrous mask of itself," invisible except insofar as in conformity to the female model.[8] "Wittig," to prove to a few of the hostile lost souls that "her intentions are peaceful" and her body is similar to theirs in the most ordinary way, undresses in the middle of a laundromat: "Since no word seems to penetrate their understanding, I strip naked between two rows of washing-machines and advance among them, not like Venus emerging from the waves, nor even as my mother bore me, but in short, with two shoulders, a torso, a belly, legs and the rest" (A, 14).

She does not succeed, however, in making herself seen any more than in making herself heard. Her naked body, as the reference to Venus suggests, is masked by traditional images of a female body. Whereas the heroine knows that she has "nothing special to display," her body does not appear to be a faithful copy of woman. It is perceived as a threat by the laundromat's customers, who shout "rape"; her body is transformed, enveloped by clichés whose dominant discourse clothes female homosexuals. "Wittig," in this humorous scene, is soon seen covered with hair, and she congratulates herself on it. The hair gives way to scales, and finally her clitoris becomes longer. "Look, it's as long as a middle finger. Cut it off. Cut it off" (A, 16).

Lesbians in Color

In *Across the Acheron,* as under what Wittig calls elsewhere the heterosexual "political regime," the alternative "offered" to women is to accept, giving up the position of subject and subsuming their bodies to a single phallic signifier for which it is the necessary other. Or, they can take to their heels and flee hell for purgatory, an intermediate zone between hell and heaven.[9] Purgatory is a narrow, precarious place where one has "nothing to eat" but can refuse to be a woman (i.e., look like one). Muscular, heads shaved, tattooed, and dressed in leather, the souls of purgatory take on an appearance that makes them recognizable as lesbians: "There are some who go around with shaven heads and the threat they pose engraved on their foreheads. There are some whose shoulders are girded in black leather" (A, 40).

Biceps, heaviness, and vigorous gestures indicate that just as "lesbians are not women" (SM, 32), inhabitants of purgatory are not—or are no longer—lost souls. Their martial appearance recalls that of the proud guérillères, but, "Unlike the warriors of *Les guérillères,* they fail to see the perils of self-admiration and the sterility of vindictive attacks upon individual men, when the real enemy is difference."[10]

Thus, in *Across the Acheron* Monique Wittig denounces, although with humor and tenderness, the antiprogressive attitude of the lesbian community. In comparison, the guérillères, engaged in total revolution, adopt with enormous freedom and a deep sense of play the clothing, postures, and makeup whose diversity implies an ongoing attempt at self-invention. Sometimes they paint their faces and legs in bright colors, sometimes they cover their faces with shiny powder, sometimes they gather up their hair in a silk headband, and sometimes they let their black hair flow onto their shoulders and shake it "like bacchantes who make their thyrsi move" (*G*, 102, 99, 93). They wear blue or red garments or black tunics and masks and carry clubs (*G*, 138, 140). Sometimes they battle in futuristic outfits: "They wear garments all of one piece, made of some variety of metal. Their faces, intermittently lit up by the spheres and their rays, resemble great insect heads with antennae and stalked eyes" (*G*, 108).

Further progression is exhibited as the bodies of female lovers in *The Lesbian Body* mutate and take shape, becoming gigantic, monstrous, and endowed with ten thousand eyes or thousands of arms. Plethoric bodies result from the explosion of the univocal female body and can only take shape in that "privileged field" that literature constitutes.[11]

Bodies in Fragments

Let us consider little Catherine Legrand, so uncomfortable in her pants: "You don't wear pants when you are a little girl. You don't like them because they divide you in two. Perhaps Catherine Legrand is the only little girl who wears pants and who is not exactly a little girl."[12]

In the shackles of the social universe, being a little girl who is not exactly a little girl means physically feeling the discomfort of a division. Catherine Legrand's pants stick "between her legs, the seam keeps her from walking." It is not her garment, although we see how it imprisons her, but the writing of desire, the practice of quoting, and the encounter with the other that will permit the little girl, uttering in her turn phrases written elsewhere by Baudelaire and Scève, to reach that world beyond the sexes; it is a world without which, according to Wittig, there can be no subjectivity.

Literature is the only place where the semantic system, and hence the structures of thought and habits of perception, can lose their evidential character. Treating the lesbian body [*le corps, corpus, lesbien*] as the language she wishes to extract from the univocity that earlier usages have imposed on it,

Wittig fragments it, dissects it, disintegrates it, and recomposes it endlessly until the point where, freed from the female straitjacket or heterosexual reading, it bursts, open to infinite mutations and liberating a subjectivity that is not dual but plural, well beyond the binary model of sexual gender.

Through writing, Wittig transgresses, overturns, and goes beyond the question of sexual identity. She carries out a reversal of grammatical gender, "the linguistic indication of the political opposition between the sexes."[13] She either feminizes the divine and paternal figures of Zeus or the God of the Christians or she apposes a masculine substantive [masculine in the French text] such as "our great predecessor" to the name of Sappho.[14] She even institutes a monosexual world in which the feminine that does not alternate with any masculine loses all character that is particularizing or sexualizing.

Wittig's poetic texts, far from being simple illustrations of the viewpoint she has defended in theoretical essays—to which they were often posterior—reveal the fertility and original character of her concept of the subject. Assiduously exploring the relationship between the unnamed and language, the poetic texts extract considerations of difference from the valorization of the feminine, breaking the impulsive/symbolic, female/male parallel and in so doing allowing emergence of a subjectivity that tends to efface genders without returning (as reading the political essays leads Judith Butler to believe) to the monolithic subject of humanist thinking.[15]

In *The Lesbian Body,* which announces from its very first sentence the intention to break with the feminine ("In this dark adored adorned Gehenna, say your farewells m/y very beautiful one . . . to what they . . . call affection, tenderness or gracious abandon" [15]), the bodies of two lovers are constantly dismembered, dissected, and devoured. They are the subject of the most diverse metamorphoses; they are liquefied, petrified, spread out, or diminished. Through a long listing in bold letters of humors, viscera, and bones that alternates with poetic fragments and echoes many scenes of dismemberment, the female body, having become unrecognizable, is literally pulverized. The magic of Wittig's poetry, as Teresa de Lauretis remarks, "transcends sex as well as sexual gender and recreates the body in another way at the risk of being monstrous, grotesque, mortal, violent."[16]

Even if there is no "appropriation and redeployment of sexual categories" there is perpetual redeployment of the oppositions between the named and the unnamable, between the particular and the general.[17] It is a constant movement from the situation of the unique speaker, "glittering maybe but sombre nonetheless" (*LB,* 145), to that of the "I," dumbfounded, threatened, desirous, desired, and cleaved but in the end the subject. The bodies of the lovers that are constantly in mutation in *The Lesbian Body*—like the variety of erotic positions they adopt, sometimes swallowed and penetrated, infiltrated and liquefied, straddled, or adulated—shape a subject that is both shattered and brilliant.

By shifting the question of travesty, of the metamorphosis of bodies, into the literary field, Wittig opens a space in which movements from one appearance to another, like the fundamental relationship between I and you, are named and presented independent of any reference to sexuation. In *The Lesbian Body*, a "musing on the beautiful analysis of the pronouns 'I' and 'you' by the linguist Emile Benveniste" (*SM*, 87) because the verbal exchange appears as a necessary condition for the emergence of subjectivity, the person speaking and the person spoken to are constituted by each other. Nevertheless, the lovers who explore the reversibility of "I" and "you" to the point of orgasm are absolutely not identical to each other. The absence of the person spoken to as well as her ferociousness are sometimes vividly felt, and in this quest for subjectivity the person who speaks feels threatened by the other: "I explode the small units of m/y ego, am threatened, am desired by you" (*LB*, 98).

Threatened by losing oneself in the other? Threatened by being separated from her? All of the fragments relate how lovers go from separation to fusion, from I to you, and from you to me. The conquest of a subjectivity is carried out through this movement from one to the other, which is an exercise of the subject and fills the same function as the movement from one sex to the other in Cixous's texts. Thus this musing, starting with the pronouns *I* and *you*, continues to the materialization of the other of the same sex (i.e., equally subject). It is a materialization that deals a decisive blow to the sexual opposition established by psychoanalysis as pivotal to the relationship with language because between the one and the other, between Zeyna and Ganymede the cup-bearer, between Artemis and Sappho, sexual opposition is not what creates difference, nor does it signify.

Sprinkled with quotations and rich in borrowed figures, Wittig's writing parodies, travesties, and creates a pastiche of earlier texts more often than a cliché of femininity or masculinity. When the speaker of *The Lesbian Body* utters the words of Christ or the guérillères take on the heroic postures of *The Iliad*'s hero, the myth of sexed identity as well as the claim to universality of the male subject are obliterated in favor of a subject that is unaware of sexual difference while displaying the dialogical nature of its discourse. Through the travesty of the secular discourse, repeated but transformed by the lesbian viewpoint, the minority subject succeeds in circumventing a language that reduces it to silence.

186   Catherine Rognon Ecarnot

NOTES

This essay is a revised version of "Politique et poétique du travestissement dans les fictions de Monique Wittig," *Clio: Historie, Femmes et Sociétés* 10 (1999): 185–95. *Editor's note:* Because "cross-dressing" and "travesty" exist in our language as separate terms, it is impossible to render in English the versatility of the French word *travestissement,* whose polysemy provides the basis for much of the author's argument. The broader semantic spectrum of the French transitive verb *travestir, déformer, falsifier* (to "travesty," deform, falsify) more accurately renders the Wittigian concept of the effect of the gender system.

1. Je parle d'une écriture, celle de Monique Wittig, si radicalement sceptique qu'elle donne espoir, sceptique non seulement au sens de la suspicion profonde, du tracage de tout cliché, doute cartésien et ère du soupçon ne cessant de se croiser fulgureusement, mais aussi au sens où citations et répétitions ne cessent de miner l'illusion de l'énoncé personnel.

2. Ingeborg M. Kohn, "The United States in Contemporary French Fiction: A Geography of the Fantastic." In *Contours of the Fantastic: Selected Essays from the Eighth International Conference on the Fantastic in the Arts,* ed. Michele K. Langford (Westport: Greenwood Press, 1994), 187–89.

3. In Djuna Barnes, *La passion,* trans. Monique Wittig, with Avant-Note (Paris: Flammarion, 1982), 17.

4. Monique Wittig, *Across the Acheron,* trans. David Le Vay and Margaret Crosland (London: Peter Owen, 1987), 36. Cited hereafter as *A.*

5. Pierre Bourdieu, *La domination masculine* (Paris: Seuil, 1998), 35.

6. Monique Wittig, "Les tchiches et les tchouches," *Le Genre Humain,* no. 6 (1983): 136–47.

7. Monique Wittig, *Les Guérillères,* trans. David Le Vay (New York: Avon, 1973), 100, 31. Hereafter cited as *G.*

8. Leah D. Hewitt, "Confusing the Genres: Autobiographical Parody and Utopia in Monique Wittig's *Across the Acheron,*" in *Autobiographical Tightropes,* ed. Leah D. Hewitt (Lincoln: University of Nebraska Press, 1990), 148.

9. Monique Wittig, *The Straight Mind and Other Essays* (Boston: Beacon Press, 1992), 43. Hereafter cited as *SM.*

10. Jean H. Duffy, "Monique Wittig," in *Beyond the Nouveau Roman: Essays on the Contemporary Novel,* ed. Michael Tilby (New York: Berg, 1990), 210.

11. Wittig, "Avant-Note," 10.

12. Monique Wittig, *L'opoponax* (Paris: Éditions Minuit, 1964), trans. Helen Weaver (New York: Simon and Schuster, 1966), 16. I have emended Weaver's erroneous rendering of "une petite fille" and "pantalon."

13. Wittig, "Avant-Note," 9.

14. Monique Wittig, *The Lesbian Body,* trans. David Le Vay (Boston: Beacon Press, 1986), 42, 145 (hereafter cited as *LB*); Monique Wittig, *Virgile, non* (Paris: Éditions Minuit, 1985), 16.

15. Judith Butler, *Gender Trouble: Feminism and the Subversion of Identity* (New York: Routledge, 1990).

16. Teresa de Lauretis, *Differenza e indifferenza sessuale* (Florence: Estro Strumenti, 1989), 46.

17. Butler, *Gender Trouble,* 122.

13 *Wittig la Politique*

Marie-Hélène Bourcier

Translated by Sabrina Draï and Victoria Kopcik

> Leaving or giving up a place that is safe, that is "home"—physically, emotionally, linguistically, and epistemologically—for another place that is unknown and risky, that is not only emotionally but also conceptually other; a place of discourse from which speaking and thinking are at best tentative, uncertain, unguaranteed. But the leaving is not a choice: one could not live here in the first place. Thus, both aspects of the displacement, the personal and the conceptual, are painful: they are either, and often both, the cause or the result of pain and risk, and a real stake with a high price. For this is "theory in the flesh," as Cherríe Moraga has called it, a constant crossing of the border, . . . a remapping of boundaries between bodies and discourses, identities and communities—which may be a reason why it is primarily feminists of color and lesbian feminists who have taken the risk.
>
> —Teresa de Lauretis

Tucson, Arizona, 1999. Here the wind is as sharp as razor blades slamming at the bottom of the canyon. I am in a Mexican restaurant not far from the university where Monique Wittig teaches. I am waiting for Manastabal, "Wittig"'s guide when she traveled across the Acheron after leaving France in 1976.[1] I can barely see a thing with the dust masking desert horizon and city edges. Manastabal is coming to give me a hand in translating *The Straight Mind* into French.[2]

You may wonder what am I doing translating Wittig into French. In spite of Wittig's success in France as a fiction writer after publication of *L'oponax* in 1964, her political texts were not welcomed into French editorial houses. The winner of the prestigious Prix Médicis wrote her feminist political reflections in a language foreign to her. "The Category of Sex," "On the Social Contract," "Homo Sum," and "The Straight Mind" were originally written in English.

For years only "The Straight Mind" and "One Is Not Born a Woman" were available in French. This collection of political and literary essays became a classic for Canadian radical lesbian thought fifteen years before its translation into French while simultaneously starting a wave of comment among American postfeminist and queer theorists. But what does it mean to translate a French author into French twenty years later, when the political context of her work has radically changed?

Manastabal was huge. We had communicated by email, by telephone, and by fax, and now she was here. "Have a seat, Mr. Bourcier," she said, addressing me as if I were a man, while extending her hand. Manastabal allowed her hand to be taken and briefly shaken. Her palm felt like that of a prehistoric amazon or a blue-collar worker.

"You are the translator, right?" said Manastabal looking at me with pity. "No hope for you. Don't expect to find the original text. There is no original, amigo—you translate a translation. Translation was the very condition of the possibility of 'The Straight Mind' from the beginning. Didn't you know that 'The Straight Mind' was written in a language foreign both to French and to straight language?[3] Forget the original. The political thickness of these texts lies in their circulation in America, in English; that it is inseparable from their translation between France and the United States, and from the delocalization of both national and sexual writing."

"Are you suggesting that I should abandon the translation project? If that's all you have to say, then I'd better leave. Thank you for your help." I was devastated. I was ready to get up and walk away.

"No. On the contrary. I am just saying that there are choices to be made." After some thought, as if she was about to reveal a secret, Manastabal added, "I know that Wittig told you to keep the English word *straight* for the title in the French translation. Straight rather than heterosexual." She moved forward, and I saw for the first time a scar on her face. "But I think she was wrong. *La pensée hétéro, c'est ça.* When are you French people going to stop hiding your fear of identity politics behind universalism, *quand ça?*"

I realized then that she spoke perfect French. Where was she coming from? What was the native language camouflaged behind her American accent? I didn't say anything. I was afraid to ask the wrong question.

"Don't you know what happened when Monique Wittig gave the lecture 'The Straight Mind' at the MLA in New York in 1978?" she continued. "You don't know how the audience reacted when she concluded with a now-famous sentence: 'Lesbians are not women'? During the conference, Hélène Cixous declared that French women who like women do not use the word *lesbian* because it bears negative connotations.[4] Wittig cried out, 'Which France?

This is a scandal!' Suddenly, the American feminist audience became aware of the profound divergences that existed between the French group Féministes Révolutionnaires and Psych et Po (Psychoanalysis and Politics), between the materialist feminists who followed Christine Delphy and Monique Wittig after October 1970 and those who gathered around the essentialist Antoinette Fouque.

"Probably," Manastabal continued, "the most gifted of Fouque's followers was Hélène Cixous, who published in 1975 'The Laugh of the Medusa.' The book soon became the manifesto of the 'feminine writing' movement. To end phallocentrism the book promoted exploration of the feminine body through writing by valorizing the irreducible nature of biological sexual difference between man and woman. The subversive value of this method was rapidly questioned by materialist feminists who exposed the essentialist and biologizing character of a literature celebrating the breasts, the uterus, or the vagina of a conceiving woman, mother, or lover—in other words, the image of the traditional woman."

"Not so fast. Let's go back to the beginning. What happened in October 1970?" I implored.

"As early as 1970, tensions existed between lesbians and feminists in France. Whenever lesbians raised the question of their political invisibility and decided to work on something other than feminist questions (e.g., legalization of abortion, control of undesired pregnancies, remuneration of domestic work, and men-women relationships), 'heterofeminists,' as we used to called them, relegated them to a minority."

I had read about that before. That was the history of lesbians within European and American feminism alike. But Manastabal told me these things in the strictest of confidence, as if it were a yet-unrevealed mystery, her voice a secretive whisper at first but growing louder as she went deeper into the story.

"At the beginning of the French feminist movement there was a nonhierarchical structure. It had neither a leader nor a name," she continued. "Some women who took part in the students' movement of 1968 felt the urgency to mark the specificity of their social concerns, their language, and their political fight. They gathered in the group Feminisme, Marxisme, Action. The same year Wittig translated Marcuse's *One Dimensional Man* into French. You see, there is always some translation work going on." Manastabal laughed for a second, making me feel ridiculous about my translation anxiety, and continued.

"In May 1970 the first volume of a French leftist journal, *L'Idiot International,* was dedicated to the women's movement. Inside, you can find the text 'Fighting for Women's Liberation' written by Monique Wittig along with her sister, Gille Wittig, Margaret Stephenson (Namascar Shaktini), and Marcia Rothenberg. In August 1970 a dozen women, including Wittig, met at the Arc de Triomphe to bring a wreath to the 'wife of the unknown soldier.' For the first time a feminist action hit the Parisian media. Suddenly, they needed a name, and the group was artificially called the MLF (Mouvement de Libération des Femmes). But it was not a single movement. There were many different groups, like the Red Dykes or the Sausage Commando."[5]

"The sausage commando?" I asked, astonished by the name.

"Yes. That was the name of a group of lesbians who, armed with big sausages, attacked a radio program dealing with the question of 'The Painful Issue of Homosexuality' in 1971."[6]

"But why then did they choose to call the movement MLF?" I asked.

"Sufficiently totalizing, the acronym MLF should have allowed for resistance to any appellation from the outside and avoided a restricted and nonrepresentative appropriation of the multiple tendencies in French feminism. From an anarcho-Marxist point of view, the vagueness of the appellation was a strategy for rupture with institutions and their naming 'power.' The political shock was all the more violent when Antoinette Fouque from Psych et Po arrogated the acronym MLF by depositing it as a brand name at the National Institute of Industrial Property in 1979. Do you understand now? Lesbians experienced a similar feeling of betrayal a year later with the barely dissimulated reshaping of *Questions Feministes* into *Nouvelles Questions Feministes* while the publishing contract between the editorial staff of the materialist feminist journal specified that no one would use the name of the journal. History was repeating itself."

Suddenly, pieces of the story began to fall into place. Manastabal couldn't stop talking. Somehow, her desire to talk was greater than her fidelity to a supposed confidentiality agreement signed probably twenty years earlier, as a mute that suddenly recovers the capacity to speak: "As early as 1979, Wittig contested in France the epistemological and political privilege of 'the discourses which particularly oppress all of us, lesbians, women, and homosexual men, . . . those which take for granted that what founds society, any society, is heterosexuality.' These discourses oppress us in the sense that they prevent us from speaking unless we speak in their terms. They deny us every possibility of creating our own categories" (*SM*, 24–25).

"Unfortunately, twenty years later we are still confronted with the same disciplinary discourses in France. During the vote for legal recognition of gay and lesbian partnership in 1999, guardians of the symbolic order and sexual difference invoked Lacan and Lévi-Strauss at the French Parliament," I responded, trying to add some of my own information to her, by now endless, story.

"I have been waiting for a long time to read *The Straight Mind* in the language of Proust." Manastabal added. "Wittig proposes in this text, as in her literary texts, epistemopolitical strategies and modes of subjectivization that are still to be discovered in France: the development of a theory of oppression, a sort of 'queer theory' before its time, a theory from the point of view of the oppressed, what she calls 'the science of the oppressed' (*SM*, 31). Read again the description of the first drafts of *Les guérillères* in the text I faxed you the other day.[7] Her writing strategy directly opposes the straight mind and the new theory of oppression. Wittig's text unfolds straight history: Freud, Mao, and a dictionary of sexuality, among others, on the right page, onto which the words for a new science of the oppressed are grafted. In *Les guérillères* one goes from one language to the other, from one page to the other, from one referential universe to the other, one shifts in it, one resignifies, retranslates, undoing the arbitrary character of gender."

"You sound like Barthes in his semioclast and semiopolitical period," I said, thinking it a compliment.

"Wittig knows her politics, which was never the case of Barthes, who was bored by politics," said Manastabal, tearing down my idealized image of Barthes. "Don't forget that the Wittigian analyses and strategies I am talking about spread themselves out against the 'seminaries' as well as against the 'ovularies' and 'feminaries' of all sorts that proliferated in France after 1968. The straight mind is also the 1980s' French straight feminism or any hetero-centered feminism that seeks to impose the identification of woman at the expense of the lesbian point of view and produces straight bodies and straight politics. Wittig's political writings make manifest the intellectual rupture of lesbian politics from French heterofeminist thought from the usurpers of the MLF to the revolutionary feminists in the closet."

"Is that why Wittig is never considered as part of the so-called French feminism?" I asked.

"Of course Wittig's radical materialist constructivism could not accommodate the retrospective illusions of the 'feminists of difference' who viewed themselves through several fictions that celebrated the woman's body or the mother's uterus and 'feminine writing.' It accommodated even less when those feminists relied on the psychoanalytical discourse, which anchored feminist political semiotics in the pre-Oedipal or the pre-symbolic, as in Kristeva. Everybody is well aware that they were only reinforcing and reifying what they called *la féminitude*. How subversive was that? What you call 'French feminism' was fabricated in the U.S. academic milieu to designate a troika: Cixous-Kristeva-Irigaray. This must be the only thing on which I agree with Christine Delphy.[8] This label contributed to eliding the political multiplicity of different French movements and rendering the materialist feminist trend invisible. Ah, how efficient this elitist 'French feminism' proved to be to de-politicize feminism in France!"

"Interesting. Wittig appears somehow to be non-French and nonfeminist," I suggested timidly.

"It is not as easy as it seems. There were also heterofeminists among the materialists, like Delphy herself, who did not dare, or was even literally prevented from openly formulating lesbian politics. But that is a long story, and I think that I am already talking too much," she said and turned around to ask for another drink.

"Wait a minute," I urged, hoping to find out something else, a clue, a piece of the puzzle. "How do you want me to translate *The Straight Mind* without knowing what happened with straight feminism in France? I haven't traveled up to here to come back home without a single finding. This translation is starting to drive me mad. After all, your history is also my history, and I have the right to know."

"You, little man, you want to know too much," said Manastabal, insisting upon my male linguistic identity. "Listen, in 1977 five radical feminists, Colette Capitan Peter, Christine Delphy, Emmanuèle de Lesseps, Nicole-Claude Mathieu, and Monique Plaza, founded *Questions Feministes* and asked Sim-one de Beauvoir to be editor-in-chief of the journal. Number 1, published in February 1980, included two texts that will trigger the debate on the place of 'lesbian politics' within the journal: 'The Straight Mind' by Monique Wittig and 'Heterosexuality and Feminism' by Emmanuèle de Lesseps. Monique Wittig's 'On ne naît pas femme,' published in May, was the *coup de grâce.* The political lesbians were accused of dividing the movement and promoting separatism. During that summer an anglophone version of the journal, *Feminist Issues,* was launched in the United States by editors Mary Jo Lakeland and Susan Ellis Wolf with Monique Wittig as advisory editor. The first issue included 'The Straight Mind' and 'The Point of View, Universal or Particular.'

"It had been decided by consensus that number 8 of *Questions Feministes* would be the last and would continue the debate about normative heterosexual-ity. That was not to be the case. In October the group of *Questions Feministes,* as well as the *Homonym Journal,* was officially dissolved due to disagreements about the relationship among lesbianism, heterosexuality, and feminism. In 1981 publication of the first issue of *Nouvelles Questions Feministes,* still un-der Simone de Beauvoir's supervision, would be experienced as a political betrayal, all the more for having this lesbian founder of *Questions Feministes* who chased lesbians out of the journal. From then on, radical political lesbians, Colette Guillaumin, Nicole-Claude Matthieu, Monique Plaza, Joëlle Bisseret, and Monique Wittig would publish their texts in *Feminist Issues.*"

"Why do you care that a lesbian founder of the journal was chasing the lesbians out? It was supposed to be a dispute between lesbians and straight women, right?" I asked.

"You keep asking too many questions. Don't tell me that you are going to fall into a form of lesbian essentialism?" Manastabal retorted.

"So, tell me, what happened? What was Wittig doing in the middle of this hassle?" I asked.

"Wittig responded to the conflict with the article entitled "Les questions féministes ne sont pas des questions lesbiennes" (Feminist Issues Are Not Lesbian Issues), published in the Canadian lesbian journal *Amazones d'Hier, Lesbiennes d'Aujourd'hui.*[9] In the article, Wittig, who claimed that heterosexuality was a political regime, accused heterofeminists of reducing lesbian politics to a sexual orientation and therefore to a private question. It was sad; it was also the end of a political love story between Wittig and—I am definitely talking too much today," said Manastabal, giggling nervously.

"Did you say love story? What do you mean? I've heard before of the violence of the split between feminists and lesbians, but are you implying that heartbreak was the reason of Wittig's exile to the States?" I asked. I couldn't wait to know but felt, seeing Manastabal's embarrassment, that the story had reached a limit.

"Lesbian politics had to pay the price of delocalization, of displacement, of travel. Exile is just the result of what Teresa de Lauretis calls 'the eccentricity of the subject.' Weren't you the one who was quoting her on your email the other day?" Manastabal said, trying to change the topic.

"If I understand well, you are telling me that Monique Wittig's 'bilingualism' implies that 'to be' a lesbian is to always be exposed to translation in order to be heard," I add.

"You can say that. Besides, from this point of view Wittig is close to the feminist politics of women and lesbians of color of the 1980s, to the *chicanas* who undid a feminism that invited them to an undifferentiated sorority.[10] The more they approached the center, the more they delocalized, to the point of understanding that a political discourse could not be conceived of without radical politics of situation.[11] It was a 'situated knowledge,' Haraway would have said. After all these years this is my only political truth: We should rethink transversal differences, sex, gender, class, and race. If Marxism could not sacrifice everything to class oppression, feminism could not content itself with privileging the criterion of sex or of gender. You can understand this resistance to homogenization as postmodern and postcolonial momentum, but I cannot help recognizing in it a typical delocalization of lesbians, who are always situated between gay and lesbian feminism and politics, between lesbian politics and feminism, between Marxism and feminism. After Stonewall, in Paris as well as in New York, political lesbians were part of feminist and gay movements, founding the very movements from which they will be finally withdrawn."[12]

"Talking about lesbophobic feminists, you had Friedan, we had Beauvoir," I said.[13] "One has only to reread the chapter devoted to 'the lesbian' in *The Second Sex* to convince oneself of her lesbophobia. After what you told me I understand better Simone de Beauvoir's commitment to hetero-feminists who opposed lesbian politics during the *Questions Feministes vs. Nouvelles Questions Feministes* lawsuit."

"In France," Manastabal replied, "at the time of the MLF, one had the right to be a lesbian feminist—the order of the concatenation of the terms means what it means—but not a political lesbian. In fact, Monique Wittig allowed for the disposal of the appropriations and constructions of 'the lesbian' by feminists who never questioned their heterosexual position themselves. Feminists often thought they were doing sexologic charity by concluding that feminine homosexuality was innate or by approaching the question with psychoanalytical prevention. In her literary and political work Wittig proposes a resolutely alternative representation of lesbians that is neither medical nor psychological but political. You know, I am particularly grateful to her for accepting me as her guide in San Francisco during our trip in 1976, me who used to walk with my hands in the pockets of my jeans as in a silent movie.[14] Wittig completely abandoned the paradigm of identification with women who were very fashionable at the time in heterofeminist and lesbian feminist milieus. Even American radicals did not dare say that lesbians were not women. Remember when the radicals of the Lavender Menace split from the feminists of the National Organization for Women (NOW)?[15] In her resignation letter from NOW, Rita Mae Brown reproached the executive members for lesbophobia, sexism, racism, and class prejudices. 'The mere word *lesbian,* she told me once, 'triggered a collective heart attack in the executive committee.'"

"Are you talking about the demonstration of May 1970?" I asked.

"Yes. Twenty of them in the limelight, Rita Mae Brown leading. They distributed pamphlets which would later become part of *The Woman-Identified Woman.* 'Take a lesbian to lunch,' they said, 'Superdyke loves you'; 'Women's liberation is a lesbian plot'; 'We are your worst nightmare, your best fantasy'; striking paragraphs for one of the first manifestos in the history of the emancipation of lesbians. Unlike Wittig, they didn't give up the identification with woman. Moreover, the text is desexualizing in the sense that the discriminating political criterion is not sexual practice. It is monogendered. The woman versus the lesbian is constructed in opposition to the male and to the potential male within ourselves. Almost simultaneously, Adrienne Rich reacted against feminists by sketching a demarcation based on lesbian identity, but she promoted the lesbian-feminine continuum for all women.[16] Only Wittig stopped prescribing identification to woman and opened up the way for the bearded lesbians."

"Are you saying that Wittig is into identity politics?" I asked with surprise. I always thought that she was rather reluctant to engage identity politics.

"Wittig would not call herself pro-identity, but she inscribes lesbian identity permanently, ironically, and efficiently. Remember what she said about the way she came up with the title 'Le Corps Lesbien': 'When I found the title *Lesbian Body*, the association of those two words made me laugh. It was absurdly sarcastic.'[17] She symbolizes the criticism of a totalizing feminist identity, and in this respect her position enables us to take advantage of identity politics resources. Irony is a major figure in Wittig's politics. Irony enables her to create a productive imbalance in relation to lesbian identity. Her *détournements* happened at the level of resignification. Listen to the titles: *Lesbian Body, Straight Mind, Les guérillères*. Wittig changed the words and added the ones that were missing. It does not surprise me at all that her text is a relay in the poststructural criticism of identity. She knew the song, and she played with the karaoke of heterosexuality," Manastabal said, looking at the jukebox behind her playing Bowie's XXX.

It was starting to get dark outside, but Manastabal seemed unaware of passing time. "Wittig," she continued, "opened a lesbian identity space by making the lesbian a radical site of de-nomination and dis-identification. This was a paradoxical gesture that can be useful for many identity politics and a gesture that one would be wrong to understand as a simple reaction to the lesbophobic feminist context of the 1980s. Obviously, it helped. She broke the heterofeminist silence on lesbians, but she also put feminism and its fixed identity in crisis. Second-wave feminism and French feminism that became dominant at the beginning of the 1980s largely privileged the point of view of the heterosexual white, middle-class women. Not only are lesbians not women, but it is also not an accident if Wittig renames them *maronnes* in another language than that of the French white woman.[18] Wittig and radical lesbians asked French feminism to go through a critical phase and to realize that the promotion of Woman as emancipating subject of sexual politics has normative effects. Not only does Wittig react against the political instrumen-

talization of 'the lesbian' by feminism, but she also asks feminism to reconsider the gender and sexual categories upon which its foundations are built.
This feminism promotes a type of difference, whether essentialist or strictly
articulated in terms of gender by opposition to man and patriarchy, and not
in relation to a political opposition between hetero- and homosexuality. One
can never repeat enough that this kind of valorization of difference ends up
neglecting the differences of sexual identity as well as class and race between
women. Wittig used to say, 'feminism, an embarrassing word not because of
the suffragettes (no) but because of the concept of woman around which it is
constructed.'"[19]

She asked if I wanted another drink. I was feeling drunk, intoxicated by
her stories.

"No thank you," I said, "after two Margaritas, I see cats as big as lynxes."

"It is not the tequila. In the West the bobcats are imposing wild cats.
People around here say that they have seen two bobcats guarding Wittig's door
during the night. It seems that Wittig is not afraid of them. I heard that some
nights, when she cannot sleep, she walks with them to the end of the desert."
Manastabal took her breath again and flagged the waiter. He was approaching
our table to bring us the bill and murmured, "Tortilleras."[20]

"Yes, bring us some spicy tortillas for the dykes, thank you," Manastabal
retorted. And seeing that I had not understood, she added, "When I was
traveling with Wittig, it happened to us all the time. They thought they would
affect us or scare us home by saying 'dirty dykes' or by telling us that we were
not women. What was an insult for them became for us a compliment and a
political program. Not only is a lesbian not a woman, but she doesn't have to
become one."

"Excuse me now. I have to leave. It was a pleasure talking to you. And
don't forget your copy of *The Straight Mind.*" She shook my hand again and
walked out.

NOTES

Editor's note: This parodic queer fantastic text departs from the academic rigor of the
previous twelve chapters.

1. Manastabal and "Wittig" are characters in *Virgile, non* (Paris: Éditions Minuit,
1985).

2. Monique Wittig, *The Straight Mind and Other Essays* (Boston: Beacon Press, 1992).
Hereafter cited as *SM*.

3. The "Straight Mind" transited from Paris to Berkeley via New York. Monique Wittig's
lecture was entitled "On ne naît pas femme." The text was published in France in *Questions
Feministes* (1980) and then in the United States in *Feminist Issues* (1981).

4. *Editor's note:* Bourcier conflates two different New York conferences, the 1978 MLA conference at which Wittig affirmed that "lesbians are not women," and the 1979 conference "The Second Sex, Thirty Years After," where Hélène Cixous declared that in France the word *lesbian* isn't used. Her statement caused Wittig to exclaim from the back of the hall "Which France? This is a scandal."]

5. "Les Gouines Rouges" was created in 1971.

6. The "sausage commando" was, in reality, the first action of the FHAR. Wittig did not participate in it.

7. Monique Wittig, *Les guérillères* (Paris: Éditions Minuit, 1969) (hereafter cited as *G*).

8. Christine Delphy, "L'invention du 'French feminism': Une démarche essentielle," in *L'ennemi principal,* vol. 2: *Penser le genre* (Paris: Éditions Syllepse, 2001), 319–58.

9. Monique Wittig, "Les questions féministes ne sont pas des questions lesbiennes," in *Amazones d'Hier, Lesbiennes d'Aujourd'hui* 2, no. 1 (1983): 10–14.

10. See "A Black Feminist Statement," the manifesto of the Combahee River Collective, a black lesbian activist group that mobilizes itself against heterosexual, racial, and economic oppression, in *All the Women Are White, All the Blacks Are Men, but Some of Us Are Brave: Black Women's Studies,* ed. Gloria T. Hull, Patricia Bell Scott, and Barbara Smith (Old Westbury: Feminist Press, 1982), 13–22. Cherrie Moraga and Gloria Anzaldúa, eds., *This Bridge Called My Back: Writings by Radical Women of Colour* (New York: Kitchen Table: Women of Color Press, 1983).

11. Gloria Anzaldúa, *Borderlands/La Frontera: The New Mestiza* (San Francisco: Spinsters/Aunt Lute Press, 1971).

12. Lesbians and feminists launched the FHAR.

13. Betty Friedan, the second-wave feminist author of *The Feminine Mystique* (Harmondsworth: Penguin, 1963), coined in 1970 the expression *lavender menace* to describe a budding lesbian movement that had the potential to harm the feminist agenda.

14. The trip is described in *Virgile, non.*

15. Lavender Menace is the first post-Stonewall group to focus on lesbian questions.

16. Adrienne Rich, "La contrainte à l'hétérosexualité et l'existence lesbienne," *Nouvelles Questions Feministes* (March 1981): 15–43.

17. Monique Wittig in *Libération,* June 17, 1999.

18. *Maronnes,* a Creole term, is an alteration of the hispano American *cimarron* (fugitive slave).

19. Wittig, "Les questions feministes," 10.

20. The word *tortillera* is Spanish for "dyke."

BIBLIOGRAPHY OF WORKS BY MONIQUE WITTIG

BOOKS

Wittig, Monique. *Across the Acheron*. Translated by David Le Vay and Margaret Crosland. London: Peter Owen, 1987.

———. *Le corps lesbien*. Paris: Éditions Minuit, 1973.

———. *Les guérillères*. Paris: Éditions Minuit, 1969.

———. *Les Guérillères*. Translated by David Le Vay. London: Peter Owen, 1971. Reprint. Boston: Beacon Press, 1985.

———. *The Lesbian Body*. Translated by David Le Vay. London: Peter Owen, 1975. Reprint. New York: William Morrow, 1975; New York: Bard/Avon, 1976; Boston: Beacon Press, 1986.

———. *L'opoponax*. Paris: Éditions Minuit, 1964.

———. *The Opoponax*. Translated by Helen Weaver. New York: Simon and Schuster, 1966.

———. *Paris-la-politique et autres histoires*. Paris: P.O.L., 1999.

———. *La pensée straight*. Translated by Marie-Hélène Bourcier. Paris: Balland, 2001.

———. *The Straight Mind and Other Essays*. Boston: Beacon Press, 1992.

———. *Virgile, non*. Paris: Éditions Minuit, 1985.

COEDITED JOURNALS/COAUTHORED BOOKS

Wittig, Monique, with Lise Leibacher-Ouvrard. "Nathalie Sarraute, ou le texte du for intérieur." *L'Esprit Créateur* 36 (Summer 1996). Special issue on Nathalie Sarraute.

———, with Sande Zeig. *Brouillon pour un dictionnaire des amantes*. Paris: Grasset, 1976.

———, with Sande Zeig. *Lesbian Peoples: Material for a Dictionary*. New York: Avon, 1979.

TRANSLATIONS OF BOOKS

Wittig, Monique, with Avant-Note. *L'homme unidimensionnel*. Translation of *The One Dimensional Man* by Herbert Marcuse. Paris: Éditions Minuit, 1968.

———, with Evelyne Le Garrec and Vera Prado. *Les nouvelles lettres Portugaises*. Translation of *Novas cartões Portuguesas* by the Three Marias (Isabel Barreno, Teresa Horta, and Fatima Velho Da Costa). Paris: Seuil, 1974.

————, with Avant-Note. *La passion.* Translation of *Spillway* by Djuna Barnes. Paris: Flammarion, 1982.

ARTICLES

Wittig, Monique. "Avatars." *L'Esprit Créateur* 36, no. 2 (1996): 109–16.

————. "Banlieues." *Nouveau Commerce*, no. 5 (1965): 113–17.

————. "The Category of Sex." *Feminist Issues* 2, no. 2 (1982): 63–68.

————. "Le cheval de Troie." *Vlasta*, no. 4 (1985): 36–41.

————. *"The Constant Journey:* An Introduction and a Prefatory Note." *Modern Drama* 39, no. 1 (1996): 156–59.

————. "Le déambulatoire: Entretien avec Nathalie Sarraute." *L'Esprit Créateur* 36, no. 2 (1996): 3–8.

————. "Homo Sum." *Feminist Issues* 10, no. 1 (1990): 3– .

————. "Un jour mon prince viendra." *Questions Feministes*, no. 2 (1978): 31–39.

————. "Lacunary Films (on Jean-Luc Godard)." *New Statesman*, July 15, 1966, 102.

————. "Le lieu de l'action." *Digraphe*, no. 32 (1984): 69–75.

————. "Une moie est apparue." *Le Torchon Brûle*, no. 5 (1972): 3.

————. "On ne naît pas femme." *Questions Feministes*, no. 8 (1980): 75–84.

————. "On the Social Contract." *Feminist Issues* 9, no. 1 (1989): 3–12.

————. "Paris-la-politique." *Vlasta*, no. 4 (1985): 8–35.

————. "Une partie de campagne." *Le Nouveau Commerce*, no. 26 (1973): 13–31.

————. "La pensée straight." *Questions Feministes*, no. 7 (1980): 5–18.

————. "A propos de Bouvard et Pécuchet." *Cahiers de la Compagnie Madeleine Renaud-Jean Louis Barrault*, no. 59 (1967): 113–22.

————. "Quelques remarques sur *Les guérillères.*" *L'Esprit Créateur* 34, no. 4 (1994): 116–22.

————. "Les questions féministes ne sont pas des questions lesbiennes." *Amazones d'Hier, Lesbiennes d'Aujourd'hui* 2, no. 1 (1983): 10–14.

————. "The Straight Mind." *Feminist Issues* 1, no. 1 (1980): 103–11.

————. "Les tchiches et les tchouches." *Le Genre Humain*, no. 6 (1983): 136–47.

————. "The Trojan Horse." *Feminist Issues* 4, no. 2 (1984): 45–49.

————. "Voyage: Yallankoro." *Nouveau Commerce*, no. 177 (1967): 558–63.

CHAPTERS IN BOOKS

Wittig, Monique. "The Mark of Gender." In *The Poetics of Gender,* edited by Nancy K. Miller, 63–73. New York: Columbia University Press, 1986.

————. "One Is Not Born a Woman." In *Writing on the Body: Female Embodiment and Feminist Theory,* edited by Katie Conboy, Nadia Medina, and Sarah Stanbury, 309–17. New York: Columbia University Press, 1997.

————. "On the Social Contract." In *Feminist Interpretations of Jean-Jacques Rousseau,* edited by Lynda Lange, 383–92. University Park: Pennsylvania State University Press, 2002.

————. "L'ordre du poème." In *Narrative Voices in Modern French Fiction: Studies in Honor of Valerie Minogue on Her Retirement*, edited by Michael Cardy, George Evans, and Gabriel Jacobs, 7–12. Cardiff: University of Wales Press, 1997.

————. "Paradigm." In *Homosexualities and French Literature: Cultural Contexts, Criti-*

cal Texts, edited by Elaine Marks and George Stambolian, 114–21. Ithaca: Cornell University Press, 1979.

———. "The Place of the Action." In *Three Decades of the French New Novel,* edited by Lois Oppenheim. Translated by Lois Oppenheim and Evelyn de Costa Beauregard, 132–40. Urbana: University of Illinois Press, 1986.

———. "The Point of View: Universal or Particular." In *Women, Creativity, and the Arts: Critical and Autobiographical Perspectives,* edited by Diane Apostolos-Cappadona and Lucinda Ebersole, 87–93. New York: Continuum, 1997.

MANIFESTO

Wittig, Monique, with Gille Wittig, Marcia Rothenberg, and Margaret Stephenson (Namascar Shaktini). "Combat pour la libération de la femme." *L'Idiot International* 6 (May 1970): 13–16.

RADIO PLAY

Wittig, Monique. *Le grand-cric-Jules, Récréation,* and *Dialogue pour les deux frères et la soeur.* 1972.

PUBLISHED PLAY

Wittig, Monique. "Le voyage sans fin," *Vlasta,* 1985. Supplement to *Vlasta* 4, a special issue on Wittig.

UNPUBLISHED PLAY

Wittig, Monique. "L'amant vert (pièce de théâtre)." 1967.

ROUNDTABLE PARTICIPATION

Wittig, Monique, with Alain Robbe-Grillet, Claude Simon, Nathalie Sarraute, Robert Pinget, François Jost, Michel Rybalka, and Tom Bishop. "The New Novel—Past, Present, Future: A Roundtable." Published in *Three Decades of the French New Novel,* edited and translated by Lois Oppenheim and Evelyn de Costa Beauregard. Urbana: University of Illinois Press, 1986.

COAUTHERED FILM SCENARIO

Wittig, Monique, with Sande Zeig. *The Girl.* 2001.

SELECTED BIBLIOGRAPHY OF
MONIQUE WITTIG CRITICISM

BOOKS

Bourcier, Marie-Hélène, and Suzette Robichon, eds. *Parce que les lesbiennes ne sont pas des femmes: Autour de l'oeuvre politique, théorique et littéraire de Monique Wittig.* Paris: Éditions Gaies et Lesbiennes, 2002.

Ecarnot, Catherine. *L'écriture de Monique Wittig à la couleur de Sappho.* Paris: L'Harmattan, 2002.

Ostrovsky, Erika. *A Constant Journey: The Fiction of Monique Wittig.* Carbondale: Southern Illinois University Press, 1991.

Robichon, Suzette, ed. *Vlasta,* no. 4. Paris: Voix Off, 1985. Special issue on Monique Wittig.

PARTS OF BOOKS

Allen, Jeffner. "Poetic Politics: How the Amazons Took the Acropolis." In *Sexual Practice, Textual Theory: Lesbian Cultural Criticism,* edited by Susan J. Wolfe and Julia Penelope, 307–21. Cambridge: Blackwell, 1993.

———. "Women Who Beget Women Must Thwart Major Sophisms." In *Women, Knowledge and Reality: Explorations in Feminist Philosophy,* edited by Ann Gary and Marilyn Pearsall, 37–46. Boston: Unwin-Hyman, 1989.

Armengaud, Françoise. "L'entreprise littéraire de Monique Wittig: Une réélaboration utopiste du contrat social?" In *Parce que les lesbiennes ne sont pas des femmes: Autour de l'oeuvre politique, théorique et littéraire de Monique Wittig,* edited by Marie-Hélène Bourcier and Suzette Robichon, 137–62. Paris: Éditions Gaies et Lesbiennes, 2002.

Arsène, Cécile. "Christiane Rochefort: The Privilege of Consciousness." In *Homosexualities and French Literature: Cultural Contexts, Critical Texts,* edited by George Stambolian and Elaine Marks, 101–13. Ithaca: Cornell University Press, 1979.

Atack, Margaret, and Phil Powrie. "Introduction." In *Contemporary French Fiction by Women: Feminist Perspectives,* edited by Margaret Atack and Phil Powrie, 1–11. Manchester: Manchester University Press, 1990.

Ayres, Susan. "The Straight Mind in Russ's *The Female Man.*" In *Critical Studies on the Feminist Subject,* edited by Giovanna Covi, 165–84. Trento, Italy: Department of Philological and Historical Sciences, 1997.

Baruch, Elaine Hoffman. "Women and Love: Some Dying Myths." In *The Analysis of Literary Texts: Current Trends in Methodology,* edited by Randolph D. Pope, 51–65. Ypsilanti: Bilingual Press, 1980.

Bersani, Leo. *Homos,* 37–66. Cambridge: Harvard University Press, 1995.

Birkett, Jennifer. "Sophie Menade: The Writing of Monique Wittig." In *French Erotic Fiction: Women's Desiring Writing, 1880–1990,* edited by Alex Hughes and Kate Ince, 93–119. Oxford: Berg, 1996.

Bourcier, Marie-Hélène. "Les ruses de la raison straight." In *Parce que les lesbiennes ne sont pas des femmes: Autour de l'oeuvre politique, théorique et littéraire de Monique Wittig,* edited by Marie-Hélène Bourcier and Suzette Robichon, 23–34. Paris: Éditions Gaies et Lesbiennes, 2002.

Bourque, Dominique. "Dire l'interdit: La subversion dialogique chez Monique Wittig." In *Parce que les lesbiennes ne sont pas des femmes: Autour de l'oeuvre politique, théorique et littéraire de Monique Wittig,* edited by Marie-Hélène Bourcier and Suzette Robichon, 111–36. Paris: Éditions Gaies et Lesbiennes, 2002.

Braidotti, Rosi. "Essentialism." In *Feminism and Psychoanalysis: A Critical Dictionary,* edited by Elizabeth Wright, 77–83. Oxford: Blackwell, 1992.

Brée, Germaine. "Experimental Novels? Yes, but Perhaps Otherwise: Nathalie Sarraute, Monique Wittig." In *Breaking the Sequence: Women's Experimental Fiction,* edited by Ellen G. Friedman and Miriam Fuchs, 267–83. Princeton: Princeton University Press, 1989.

Butler, Judith. Brief reference under "Gender." In *Feminism and Psychoanalysis: A Critical Dictionary,* edited by Elizabeth Wright, 140–45. Oxford: Blackwell, 1992.

———. "Gender Trouble, Feminist Theory, and Psychoanalytic Discourse New York." In *Feminism/Postmodernism,* edited by Linda J. Nicholson, 324–40. New York: Routledge, 1990.

———. "Monique Wittig: Bodily Disintegration and Fictive Sex." In *Gender Trouble: Feminism and the Subversion of Identity,* edited by Judith Butler, 111–28. New York: Routledge, 1990.

———. "Variations on Sex and Gender: Beauvoir, Wittig and Foucault." *Praxis International* 5 (1984): 505–16. Also published in *Contemporary Literary Criticism: Literary and Cultural Studies,* edited by Robert Con Davis and Ronald Schleifer, 612–23. New York: Longman, 1998.

———, and Rosi Braidotti. "Feminism by Any Other Name." *differences: A Journal of Feminist Cultural Studies* 6, no. 23 (1994): 1–26.

Causse, Michèle. "The World as Will and Representation." In *Lesbian Philosophies and Cultures,* edited by Jeffner Allen, 259–74. Albany: SUNY Press, 1990.

Chisholm, Dianne. "Lesbianizing Love's Body: Interventionist Imag(in)ings of Monique Wittig." In *Reimagining Women: Representations of Women in Culture,* edited by Shirley Neuman and Glennis Stephenson, 196–216. Toronto: University of Toronto Press, 1993.

———. "Woman-Identified Woman/Radical Lesbianism." In *Feminism and Psychoanalysis: A Critical Dictionary,* edited by Elizabeth Wright and Juliet Flower MacCannell; advisory eds. Dianne Chisholm and Margaret Whitford, 451–53. Oxford: Blackwell, 1992.

Cooper, Sarah. "Becoming Readers of Lesbian Desire: Engaging with Monique Wittig." In *Working Papers on Contemporary France,* vol. 4: *Gender and Identities in France,* edited by Brigitte Rollet and Emily Salines, 37–44. Portsmouth: University of Portsmouth, 1999.

──────. In Cooper, *Relating to Queer Theory: Rereading Sexual Self-Definition with Irigaray, Kristeva, Wittig and Cixous*. Bern: Peter Lang, 2000.

Crosland, Margaret. "The Two-Breasted Amazon." In *Women of Iron and Velvet*, edited by Margaret Crosland, 211–17. New York: Taplinger, 1976.

Crowder, Diane Griffin. "De la pensée straight à la théorie queer: implications pour un mouvement politique." In *Parce que les lesbiennes ne sont pas des femmes: Autour de l'oeuvre politique, théorique et littéraire de Monique Wittig*, edited by Marie-Hélène Bourcier and Suzette Robichon, 163–78. Paris: Éditions Gaies et Lesbiennes, 2002.

──────. "Lesbians and the (Re/De) Construction of the Female Body." In *Reading the Social Body*, edited by Catherine Burroughs and Jeffrey Ehrenreich, 61–84. Iowa City: University of Iowa Press, 1993.

──────. "Separatism and Feminist Utopian Fiction." In *Sexual Practice, Textual Theory: Lesbian Cultural Criticism*, edited by Susan J. Wolfe and Julia Penelope, 237–50. Cambridge: Blackwell.

Dallery, Arlene B. "The Politics of Writing (the) Body: Ecriture Feminine." In *Gender/Body/Knowledge*, edited by Allison Jaggar and Susan Bordo, 52–67. New Brunswick: Rutgers University Press, 1989.

Dehler, Johanna. "Monique Wittig." In Dehler, *Fragments of Desire: Sapphic Fictions in Works by H.D., Judy Grahn and Monique Wittig*, 129–40. New York: Peter Lang, 1999.

De Koven, Marianne. "Male Signature, Female Aesthetic: The Gender Politics of Experimental Writing." In *Breaking the Sequence: Women's Experimental Fiction*, edited by Ellen G. Friedman and Miriam Fuchs, 72–81. Princeton: Princeton University Press, 1989.

de Lauretis, Teresa. "Quand les lesbiennes n'étaient pas des femmes: sur la portée épistémologique de la Pensée Straight et du Corps Lesbien des années 80 à nos jours." In *Parce que les lesbiennes ne sont pas des femmes: Autour de l'oeuvre politique, théorique et littéraire de Monique Wittig*, edited by Marie-Hélène Bourcier and Suzette Robichon, 35–54. Paris: Éditions Gaies et Lesbiennes, 2002.

──────. "The Technology of Gender." In *Technologies of Gender*, edited by Teresa de Lauretis, 1–30. Bloomington: Indiana University Press, 1987.

──────. "When Lesbians Were Not Women." Available online at http://www.unb.br/ih/his/geferm/special/artigos.htm.

Deudon, Catherine. *Un mouvement à soi: Images du mouvement des femmes, 1970–2001*, 6, 30, 31, 212, 213. Paris: Syllepse, 2003.

Deutscher, Penelope. Brief references in Deutscher, *Yielding Gender: Feminism, Deconstruction, and the History of Philosophy*, 11, 20–21, 23–31. New York: Routledge, 1997.

Doan, Laura. "Jeannette Winterson's Sexing the Postmodern." In *The Lesbian Postmodern*, edited by Laura Doan, 137–55. New York: Columbia University Press, 1994.

Duffy, Jean H. "Monique Wittig." In *Beyond the Nouveau Roman: Essays on the Contemporary Novel*, edited by Michael Tilby, 201–28. New York: Berg, 1990.

Duquesne, Dominique. "Essai de lecture symbolique: *Le corps lesbien* de Monique Wittig." In *Recherches sur l'Imaginaire Cahier X*, 121–33. Angers: University d'Angers, 1983.

Eberbach, Margaret. "Roland Barthes's Pleasure Primer." In *Twentieth-Century French Fiction: Essays for Germaine Brée*, edited by George Stambolian, 252–65. New Brunswick: Rutgers University Press, 1975.

Ecarnot, Catherine. "L'interlocutrice du corps lesbien: Menaçante, désirée, constituante." In *Parce que les lesbiennes ne sont pas des femmes: Autour de l'oeuvre politique, théorique et littéraire de Monique Wittig,* edited by Marie-Hélène Bourcier and Suzette Robichon, 99–110. Paris: Éditions Gaies et Lesbiennes, 2002.

———. "La monstrueuse sexualité d'au-delà du verbe dans les fictions de Monique Wittig." In *Le sexe sur le bout de la langue,* edited by Jacqueline Julien et Brigitte Boucheron, 157–70. Toulouse: Espace Lesbien, 2002.

Evans, Martha Noel. "Monique Wittig: The Lesbian." In *Masks of Tradition: Women and the Politics of Writing in Twentieth-Century France,* edited by Martha Noel Evans, 185–200. Ithaca: Cornell University Press, 1987.

Fallaize, Elizabeth. Brief references in *Simone de Beauvoir: A Critical Reader,* edited by Elizabeth Fallaize, 10, 30, 40. London: Routledge, 1998.

Fariña Busto, María Jesús. "Una cuestión de géneros: Inversión y dramatización del Quijote en *Le voyage sans fin* de Monique Wittig." In *Problemata Theatralia I: El signo teatral: Texto y representación,* edited by Jesús G. Maestro, 91–103. Vigo, Spain: Universidade de Vigo, 1996.

Farwell, Marilyn R. "Heterosexual Plots and Lesbian Subtexts: Toward a Theory of Lesbian Narrative Space." In *Lesbian Texts and Contexts: Radical Revisions,* edited by Karla Jay and Joanne Glasgow, 91–103. New York: New York University Press, 1990.

———. "Heterosexual Plots and Lesbian Narratives." In *The Cutting Edge: Lesbian Life and Literature,* edited by Karla Jay. New York: New York University Press, 1996.

———. "The Lesbian Narrative: 'The Pursuit of the Inedible by the Unspeakable.'" In *Professions of Desire: Lesbian and Gay Studies in Literature,* edited by George E. Haggerty and Bonnie Zimmerman, 156–68. New York: Modern Language Association of America, 1995.

———. "Toward a Definition of the Lesbian Literary Imagination." In *Sexual Practice, Textual Theory: Lesbian Cultural Criticism,* edited by Susan J. Wolfe and Julia Penelope, 66–84. Cambridge: Blackwell, 1993.

Ferguson, Ann. "Is There a Lesbian Culture?" In *Lesbian Philosophies and Cultures,* edited by Jeffner Allen, 63–88. Albany: SUNY Press, 1990.

Ferguson, Mary Anne. "The Female Novel of Development and the Myth of Psyche." In *The Voyage In: Fictions of Female Development,* edited by Marianne Hirsch, Elizabeth Abel, and Elizabeth Langland, 228–43. Hanover: University Press of New England, 1983.

Findlay, Heather. "Is There a Lesbian in This Text? Derrida, Wittig, and the Politics of the Three Women." In *Coming to Terms: Feminism, Theory, Politics,* edited by Elizabeth Weed, 59–69. New York: Routledge, 1989.

Fouque, Antoinette. Brief references in Fouque, *Il y a deux sexes: Essais de féminologie, 1989–1995,* 24, 31–32, 133. Paris: Gallimard, 1995.

Friedman, Ellen G., and Miriam Fuchs. Brief references in *Breaking the Sequence: Women's Experimental Fiction,* xi–xvi. Princeton: Princeton University Press, 1989.

Fullbrook, Edward, and Kate Fullbrook. Brief references in Fullbrook and Fullbrook, *Simone de Beauvoir: A Critical Introduction,* 132–34. Cambridge: Polity Press, 1998.

Furman, Nelly. "The Politics of Language: Beyond the Gender Principle?" In *Making a Difference: Feminist Literary Criticism,* edited by Gayle Greene and Coppelia Kahn, 59–79. London: Methuen, 1985.

Fuss, Diana J. "'Essentially Speaking': Luce Irigaray's Language of Essence." In *Revaluing French Feminism: Critical Essays on Difference, Agency, and Culture,* edited by Nancy Fraser and Sandra Lee Bartky, 94–112. Bloomington: Indiana University Press, 1992.

———. "Monique Wittig's Anti-Essentialist Materialism." In *Essentially Speaking: Feminism, Nature and Difference,* edited by Diana J. Fuss, 39–53. New York: Routledge, 1989.

Gaudet, Jeannette. "Monique Wittig: Virgile, non." In *Writing Otherwise: Atlan, Duras, Giraudon, Redonnet and Wittig*, edited by Jeannette Gaudet, 162–203. Amsterdam: Rodopi, 1999.

Gilmore, Leigh. "An Anatomy of Absence: Written on the Body, the Lesbian Body, and Autobiography without Names." In *The Gay Nineties: Disciplinary and Interdisciplinary Formations in Queer Studies*, edited by Thomas Foster, Carol Siegel, and Ellen E. Berry, 224–51. New York: New York University Press, 1997.

Greene, Gayle, and Coppélia Kahn. "Feminist Scholarship and the Social Construction of Woman." In *Making a Difference: Feminist Literary Criticism*, edited by Gayle Greene and Coppélia Kahn, 1–36. London: Methuen, 1985.

Grice, Helena, and Tim Woods. *"I'm Telling You Stories": Jeanette Winterson and the Politics of Reading.* Amsterdam: Rodopi, 1998.

Gunther, Renate. "Are Lesbians Women? The Relationship between Lesbianism and Feminism in the Work of Luce Irigaray and Monique Wittig." In *Gay Signatures: Gay and Lesbian Theory, Fiction and Film in France, 1945–1995*, edited by Owen Heathcote, Alex Hughes, and James S. Williams. New York: Berg, 1998.

Haraway, Donna J. *Simians, Cyborgs, and Women: The Reinvention of Nature*, 137–38, 73–74, 243. New York: Routledge, 1991.

Hewitt, Leah D. "Confusing the Genres: Autobiographical Parody and Utopia in Monique Wittig's *Across the Acheron*." In *Autobiographical Tightropes: Simone de Beauvoir, Nathalie Sarraute, Marguerite Duras, Monique Wittig, and Maryse Conde*, edited by Leah D. Hewitt, 127–58. Lincoln: University of Nebraska Press, 1990.

Hoagland, Sarah Lucia. "Lesbian Ethics and 'Female Agency.'" In *Lesbian Philosophies and Cultures*, edited by Jeffner Allen, 275–91. Albany: SUNY Press, 1990.

Huston, Nancy. "The Matrix of War, Mothers and Heroes." In *The Female Body in Western Culture*, edited by Susan Rubin Suleiman, 119–36. Cambridge: Harvard University Press, 1986.

Jardine, Alice A., and Anne M. Menke. "Exploding the Issue: 'French' 'Women' 'Writers' and 'The Canon.'" In *Displacements: Women, Tradition, Literatures in French*, edited by Joan DeJean and Nancy K. Miller, 275–307. Baltimore: Johns Hopkins University Press, 1991.

———. "Monique Wittig." In *Shifting Scenes: Interviews on Women, Writing, and Politics in Post-68 France*, edited by Alice A. Jardine and Anne M. Menke, 192–95. New York: Columbia University Press, 1991.

Jean, Raymond. "Le 'féminaire' de Monique Wittig." In *Pratique de la littérature*, edited by Raymond Jean, 130–32. Paris: Seuil, 1978.

Jones, Ann Rosalind. "Inscribing Femininity: French Theories of the Feminine." In *Making a Difference: Feminist Literary Criticism*, edited by Gayle Greene and Coppélia Kahn, 80–112. London: Methuen, 1985.

Jouve, Nicole Ward. "'Bliss was it in that dawn . . .' Contemporary Women's Writing in France and the Éditions des Femmes." In *Contemporary French Fiction by Women: Feminist Perspectives*, edited by Margaret Atack and Phil Powrie, 128–40. Manchester: Manchester University Press, 1990.

Kohn, Ingeborg M. "The United States in Contemporary French Fiction: A Geography of the Fantastic." In *Contours of the Fantastic: Selected Essays from the Eighth International Conference on the Fantastic in the Arts*, edited by Michele K. Langford, 187–96. Westport: Greenwood Press, 1994.

Kramarae, Cheris, and Paula A. Treichler. *A Feminist Dictionary.* London: Pandora Press, 1985.

Kutzer, M. Daphne. "The Cartography of Passion: Cixous, Wittig and Winterson." In *Re-Naming the Landscape,* edited by Jurgen Kleist and Bruce A. Butterfield, 133–45. New York: Peter Lang, 1994.

Lanser, Susan Sniader. *Fictions of Authority: Women Writers and Narrative Voice.* Ithaca: Cornell University Press, 1992.

MacCannell, Juliet Flower. "Lack." In *Feminism and Psychoanalysis: A Critical Dictionary,* edited by Elizabeth Wright, 207–9. Oxford: Blackwell, 1992.

Marks, Elaine. "Lesbian Intertextuality." In *Homosexualities and French Literature: Cultural Contexts, Critical Texts,* edited by George Stambolian and Elaine Marks, 353–77. Ithaca: Cornell University Press, 1979.

———, and Isabelle de Courtivron. *New French Feminisms: An Anthology,* edited by Elaine Marks and Isabelle de Courtivron. New York: Schocken Books, 1981.

Mathieu, Nicole-Claude. *L'anatomie politique: Catégorisations et idéologies du sexe.* Paris: Côté-Femmes Éditions, 1991.

Meese, Elizabeth A. Brief references in Meese, *Crossing the Double-Cross: The Practice of Feminist Criticism,* 70–87. Chapel Hill: University of North Carolina Press, 1986.

———. "Theorizing Lesbian: Writing—A Love Letter." In *Lesbian Texts and Contexts: Radical Revisions,* edited by Karla Jay and Joanne Glasgow. New York: New York University Press, 1990.

Mohanty, Chandra Talpadi. "Feminist Encounters: Locating the Politics of Experience." In *Destabilizing Theory: Contemporary Feminist Debates,* edited by Michele Barrett and Anne Philips, 74–92. Stanford: Stanford University Press, 1992.

Moi, Toril. Brief references in Moi, *What Is a Woman? And Other Essays,* 5, 74. New York: Oxford University Press, 1999.

Montefiore, Jan. "Textual Erotics: Irigaray and Wittig." In *Feminism and Poetry,* edited by Jan Montefiore, 153–58. New York: Pandora, 1987.

Oppenheim, Lois. "The Ontology of Language in a Post-Structuralist Feminist Perspective: Explosive Discourse in Monique Wittig." In *Poetics of the Elements in the Human Condition,* part 2: *The Airy Elements in Poetic Imagination,* edited by Anna-Teresa Tymieniecka. Boston: Kluwer Academic, 1988.

Ostrovsky, Erika. "A Cosmogony of O: Wittig's *Les guérillères.*" In *Twentieth Century French Fiction,* edited by George Stambolian, 241–61. New Brunswick: Rutgers University Press, 1975.

———. "Religion in the Fiction of Monique Wittig." In *Religion in French Feminist Thought: Critical Perspectives,* edited by Morny Joy, Kathleen O'Grady, and Judith L. Poxon, 191–202. London: Routledge, 2003.

Palmer, Paulina. "The Passion: Storytelling, Fantasy, Desire." In *"I'm Telling You Stories": Jeanette Winterson and the Politics of Reading,* edited by Helena Grice and Tim Woods, 103–16. Amsterdam: Rodopi, 1998.

Parker, Alice. "Nicole Brossard: A Differential Equation of Lesbian Love." In *Lesbian Texts and Contexts: Radical Revisions,* edited by Karla Jay and Joanne Glasgow, 304–29. New York: New York University Press, 1990.

Peel, Ellen. *Politics, Persuasion, and Pragmatism: A Rhetoric of Feminist Utopian Fiction.* Columbus: Ohio State University Press, 2002.

———. "Utopian Feminism, Skeptical Feminism, and Narrative Energy." In *Feminism, Utopia and Narrative,* edited by Libby Falk Jones, Sarah Webster Goodwin, Jean Pfaelzer, and Jean Bethke Elshtain, 34–49. Knoxville: University of Tennessee Press, 1990.

Penelope, Julia. "The Lesbian Perspective." In *Lesbian Philosophies and Cultures,* edited by Jeffner Allen, 89–108. Albany: SUNY Press, 1990.

Phillips, Catherine. "L'ecart soude le projet: Subjectivité textuelle et sexualité narratrice chez Hélène Cixous et Monique Wittig." In *Repenser les processus créateurs/Rethinking Creative Processes,* edited by Françoise Grauby and Michelle Royer, 263–73. Bern, Switzerland: Peter Lang, 2001.

Plate, Liedeke. "Dis/Remembering the Classics: Female Identity and the Act of Rewriting." In *Gendered Memories,* edited by John Neubauer and Helga Geyer-Ryan, 65–75. Amsterdam: Rodopi, 2000.

Porter, Laurence M. "Monique Wittig." In *The Contemporary Novel in France,* edited by William Thompson, 279–92. Gainesville: University Press of Florida, 1995.

Porter, Melinda Camber. "Decisive Women: Marguerite Duras, Delphine Seyrig, Roger Vadim, Monique Wittig, Françoise Giroud." In *Through Parisian Eyes: Reflections on Contemporary French Arts and Culture,* edited by Melinda C. Porter, 105–32. New York: Oxford University Press, 1986.

Preciado, Beatriz. "Gare à la gouine garou! Ou comment se faire un corps queer à partir de la pensée straight?" In *Parce que les lesbiennes ne sont pas des femmes: Autour de l'oeuvre politique, théorique et littéraire de Monique Wittig,* edited by Marie-Hélène Bourcier and Suzette Robichon, 179–216. Paris: Éditions Gaies et Lesbiennes, 2002.

Ragland-Sullivan, Ellie. "Lacan, Jacques." In *Feminism and Psychoanalysis: A Critical Dictionary,* edited by Elizabeth Wright, 201–9. Oxford: Blackwell, 1992.

Riley, Anthony W. "Der Volksschriftsteller Joseph Wittig (1879–1949): Ausklang vom 19. oder Weckruf zum 20. Jahrhundert?" In *Bildung und Konfession: Politik, Religion und literarische Identitatsbildung 1850–1918,* edited by Martin Huber and Gerhard Lauer, 147–61. Tubingen: Niemeyer, 1996.

Robichon, Suzette. "Monique Wittig, une oeuvre pionnière." In *Parce que les lesbiennes ne sont pas des femmes: Autour de l'oeuvre politique, théorique et littéraire de Monique Wittig,* edited by Marie-Hélène Bourcier and Suzette Robichon, 15–22. Paris: Éditions Gaies et Lesbiennes, 2002.

Roof, Judith. "Lesbians and Lyotard: Legitimation and the Politics of the Name." In *The Lesbian Postmodern,* edited by Laura Doan, 47–66. New York: Columbia University Press, 1994.

———. "The Match in the Crocus: Representation of Lesbian Sexuality." In *Discontented Discourses: Feminism/Textual Intervention/Psychoanalysis,* edited by Marleen S. Barr and Richard Feldstein, 100–117. Chicago: University of Chicago Press, 1989.

Rosenfeld, Marthe. "Monique Wittig (1935–)." In *Postmodern Fiction: A Biobibliographical Guide,* edited by Larry McCaffery, 548–51. Westport: Greenwood Press, 1986.

Rossum-Guyon, Françoise van. "Le collage comme concept et comme pratique dans l'avant-garde et le roman français contemporain." In *Vitalité et contradictions de l'avant-garde Italie-France 1909–1924,* edited by Sandro Briosi and Henk Hillenaar, 85–93. Paris: José Corti, 1968.

Rubin, Gayle. "The Traffic in Women: Notes on the 'Political Economy' of Sex." In *The Second Wave: A Reader in Feminist Theory,* edited by Linda Nicholson, 27–62. New York: Routledge, 1997.

Russ, Joanna. "Recent Feminist Utopias." In *Future Females: A Critical Anthology,* edited by Marleen S. Barr, 71–85. Bowling Green: Bowling Green State University Popular Press, 1981.

Shaktini, Namascar. "*Brouillon pour un dictionnaire des amantes:* Wittig et Zeig lesbianisent la langue," translated by Anne-Marie Livoti. In *Le sexe sur le bout de la langue,* edited by Jacqueline Julien and Brigitte Boucheron, 21–29. Toulouse: Espace Lesbien, 2002.

———. *"Elles* and the Ladies of Orange: Monique Wittig's Deconstructive Use of Epic." In *Romance Languages Annual* 4, edited by Jeanette Beer, Charles Ganelin, and Anthony Julian Tamburri, 152–55. West Lafayette: Purdue Research Foundation, 1993.

———. "Figuring Circulation: Claude Lévi-Strauss and Monique Wittig." In *Contemporary French Women's Fiction,* edited by Margaret Atack and Phillip Powrie, 141–50. Manchester: Manchester University Press, 1990.

———. "Lire *Le corps lesbien:* Sur la réception critique de l'oeuvre de Monique Wittig." In *Parce que les lesbiennes ne sont pas des femmes: Autour de l'oeuvre politique, théorique et littéraire de Monique Wittig,* edited by Marie-Hélène Bourcier and Suzette Robichon, 67–82. Paris: Éditions Gaies et Lesbiennes, 2002.

———. "Le point de vue universel dans *le brouillon pour un dictionnaire des amantes."* In *Lesbianisme/féminisme: Histoires, politiques,* edited by Natacha Chetkuti and Claire Michard, 131–43. Paris: L'Harmattan, 2003.

———. "A Revolutionary Signifier: The Lesbian Body." In *Lesbian Texts and Contexts: Radical Revisions,* edited by Karla Jay and Joanne Glasgow, 291–303. New York: New York University Press, 1990.

Sherzer, Dina. *Representation in Contemporary French Fiction,* 123–32. Lincoln: University of Nebraska Press, 1987.

Spinelli, Simonetta. "L'espace du désir: La réception de l'oeuvre de Wittig en Italie." In *Parce que les lesbiennes ne sont pas des femmes: Autour de l'oeuvre politique, théorique et littéraire de Monique Wittig,* edited by Marie-Hélène Bourcier and Suzette Robichon, 83–98. Paris: Éditions Gaies et Lesbiennes, 2002.

Still, Judith. "Literature." In *Feminism and Psychoanalysis: A Critical Dictionary,* edited by Elizabeth Wright, 228–35. Oxford: Blackwell, 1992.

Stimpson, Catharine R. "Ad/d Feminam: Women, Literature and Society." In *Literature and Society: Selected Papers from the English Institute,* edited by Edward W. Said, 174–92. Baltimore: Johns Hopkins University Press, 1980.

Suleiman. "Mothers and the Avant-Garde: A Case of Mistaken Identity?" In *Femmes = Frauen = Women,* edited by Françoise van Rossum-Guyon, 135–46. Amsterdam: Rodopi, 1990.

Suleiman, Susan Rubin. Brief reference in Suleiman, *Subversive Intent: Gender, Politics, and the Avant-Garde,* 133–34. Cambridge: Harvard University Press, 1990.

———. "(Re)Writing the Body: The Politics and Poetics of Female Eroticism." In *The Female Body in Western Culture: Contemporary Perspectives,* edited by Susan Rubin Suleiman, 7–29. Cambridge: Harvard University Press, 1986.

Thiébaux, Marcelle. "A Mythology for Women: Monique Wittig's *Les guérillères."* In *The Analysis of Literary Texts: Current Trends in Methodology,* edited by Randolph D. Pope, 89–99. Ypsilani: Bilingual Press, 1980.

Turcotte, Louise. Foreword. In Monique Wittig, *The Straight Mind and Other Essays.* Boston: Beacon Press, 1992.

———. "La pensée matérialiste de Monique Wittig." In *Parce que les lesbiennes ne sont pas des femmes: Autour de l'oeuvre politique, théorique et littéraire de Monique Wittig,* edited by Marie-Hélène Bourcier and Suzette Robichon, 55–66. Paris: Éditions Gaies et Lesbiennes, 2002.

Waelti-Walters, Jennifer. *Fairy Tales and the Female Imagination.* Montreal: Eden Press, 1982.

Wakeman, John. "Monique Wittig." In *World Authors 1970–75,* edited by John Wakeman. New York: H. W. Wilson, 1980.

Woodhull, Winnie. "By Myriad Constellations: Monique Wittig and the Writing of Women's

Experience." In *Power, Gender, Values,* edited by Judith Genova, 13–30. Edmonton: Academic Printing, 1987.

Zimmerman, Bonnie. *The Safe Sea of Women: Lesbian Fiction 1969–1989.* Boston: Beacon Press, 1990.

———. "Exiting from Patriarchy: The Lesbian Novel of Development." In *The Voyage In: Fictions of Female Development,* edited by Marianne Hirsch Elizabeth Abel, and Elizabeth Langland, 244–57. Hanover: University Press of New England, 1983.

———. "What Has Never Been: An Overview of Lesbian Feminist Criticism." In *Making a Difference: Feminist Literary Criticism,* edited by Gayle Greene and Coppélia Kahn, 195–96. New York: Methuen, 1985.

CONFERENCE PROCEEDINGS

Porter, Laurence M. "Feminist Fantasy and Open Structure in Monique Wittig's *Les guérillères.*" Presented at the "Celebration of the Fantastic: Selected Papers from the Tenth Anniversary International Conference on the Fantastic in the Arts," Westport, Conn., 1992.

ELECTRONIC SOURCES

Bonnet, Marie-Jo. "Le désir théophanique chez Monique Wittig." Available online at http://www.unb.br/ih/his/geferm/special/artigos.htm.

Causse, Michèle. "Tribute to Monique Wittig." Available online at http://www.unb.br/ih/his/geferm/special/artigos.htm.

Crowder, Diane Griffin. "Lire Wittig: Un souvenir personnel." Available online at http://www.unb.br/ih/his/geferm/special/artigos.htm.

Cleveland, Janne. *The Power of the Word: The (Unnameable) Lesbian Body.* Available online at http://www.thirdspace.ca/articles/clevland.htm.

de Lauretis, Teresa. "When Lesbians Were Not Women." Available online at http://www.unb.br/ih/his/geferm/special/artigos.htm.

Shaktini, Namascar. "Lire *Le corps lesbien.*" Available online at http://www.unb.br/ih/his/geferm/special/artigos.htm.

Spinelli, Simonetta. "Monique Wittig: Queer or Not Queer." Available online at http://www.unb.br/ih/his/geferm/special/artigos.htm.

Swain, Tania Navarro. "Monique Wittig, adieu . . . au revoir." Available online at http://www.unb.br/ih/his/geferm/special/artigos.htm.

JOURNAL ARTICLES

Allen, Hilary. "Political Lesbianism and Feminism—Space for a Sexual Politics?" *m/f* 7 (1982): 15–34.

Alter, Jean. "Monique Wittig, *Les guérillères.*" *French Review* 44 (May 1971): 1126–27.

Amat, Nuria. "La erotica del lenguaje en Alejandra Pizarnik y Monique Wittig." *Nueva Estafeta* 12 (1979): 47–54.

Andersen, Margaret. "La jouissance: Principe d'écriture." *L'Esprit Créateur* 19, no. 2 (1979): 3–12.

Anderson, Kristine J. "Encyclopedic Dictionary as Utopian Genre: Two Feminist Ventures." *Utopian Studies: Journal of the Society for Utopian Studies* 2 (1991): 124–30.

————. "Lesbianizing English: Wittig and Zeig Translate Utopia." *L'Esprit Créateur* 34, no. 4 (1994): 90–102.

Armengaud, Françoise. "La contestation des conventions du discours chez Nathalie Sarraute et chez Monique Wittig." *Nouvelles Questions Feministes* 19, no. 1 (1998): 35–64.

Balakian, Anna. "Child's World without Wonder." *Saturday Review* 49 (July 1966): 33. [Review of *The Opoponax*.]

Basch, F., Merry Blue, Agathe Cacao, Catherine Crachat, Catherine Glaviot, and Rose Prudence. "Le sexisme ordinaire." *Les Temps Modernes* 39 (1983): 2337–65.

Bazon, L. "Le Faussaire: *L'opoponax.*" *Etudes* (Feb 1965): 232–37.

Beauchamp, Jose Juan. "Guerra de los sexos y cuerpo lesbiano en la obra de Monique Wittig." *Revista del Ateneo Puertorriqueno* 4, nos. 10–11–12 (1994): 173–87.

Benegas, Noni. "Virgile, non." *Vlasta*, no. 4 (1985): 96.

Bérard, Sylvie. "Amazones de tir dans la SF côté femmes!" *Tessera*, no. 15 (1993): 42–54.

Berg, Maggie. "Luce Irigaray's 'Contradictions': Poststructuralism and Feminism." *Signs: Journal of Women in Culture and Society* 17, no. 1 (1991): 50–70.

Bondy, Francois. "Die Weld der Literatur." *Literaturbrief aus Frankreich: Die grossen Vier und Einige Andere* 1, no. 20 (1964): 685.

Bonnet, Marie-Jo. "Au commencement, s'il y eut jamais un commencement." *Lesbia*, no. 222 (2003): 24–27.

————. "De l'émancipation amoureuse des femmes dans la cité: Lesbiennes et féminités au XXème siècle." *Les Temps Modernes* 598 (March–April 1998): 85–112.

Bourdet, Denise. "Monique Wittig." *Revue de Paris* 71 (Dec. 1964): 115–19.

Braidotti, Rosi. "Feminism by Any Other Name." *differences: A Journal of Feminist Cultural Studies* 6, nos. 2–3 (1994): 27–61.

Budig-Markin, Valerie. "Vivir y escribir la lucha femenina en tres continentes: Monique Wittig, Assia Djebar y Luisa Valenzuela." *Feminaria Literaria* 5, no. 8 (1995): 4–10.

Burgess, Anthony. "New Fiction." *The Listener*, May 19, 1966, 733.

Butler, Judith. "Variations on Sex and Gender: Beauvoir, Wittig and Foucault." *Praxis International* 5 (1984): 505–16.

————, and Rosi Braidotti. "Feminism by Any Other Name." *differences: A Journal of Feminist Cultural Studies* 6, nos. 2–3 (1994): 1–26.

Byatt, A. S. "Give Me the Moonlight, Give Me the Girl." *New Review* (London), 2 (June 1975): 65–67.

Calhoun, Cheshire. "Separating Lesbian Theory from Feminist Theory." *Ethics* 104, no. 3 (1994): 558–61.

Caravaca, Francisco. "Les premios literarios franceses de 1964." *Arbor* 60 (Feb. 1965): 71–85.

Case, Sue-Ellen. "Towards a Butch-Femme Aesthetic." *Discourse* 11, no. 1 (1989): 55–73.

Chalon, Jean. "Les lectures de Monique Wittig doivent rentrer dans le 'on.'" *Le Figaro Littéraire* 13 (Dec 1964): 3. [Review of *L'opoponax*.]

Chisholm, Dianne. "Violence against Violence against Women: An Avant-Garde for the Times." *Atlantis* 17, no. 2 (1992): 59–80.

Chonez, Claudine. "Review: *Le corps lesbien.*" *Magazine Littéraire* 82 (Nov. 1973): 57–58.

Clarke, Marie-Diane. "Le monde refusé, un monde amorcé dans la vie devant soi d'Emile Ajar." *Initiales/Initials: Travaux des Etudiants de Cycle Supérieur* 10–11 (1990): 83–90.

Cluny, Claude-Michel. "La longue marche des jeunes filles en fleurs." *Les Lettres Françaises*, Nov. 22, 1969, 5–6.

Collecott, Diana. "Mirror-Images: Images of Mirrors . . . in Poems by Sylvia Plath, Adrienne
    Rich, Denise Levertov and H.D." *Revue Française D'Etudes Américaines* 11 (1986):
    149–60.
Cope, Karin. "Plastic Actions: Linguistic Strategies and *Le corps lesbien.*" *Hypatia: A Journal
    of Feminist Philosophy* 6, no. 3 (1991): 74–96.
Cornot, Michel. "Mille fleurs au courrier." *Le Nouvel Observateur,* Aug. 17, 1970, 34–35.
Courtivron, Isabelle de. "Le repos du guerrier." *L'Esprit Créateur* 19, no. 2 (1979): 23–
    35.
Coxe, Louis. "Moral Vitamins." *New Republic,* Feb. 21, 1970, 20, 22.
Creet, Julia. "Daughter of the Movements: The Psychodynamics of Lesbian S/M Fantasy."
    differences: A Journal of Feminist Cultural Studies 3, no. 2 (1991): 135–59 [special
    issue on "Queer Theory: Lesbian and Gay Sexualities"].
———. "Speaking in Lesbian Tongues: Monique Wittig and the Universal Point of View."
    Resources for Feminist Research/Documentation sur la Recherche Féministe 16, no.
    4 (1987): 16–21.
Crowder, Diane Griffin. "Amazones de . . . demain? La fiction utopique féministe et lesbi-
    enne." *AHLA* 2, no. 4 (1984): 19–27.
———. "Amazons and Mothers? Monique Wittig, Hélène Cixous, and Theories of Women's
    Writing." *Contemporary Literature* 24, no. 2 (1983): 117–44.
———. "The Semiotic Functions of Ideology in Literary Discourse." *Bucknell Review: A
    Scholarly Journal of Letters, Arts and Sciences* 27, no. 1 (1982): 157–68.
———. "Une armée d'amantes: L'image de l'amazone dans l'oeuvre de Monique Wittig."
    Vlasta, no. 4 (1985): 65–78.
Curb, Rosemary. "Re/cognition/Re/presentation, Re/creation in Woman-Conscious Drama:
  . The Seer, the Seen, the Scene." *Theater Journal* 37 (Oct. 1985): 302–16.
Dallery, Arleen B. "Sexual Embodiment: Beauvoir and French Feminism." *Women's Studies
    International Forum* 8, no. 3 (1985): 197–202.
Dalmas, André. "Contre l'ordre masculin." *Quinzaine Littéraire,* Nov. 1, 1973, 9.
———. "Un langage nouveau." *La Quinzaine Littéraire,* Nov. 16, 1969, 9. [Review of *Les
    guérillères.*]
Damon, Gene. "Lesbiana." *The Ladder* 16, nos. 5–6 (1972): 24–25.
Dargan, J. "Monique Wittig: *Across the Acheron.*" *Choice* 25 (Nov 1987): 483.
Davis, Robert Gotham. "Invaded Selves." *Hudson Review* 19, no. 4 (1966): 659–68.
Davy, Kate. "Constructing the Spectator: Reception, Context, and Address in Lesbian
    Performance." *Performing Arts Journal* 10, no. 2 (1986): 43–52.
de Lauretis, Teresa. "Eccentric Subjects: Feminist Theory and Historical Consciousness."
    Feminist Studies 16 (Spring 1990): 115–50.
———. "The Female Body and Heterosexual Presumption." *Semiotics* 67, nos. 3/4 (1987):
    259–79.
———. "Sexual Indifference and Lesbian Representation." *Theater Journal* 40, no. 2 (1988):
    155–77.
Delphy, Christine. "La passion selon Wittig." *Nouvelles Questions Feministes* 11–12 (1985):
    151–56.
———, coord. "Les origines du mouvement de libération des femmes en France." *Nouvelles
    Questions Feministes* 11, nos. 16–17–18 (1991): 1–262.
Detweiler, Robert. "Theological Trends of Postmodern Fiction." *Journal of the American
    Academy of Religion* 44, no. 2 (1976): 225–37.
Deudon, Catherine. "Monique Wittig et les lesbiennes barbues (entretien)." *Actuel* 25
    (Nov. 1977): 12–14.

Dollimore, Jonathan. "The Dominant and the Deviant: A Violent Dialectic." *Critical Quarterly* 28, nos. 1–2 (1986): 179–81.

Donnelly, Nisa, and Kris Brandenburger. "The World as It Might Be: Monique Wittig Challenges Readers." *Lambda Book Report: A Review of Contemporary Gay and Lesbian Literature* 3, no. 3 (1992): 28–29. [Review of *The Straight Mind and Other Essays.*]

Duffy, Jean. "Language and Childhood: *L'opoponax* by Monique Wittig." *Forum for Modern Language Studies* 19, no. 4 (1983): 289–300.

———. "Women and Language in *Les guérillères* by Monique Wittig." *Stanford French Review* 7, no. 3 (1983): 399–412.

Durand, Laura G. "Heroic Feminism as Art." *Novel: A Forum on Fiction* 8 (1974): 71–77.

Ecarnot, Catherine. "Pourquoi j'ai écrit ma thèse sur les fictions de Monique Wittig." *Lesbia,* no. 222 (2003): 28–29.

Ellenberger, Harriet. "From: *The Dream Is the Bridge:* In Search of Lesbian Theatre (excerpts)." *Trivia* 20 (1992): 62–66.

Engelbrecht, Penelope J. "'Lifting Belly Is a Language': The Postmodern Lesbian Subject." *Feminist Studies* 16, no. 1 (1990): 85–114.

Fauré, Christine. "Le crépuscule des déesses; ou, La crise intellectuelle en France en milieu féministe." *Les Temps Modernes* 37 (1981): 1285–91.

———. "The Twilight of the Goddesses; or, The Intellectual Crisis of French Feminism." *Signs: Journal of Women in Culture and Society* 7, no. 1 (1981): 81–86.

Feaver, William. "Typographic Tales." *The Listener* 94 (Aug 1975): 221.

Freadman, Anne. "Poeta (1st. decl., n., fem.)." *Australian Journal of French Studies* 16, no. 2 (1979): 152–65.

Froula, Christine. "Hell (and Heaven) on Earth." *Women's Review of Books* 5, no. 8 (1988): 11–12.

Gage, Carolyn. "Monique Wittig: 1935–2003: Failing to Remember, Invent." *Off Our Backs: The Feminist Newsjournal* 33, nos. 5–6 (2003): 56–57.

Gascon Vera, Elena. "Rosa Montero ante la escritura femenina." *Anales de la Literatura Espanola Contemporanea* 12, nos. 1–2 (1987): 59–77.

Gilbert, Sandra Caruso Mortola, and Susan Dreyfuss David Gubar. "Ceremonies of the Alphabet: Female Grandmatologies and the Female Autograph." *New York Literary Forum* 12, no. 3 (1984): 23–52.

———, and Susan Gubar. "Sexchanges." *College English* 50, no. 7 (1988): 768–85.

Gilbert, Sandra M. "The Battle of the Books/the Battle of the Sexes: Virginia Woolf's *Vita Nuova.*" *Michigan Quarterly Review* 23 (1984): 171–95.

Gillman, Linda. "The Looking-Glass through Alice." *Women and Literature* 1 (1980): 12–23.

Griggers, Cathy. "Lesbian Bodies in the Age of (Post)Modern Reproduction." *Postmodern Culture* 2, no. 3 (1992): 1–15.

Gruaz, Claude. "La ponctuation, c'est l'homme . . . emploi des signes de ponctuation dans cinq romans contemporains." *Langue Française* 45 (Feb. 1980): 113–24.

Halberstam, Judith. "Automating Gender: Postmodern Feminism in the Age of the Intelligent Machine." *Feminist Studies* 17, no. 3 (1991): 439–60.

Hale, Jacob. "Are Lesbians Women?" *Hypatia: A Journal of Feminist Philosophy* 11, no. 2 (1996): 94–121.

Haraway, Donna. "A Manifesto for Cyborgs: Science, Technology, and Socialist Feminism in the 1980s." *Socialist Review* 15 (1985): 65–107.

Hart, Stephen M. "Is Women's Writing in Spanish America Gender-Specific?" *Modern Language Notes* 110, no. 2 (1995): 335–52.

Hawkesworth, Mary E. "Feminist Rhetoric: Discourses on the Male Monopoly of Thought." *Political Theory* 16, no. 3 (1988): 444–67.

Hawthorne, Susan. "Dancing into the Future: A Feminist Literary Strategy." *Women's Studies International Forum* 11, no. 6 (1988): 559–68.

———. "The Politics of the Exotic: The Paradox of Cultural Voyeurism." *Meanjin* 48, no. 2 (1989): 259–68.

Heathcote, Owen. "Hermeneutic Circles and Cycles of Violence: *La fille aux yeux d'or, Histoire d'O, Les guérillères.*" *South Central Review* 19–20, nos. 4–1 (2002–2003): 44–62.

———. "Masochism, Sadism, and Women's Writing: The Examples of Marguerite Duras and Monique Wittig." *Nottingham French Studies* 32, no. 2 (1993): 71–84.

Hemmings, John. "Catholic Girlhood." *New Statesman* 71 (May 1966): 740–41.

Hennessy, Rosemary. "Queer Theory: A Review of the *differences* Special Issue and Wittig's *The Straight Mind.*" *Signs: Journal of Women in Culture and Society* 18, no. 4 (1993): 964–73 [special issue on "Theorizing Lesbian Experience"].

Herrmann, Claudine. "Une tentative de Monique Wittig pour récupérer le langage." *La Quinzaine Littéraire* 242, no. 16 (1976): 19.

Higgins, Lynn. "Nouvelle nouvelle autobiographie: Monique Wittig's *Le corps lesbien.*" *Sub-Stance,* no. 14 (1976): 160–66.

Higgins, Lynn A. "In/On Translation: Recent French Feminist Writers." *Translation Review* 17 (1985): 13–16.

Hite, M. "Writing and Reading the Body: Female Sexuality and Recent Feminist Fiction." *Feminist Studies* 14, no. 1 (1988): 121–42.

Hokenson, Jan. "The Pronouns of Gomorrha: A Lesbian Prose Tradition." *Frontiers* 10, no. 1 (1988): 62–69.

Holland, Jeanne. "Uncovering Woman's Body in Gertrude Stein's 'Subject-Cases': The Background of a Detective." *College English* 52, no. 5 (1990): 540–51.

Hollinger, Veronica. "Cybernetic Deconstructions: Cyberpunk and Postmodernism." *Mosaic* 23, no. 2 (1990): 29–44.

Homans, Margaret. "'Her Very Own Howl': The Ambiguities of Representation in Recent Women's Fiction." *Signs: Journal of Women in Culture and Society* 9, no. 2 (1983): 186–205.

Jagose, Annamarie. "Way Out: The Category 'Lesbian' and the Fantasy of the Utopic Space." *Journal of the History of Sexuality* 4, no. 2 (1993): 264–87.

Janvier, Ludovic. "Un indéfini totalisant." *Critique,* no. 20 (1964): 1084–86. [Review of *L'opoponax.*]

Jardine, Alice. "Pre-Texts for the Transatlantic Feminist." *Yale French Studies* 62 (1981): 220–36.

Jean. "*Les guérillères.*" *Women's Press* 3, no. 4 (1973): 5.

Jones, Ann Rosalind. "Writing the Body: Toward an Understanding of *l'écriture féminine.*" *Feminist Studies* 7, no. 2 (1981): 247–63.

Jordan, Clive. "Dislocations." *New Statesman* 2 (July 1971): 24.

Kanters, Robert. "'L'école des femmes.'" *Le Figaro Littéraire,* no. 29 (1964): 4. [Review of *L'opoponax.*]

Keinhorst, Annette. "Emancipatory Projection: An Introduction to Women's Critical Utopias." *Women's Studies International Forum,* no. 14 (1987): 91–99.

Komar, Kathleen L. "The Communal Self: Re-Membering Female Identity in the Works of Christa Wolf and Monique Wittig." *Comparative Literature,* no. 44 (1992): 42–58.

Lambert, Claudette. "Wittig, ou l'obsession d'un monde nouveau." *Amazones d'Hier, Lesbiennes d'Aujourd'hui* 5, no. 2 (1987): 72–73.

Lamy, Suzanne. "Retrouvailles ou premières lectures." *Spirales* 41 (March 1984): 12.

Lauter, Estella. "Leonor Fini: Preparing to Meet the Strangers of the New World." *Women's Art Journal* 1, no. 1 (1980): 44–49.

LeBlanc, Elizabeth. "The Metaphorical Lesbian: Edna Pontellier in *The Awakening.*" *Tulsa Studies in Women's Literature* 15, no. 2 (1996): 289–307.

Leduc, Sylvie. "Marguerite Yourcenar, Marguerite Duras et Monique Wittig: Parcours du discours dominant au discours." *Amazones d'Hier, Lesbiennes d'Aujourd'hui* 5, no. 2 (1987): 90–105.

Le Garrec, Evelyne. "Monique Wittig: 'Je crois aux amazones.'" *Politique Hebdo* 40 (Nov. 1973): 29 [interview].

Leibacher-Ouvrard, Lise. "Monique Wittig." *L'Esprit Créateur* 36 (Summer 1996).

Lew, Margaret. "Relocating the Hedge Transforms the House: Monique Wittig and Pueblo Architecture." *Trivia,* no. 12 (1988): 6–35.

Lewis, Valerie Hannagan. "Warriors and Runaways: Monique Wittig's *Le voyage sans fin.*" *Theatre Research International* 23, no. 3 (1998): 200–204.

Limousin, Christian. "Review: *Le corps lesbien.*" *Politique Hebdo* 40 (Nov. 1973): 28–29.

Lindsay, Cecile. "Corporality, Ethics, Experimentation: Lyotard in the Eighties." *Philosophy Today* 36 (Winter 1992): 389–401.

Lindsey, Cecile. "Body/Language: French Feminist Utopias." *French Review* 60, no. 1 (1986): 46–55.

Linstrum, Cathy. "L'asile des femmes: Subjectivity and Femininity in Breton's *Nadja* and Wittig's *Le corps lesbien.*" *Nottingham French Studies* 27, no. 1 (1988): 35–45.

Loriot, Patrick. "Feuilles d'automne." *Le Nouvel Observateur,* Sept. 1–7, 1969, 30–31.

Louppe, Laurence. "Entretien avec Monique Wittig (*Le corps lesbien*)." *L'Art Vivant* 45 (Dec. 1973–Jan. 1974): 24–25.

Makward, Christiane. "Structures du silence/du délire: Marguerite Duras/Hélène Cixous." *Poétique* 35 (1978): 314–24.

Marini, Marcelle. "Enfance en archipels: *L'opoponax* de Monique Wittig." *Revue des Sciences Humaines* 96, no. 2 (1991): 143–59.

Marks, Elaine. "Women and Literature in France." *Signs: Journal of Women in Culture and Society* 3, no. 4 (1978): 832–42.

McCarthy, Mary. "Everybody's Childhood." *New Statesman* 72 (July 1966): 90, 92–94.

McFadden, Maggie. "Anatomy of Difference: Toward a Classification of Feminist Theory." *Women's Studies International Forum* 7, no. 6 (1984): 495–504.

Melcior-Bonnet, Christiane. "Sorti des presses." *A là Page* 8 (Feb. 1965): 316–17.

Michie, Helena. "Murder in the Canon: The Dual Personality of Carolyn Heilbrun." *Massachusetts Studies in English* 9, no. 3 (1990): 1–12.

Miller, Karl. "Argument: Général de Goth." *New Statesman,* July 15, 1966, 100.

Mochet, Marie-Anne, Eliane Papo, and Christine Briere. "De l'autre côté du micro." *Cahiers du Français des Années Quatre-Vingts* 2 (1986): 199–209.

Montefiore, Jan. "Feminism and Poetry: Language, Experience, Identity in Women." *Poetics Today* 8, nos. 3–4 (1987): 737–40.

Morris, Adalaide. "The Body Politic: Body, Language, and Power." *College English* 52, no. 5 (1990): 570–78.

Nelson-McDermott, Catherine. "Postmodernism Meets the Great Beyond: *Les guérillères* and *Le corps lesbien.*" *Canadian Review of Comparative Literature/Revue Canadienne de Littérature Comparée* 21, no. 3 (1994): 325–30.

Nye, Andrea. "The Inequalities of Semantic Structure: Linguistics and Feminist Philosophy." *Metaphilosophy* 3, no. 4 (1987): 222–40.

Ouerd, Michele. "Lesbianisme et littérature: 1970 et 1980." *Masques,* nos. 9–10 (1981): 28–36.

Parker, Alice. "Madame de Tencin and the 'Mascarade' of Female Im/Personation." *Eighteenth-Century Life* 9, no. 2 (1985): 65–78.

Patterson, Yolanda Astarota, and Carol V. Richards. "Germaine Bree: Teacher, Scholar, Humanist." *Contemporary French Civilization* 4, no. 2 (1980): 243–69 [interview].

Peel, Marie. "Women's Lib in Lit." *Books and Bookmen* 17 (Nov. 1971): 14–17.

Perez Minik, Domingo. "'*Las guerrilleras*' de la narrativa francesa: Monique Wittig." *Insula: Revista Bibliografica de Ciencias y Letras* 26 (1971): 23.

Piatier, Jacqueline. "Les débuts de Monique Wittig." *Le Monde,* Nov. 14, 1964, 15. [Review of *L'opoponax.*]

Poggi, Dominique. "Une apologie des rapports de domination." *La Quinzaine Littéraire* (Aug. 1976).

Porter, Laurence M. "Writing Feminism: Myth, Epic and Utopia in Monique Wittig's *Les guérillères.*" *L'Esprit Créateur* 29 (1989): 92–100.

Rawson, C. J. "Cannibalism and Fiction. Part 2: Love and Eating in Fielding, Mailer, Genet, and Wittig." *Genre* 2, no. 2 (1978): 227–313.

Richman, Michele. "Sex and Signs: The Language of French Feminist Criticism." *Language and Style* 13, no. 4 (1980): 62–80.

Robichon, Suzette. "Monique Wittig, Ecrivain." *Lesbia,* no. 222 (2003): 21.

Rognon Ecarnot, Catherine. "Politique et poetique du travestissement dans les fictions de Monique Wittig." *Clio: Histoire, Femmes et Sociétés* 10 (1999): 185–95.

———. "Rencontre avec Monique Wittig." *Lesbia Magazine* 155 (1996): 28–30.

Roll, Walter. "Bernhard Schofferlins Vorrede zum ersten Teil der 'Romischen Historie' (1505)." *Zeitschrift fu Deutsches Altertum und Deutsche Literatur* 117, no. 3 (1988): 210–23.

Rooke, Patricia T. "Woman as Artifact: Sexual Scripts and a Female Education from the Reformation to Monique Wittig." *Journal of Educational Thought* 30, no. 1 (1996).

Rosenfeld, Marthe. "Language and the Vision of a Lesbian-Feminist Utopia in Wittig's *Les guérillères.*" *Frontiers* 6, no. 1 (1981): 6–9.

———. "The Linguistic Aspect of Sexual Conflict: Monique Wittig's *Le corps lesbien.*" *Mosaic* 17, no. 2 (1984): 235–41.

———. "Vers un langage de l'utopie amazonienne: *Le corps lesbien* de Monique Wittig." *Vlasta,* no. 4 (1985): 55–64.

Rubin, Gayle. "Sexual Traffic." *differences: A Journal of Feminist Cultural Studies* 6, nos. 2–3 (1994): 62–99.

Savona, Jeannelle Laillou. "Gender and Feminist Reading [Socio-sexuation et lecture féministe]." *Atlantis* 17, no. 2 (1992): 2–10.

———. "Lesbians on the French Stage: From Homosexuality to Monique Wittig's Lesbianization of the Theatre." *Modern Drama* 39, no. 1 (1996): 132–55.

Scanlon, Julie. "XX + XX = XX: Monique Wittig's Reproduction of the Monstrous Lesbian." *Paroles Gelées* 16, no. 1 (1998): 73–96.

Schor, Naomi. "French Feminism Is a Universalism." *differences: A Journal of Feminist Cultural Studies* 7, no. 1 (1995): 15–45.

Schuster, Marilyn R. "Strategies for Survivial: The Subtle Subversion of Jane Rule." *Feminist Studies* 7, no. 2 (1981): 431–50.

Shaktini, Namascar. "Le déplacement du sujet phallique: L'écriture lesbienne de Monique Wittig." *Vlasta*, no. 4 (1985): 65–77.

———. "Displacing the Phallic Subject: Wittig's Lesbian Writing." *Signs: Journal of Women in Culture and Society* 8, no. 1 (1982): 29–45.

———. "Je me souviens du début de mon amitié avec Monique Wittig (1935–2003)." *Lesbia*, no. 222 (2003): 22.

———. "Monique Wittig's New Language." *Pacific Coast Philology* 24, nos. 1–2 (1989): 85–95.

———. "Review of Monique Wittig's *The Straight Mind and Other Essays.*" *Hypatia: A Journal of Feminist Philosophy* 9, no. 1 (1994): 211–14.

Sherzer, Dina. "Dictionnaires/fictionnaires: Anamorphoses lexicographiques et encyclopédiques." *French Review* 63, no. 4 (1990): 642–51.

Simon, Claude. "Pour Monique Wittig." *L'Express,* Nov. 30–Dec. 16, 1964, 69–70.

Slama, Beatrice. "De la 'littérature féminine' à l'écrire-femme': Différence et institution." *Littérature* 44 (1981): 51–71.

Spraggins, Mary Pringle. "Myth and Ms: Entrapment and Liberation in Monique Wittig's *Les guérillères.*" *International French Review* 3, no. 1 (1976): 47–51.

Stamponini, Suzanna. "Un nom pour tout le monde: *L'opoponax* de Monique Wittig." *Vlasta,* no. 4 (1985): 79.

Stimpson, Catharine R. "Feminism and Feminist Criticism." *Massachussetts Review* 24, no. 2 (1983): 272–88.

Turcotte, Louise. "Lettre Ouverte à Line Chamberland." *Homosapiens* 3, no. 30 (1996): 8–9.

———. "Queer Theory: Transgression and/or Regression?" *Canadian Woman Studies/Les Cahiers de la Femme* 16, no. 2 (1996): 118–20.

Vann, Italo. "Georges Conchon: *L'état sauvage;* Jean Blanzat: *Le faussaire;* Jean-Pierre Fay: *L'écluse;* Monique Wittig: *L'opoponax.*" *Nuova Antologia* 494 (June 1965): 275–80.

Vigarello, Georges. "Le laboratoire des sciences humaines." *Esprit* 2 (1982): 90–106.

Waelti-Walters, Jennifer. "Circle Games in Monique Wittig's *Les guérillères.*" *Perspectives on Contemporary Literature* 6 (1980): 59–64.

Waldrep, Shelton. "Deleuzian Bodies: Not Thinking Straight in Capitalism and Schizophrenia." *Pre/Text: A Journal of Rhetorical Theory* 13, nos. 3–4 (1992): 137–49.

Went-Daoust, Yvette. "*L'opoponax* ou le parcours de on." *Neophilologus* 75, no. 3 (1991): 358–66.

Wenzel, Hélène Vivienne. "Le discours radical de Monique Wittig." *Vlasta,* no. 4 (1985): 43–52.

———. "The Text as Body/Politics: An Appreciation of Monique Wittig's Writings in Context." *Feminist Studies* 7, no. 2 (1981): 264–87.

Whatling, Clare. "Utopian Conceptions: Rethinking *The Straight Mind.*" *Journal of Modern Critical Theory* 20, no. 2 (1997): 174–89.

———. "Wittig's Monsters: Stretching the Lesbian Reader." *Textual Practice* 11, no. 2 (1997): 237–48.

White, Susan. "The Political Borders of Language in Marie-Claire Blais's *L'ange de la solitude.*" *Modern Language Review* 95, no. 2 (2000): 350–61.

Winter, Carla "Weipplich brust-manlich hertz: Lucretia in der 'Romischen Historie.'" *Beitrage zur Geschichte der Deutschen Sprache und Literatur* 122, no. 2 (2000): 279–91.

Zerilli, Linda M G. "I Am a Woman: Female Voice and Ambiguity in the Second Sex." *Women and Politics* 11, no. 1 (1991): 93–108.

———. "Rememoration or War? French Feminist Narrative and the Politics of Self-Representation." *differences: A Journal of Feminist Cultural Studies* 3, no. 1 (1991): 1–19.

———. "The Trojan Horse of Universalism: Language as a 'War Machine' in the Writings of Monique Wittig." *Social Text: Theory/Culture/Ideology* 25–26 (1990): 146–70.

Zimmerman, Bonnie. "Is 'Chloe Liked Olivia' a Lesbian Plot?" *Women's Studies International Forum* 6, no. 2 (1983): 169–75.

MAGAZINE ARTICLES

Anonymous. "Butch Telegraph." *Times Literary Supplement,* Jan. 4, 1974, 3748.

———. *Les guérillères* book review. *Newsweek,* Oct. 25, 1971, 122.

———. "Monstrous Regiment." *Times Literary Supplement,* April 16 1970, 3555.

———. "New Fiction." *Times of London,* May 19, 1966, 56.

———. "Review: *The Straight Mind and Other Essays.*" *Publishers Weekly,* Jan. 1 1992.

Barber, Dulan. "Human Beings and Amazons." *London Sunday Tribune,* Sept. 3, 1972, 15.

Beauman, Sally. "*Les guérillères:* Women without Men Except to Kill for Fun and Survival." *New York Times Book Review,* Oct. 10, 1971, 5, 14.

Bliven, Naomi. "Daphne in India, Catherine in France." *New Yorker,* July 2, 1966, 66, 68.

Broyard, Anatole. "Who's Winning the War?" *New York Times Book Review,* Nov. 9, 1971, 23.

Burgess, Anthony. "When She Tells Us Something Is Good, We're Quite Sure of It." *New York Times Book Review,* March 8, 1970, 4, 29.

Chapsal, Madeleine. "L'amour fou des amoureuses." *L'Express,* Nov. 26–Dec. 2, 1973, 12–13.

Cluny, Claude-Michel. "Monique Wittig et Sande Zeig: Brouillon pour un dictionnaire des amantes." *Magazine Littéraire,* March 22, 1977, 66–67.

Cunningham, Valentine. "Oh m/e oh m/y." *Times Literary Supplement,* Aug. 15, 1975, 913.

Duras, Marguerite. "Une oeuvre éclatante." *Le Nouvel Observateur,* Nov. 5, 1964, 18–19.

Eliott, Janice. "The Last Testament of Beat." *Sunday Times,* May 22, 1966, 33.

Eribon, Didier. "Le retour de Monique Wittig: La femme marron." *Le Nouvel Observateur,* June 14–20, 2001, 118. [Review of *La pensée straight.*]

Etter, Ryn. "Review: *The Straight Mind and Other Essays.*" *Booklist,* Feb. 1, 1992.

Hahn, Otto. "Du sable entre les doigts." *L'Express,* Nov. 9, 1964, 70.

Jean, R. "Review: *Les guérillères.*" *Le Monde,* June 13, 1970, 22.

Josselin, Jean-François. "Lettre à Sapho." *Le Nouvel Observateur,* Oct. 8, 1973, 59.

Kanters, Robert. "A Literary Letter from Paris." *New York Times Book Review,* Dec. 20, 1964, 14–15.

Kermode, Frank. "The Zero Answer: Frank Kermode Writes about a Women's Novel by Monique Wittig." *The Listener,* July 8, 1971, 53–54.

Martin, Graham. "French Follies." *London Magazine,* 1976, 103–6.

Patton, Cindy. "*Guérillères* Warfare: Monique Wittig, Straight Shooter." *Voice,* June 30 1992, 66–67. [Review of *The Straight Mind and Other Essays.*]

Peterson, Virgilia. "Re-entry into Childhood." *New York Times Book Review,* June 26, 1966, 4.

Piatier, Jacqueline. "Monique Wittig Sappho d'aujourd'hui." *Le Monde,* Nov. 15, 1973, 20. [Review of *Le corps lesbien.*]

Raphael, Frederic. "Sexual Conjugations." *Sunday Times,* June 15, 1975, 35. [Review of *The Lesbian Body.*]

Rolin, Dominique. "Elégie pour amazones." *Le Point,* Jan. 21, 1974, 65.

Sale, Roger. "Keeping Up with the News." *New York Review of Books,* Dec. 16, 1971, 23–24.

———. "Monique Wittig: *Les guérillères.*" *New York Review of Books,* Oct. 17, 1971, 23–24.

Simon, Pierre Henri. "Un bilan de la saison romanesque." *Le Monde,* Dec. 23, 1964, 12–13.

Sturrock, John. "The Lesbian Body." *New York Times Book Review,* Nov. 23, 1975, 18, 20, 22.

Weightman, John. "The Indeterminate I." *New York Review of Books,* Dec. 1, 1966, 24–26.

THESES AND DISSERTATIONS

Arbour, Kathryn Mary. "French Feminist Re-Visions: Wittig, Rochefort, Bersianik and D'Eaubonne Re-Write Utopia." Ph.D. diss., University of Michigan, 1984.

Bammer, Angelika. "Visions and Re-Visions: The Utopian Impulse in Feminist Fiction." Ph.D. diss., University of Wisconsin, 1983.

Bartkowsky, Frances. "Toward a Feminist Eros: Readings in Feminist Utopian Fiction." Ph.D. diss., University of Iowa, 1982.

Bauer, Michelle C. "The Development of the Lesbian Subject in the Fiction of Natalie Clifford Barney and Monique Wittig." M.A. thesis, University of South Florida, 1993.

Berube, Janet Lyon. "Feminist Polemics and the Manifesto's 'Hostile Hand.'" Ph.D. diss., University of Virginia, 1992.

Blue, Sarah Jane. "Selfhood and the Art of the Found Object: Self-Creation in Three Novels by Margaret Atwood, Colette, and Monique Wittig." Ph.D. diss, University of Georgia, 2001.

Bourque, Dominique. "De L'intertextualité mythique dans *Le corps lesbien* de Monique Wittig." M.A. thesis, University of Ottawa, 1995.

———. "Vers une théorie du contre-texte: La subversion formelle dans l'oeuvre de Monique Wittig." Ph.D. diss., University of Ottawa, 2000.

Brawn, Anna Livia Julian. "Pronoun Envy: Literary Uses of Linguistic Gender (Anne Garreta, Maureen Duffy, Monique Wittig, Marge Piercy, June Arnold)." Ph.D. diss., University of California, Berkeley, 1995.

Burwell, Jennifer Lise. "Gendered Identity and the Body Politic: Twentieth-Century Transformations of the Utopian Form." Ph.D. diss., Northwestern University, 1993.

Caruso-Haviland, Linda. "Dancing at the Juncture of Being and Knowing: Sartrean Ontology, Embodiment, Gender, and Dance." Ed.D. diss., Temple University, 1995.

Davis, James D. "(Belle)-icosity: Violence in the Narrative Fiction of Monique Wittig." Ph.D. diss., University of Georgia, 2000.

Frost, Elisabeth Ann. "The Feminist Avant-Garde in American Poetry." Ph.D. diss., University of California, Los Angeles, 1994.

Gaudet, Jeannette. "L'écriture féminine en France depuis 1985: Wittig, Duras, Redonnet, Giraudon et Atlan." Ph.D. diss., Dalhousie University, 1995.

Gray, Nancy. "Slaying the Phantom: Voices of Experience in Experimental Writing by Women (Stein, Woolf, Richardson, Shange, Wittig)." Ph.D. diss., University of Washington, 1988.

Grubb, Rachel Jane. "Monique Wittig's *The Opoponax:* A Contemporary Study of Form and Meaning." M.A. thesis, Southern Connecticut State University, 1998.

Hersh, Allison Lori. "Transgressive Intent: The Postmodern Epic and the Subversion of Generic Form (Homer, Acker Kathy, Wittig Monique, Churchill Caryl, Duffy Maureen)." Ph.D. diss., University of Michigan, 1993.

Kuzminsky, Irina. "The Language of Women? A Study of Three Women Writers: Marina Tsvetaeva, Ingeborg Bachmann and Monique Wittig." Ph.D. diss., Oxford University, 1989.

Lavilne, Laurie K. "The Functions of Female Anger in the French and Francophone Novel of the Mid-Twentieth Century (Myriam Warner Vieyra, Senegal, Anne Hebert, Marie Chauvet, Haiti)." Ph.D. diss., Rutgers, The State University of New Jersey, 1997.

Master, Tulsi Dhimant. "Niche Marketing of Feminist Writings." Ph.D. diss., Syracuse University, 1995.

Mayfield, John Nash. "Romantic Liaisons: Selves and Subjects in Novels of Female Formation (Bildungsrom, Shelley Mary, Sand George, Austen Jane, Woolf Virginia, Wittig Monique)." Ph.D. diss., University of Michigan, 1991.

Merlin, Lara Cassandra. "Body Magic: Witchcraft and Polymorphous Perversity in Women's Postcolonial Literature." Ph.D. diss., Rutgers, The State University of New Jersey, 1998.

Moore, Kendra E. "The Subject in the Writings of Kristeva, Irigaray, and Wittig: Some Political Implications." M.A. thesis, Columbia University, 1984.

Oleska, Carla Marie. "'This Is My Body Which Will Not Be Given Up for You': The Postmodern Feminist Avant-Garde and the Female Body (Acker Kathy, Wittig Monique, Finley Karen)." Ph.D. diss., University of Rhode Island, 1992.

Olson, Catherine L. "The Trojan Horse: Monique Wittig's War on Gender." M.A. thesis, Florida Atlantic University, 1996.

Pavlides, Merope. "Monique Wittig: The Constant Journey. Restructuring the Traditional: Myth in Selected Works of Cixous, Chedid, Wittig and Yourcenar." Ph.D. diss., University of Wisconsin, Madison, 1986.

Rofougaran, Fariba. "Les corps dans l'oeuvre de Monique Wittig." Ph.D. diss., University of Southern California, 1987.

Russi, Roger. "Dialogues with Epic Figures: Christa Wolf's *Kassandra,* Monique Wittig's *Les guérillères,* and Marion Zimmer Bradley's *The Firebrand.*" Ph.D. diss., University of North Carolina, Chapel Hill, 1993.

Shaktini, Namascar. "The Problem of Gender and Subjectivity Posed by the New Subject Pronoun j/e in the Writing of Monique Wittig." Ph.D. diss., University of California, Santa Cruz, 1981.

Spangler, Luita Deane. "'On Her Mouth You Kiss Your Own': Lesbian Conversations in Exile, 1924–1936." Ph.D. diss., University of New Hampshire, 1992.

Travis, Molly Abel. "Subject on Trial: The Displacement of the Reader in Modern and Postmodern Fiction." Ph.D. diss., Ohio State University, 1989.

Tyminski, Renia. "Divinity, Transcendence and Female Subjectivity in the Works of Mary Daly (Luce Irigaray, Monique Wittig, Goddess Worship)." Ph.D. diss., University of Toronto, 1996.

Van Rest, Monica. "The Revolutionary Message in *Les guérillères.*" Ph.D. diss., University of Illinois at Urbana-Champaign, 1979.

Venkatesan, Jaishree. "Patriarchy and Feminist Praxis: The Dialectics of Power and Resistance in Contemporary French Women's Theatre." Ph.d. diss., Purdue University, 1996.

Wells, Gwendolyn Marie. "Zones of Excess." Ph.D. diss., University of Pennsylvania, 1995.

Wenzel, Hélène Vivienne. "L'opoponax: I Still Live in Her." Ph.D. diss., University of California, Berkeley, 1978.

Winterhalter, Teresa Marie. "Women without Words: Narratives of Self for Absent Voices." Ph.D. diss., University of Rochester, 1994.

Woodhull, Winifred. "Politics, the Feminine, and Writing: A Study of Monique Wittig's Les guérillères and Brouillon pour un dictionnaire des amantes." Ph.D. diss., University of Wisconsin, 1980.

Yang, Linda Diane. "A là recherche de l'autre dans La maison sans racines, Les grandes desordres, Virgile, non, et Redemption." M.A. thesis, Dalhousie University, 1993.

CONTRIBUTORS

A member of the École Normale Supérieure and the École des Hautes Études en Sciences Sociales, MARIE-HÉLÈNE BOURCIER is a sociologist and queer activist. She teaches at the University of Lille III in France. Among her other work, she has written *Lesvos, oui* and *Queer Zones: Politiques des identités sexuelles, des représentations et des savoirs*. She also coordinated *The Straight Mind* in French and translated three of its essays; coorganized the first international symposium on the literary, political, and theoretical works of Monique Wittig in Paris in 2001 in the presence of Wittig; and coedited the publication of the acts of the symposium with Suzette Robichon (*Parce que les lesbiennes ne sont pas des femmes*). The founder of a queer nonprofit organization, Le Zoo (1996), she has written numerous articles on queer theory and politics, sexual subcultures, feminisms, and lesbian cultures. *Queer Zones 2* will be published in the spring of 2005. Bourcier is at work on a book on pornography and post-pornography.

Born in Quebec, DOMINIQUE BOURQUE has spent much of her life crossing physical, linguistic, and conceptual boundaries, living in Germany, Spain, and Japan and focusing on the creative work of groups such as lesbians and immigrants. She collaborated in creating the Canadian Museum of Civilization's exhibition of Arab-Canadian artists *Ces pays qui m'habitent/The Lands within Me*, as well as the museum's book about the exhibition. An associate professor in women's studies and French literature at the University of Ottawa, she has published in a number of periodicals and produced a dissertation on the formal subversion in Monique Wittig's fiction ("Towards a Theory of the Counter-Text"). A study of mythic intertextuality in *The Lesbian Body* (entitled *Les mythes en éclats: Une lecture du Corps lesbien de Monique Wittig*) is forthcoming. She is at work under a grant from the Social Sciences and Humanities Research Council on the "de-marking" of the categories of sex in French texts since the seventeenth century.

DIANE GRIFFIN CROWDER is professor of French and women's studies at Cornell College in Iowa. She did her doctorate at the University of Wisconsin-Madison, where she was among a group of graduate students working with faculty to create the women's studies program there and taught the first such course offered by the French department. At Cornell College, she cofounded a women's studies program and a lesbigay student group. She has also presented frequent papers at regional and national conferences and published articles on feminist semiotics, utopian fiction, French feminist and lesbian theory, and queer theory, as well as numerous works on Monique Wittig.

TERESA DE LAURETIS is professor of the history of consciousness, an interdisciplinary doctoral program at the University of California, Santa Cruz. Born and educated in Italy, she received her doctorate in modern languages and literatures from Bocconi University in Milan and taught Italian and comparative literature, film theory, and women's and gender studies at several American universities. She has held visiting professor appointments at universities in Canada, Germany, Italy, and The Netherlands, as well as in the United States. The author of more than a hundred essays and numerous books in both English and Italian, de Lauretis has written on semiotics, psychoanalysis, film, literature, science fiction, and feminist and cultural theory. Some of her work has been widely anthologized and translated into fourteen other languages. Her present scholarly interests concern Djuna Barnes and Freud's theory of drives.

CATHERINE ROGNON ECARNOT, who teaches at the Lycée Paul Verlaine in Paris, wrote the first doctoral dissertation in France on Monique Wittig—"L'écriture poétique de Monique Wittig"—at the Université de Paris VII, Denis Diderot (1999). Her book *L'écriture de Monique Wittig à la couleur de Sappho* (2002) was the first published in France on Monique Wittig. Other publications include "Rencontre avec Monique Wittig," "Politique et poétique du travestissement dans les fictions de Monique Wittig," "L'interlocutrice du corps lesbien: Menaçante, désirée, constituante," *Parce que les lesbiennes ne sont pas des femmes: Autour de l'oeuvre politique, théorique et littéraire de Monique Wittig,* "La monstrueuse sexualité d'au-delà du verbe dans les fictions de Monique Wittig," and "Pourquoi j'ai écrit ma thèse sur les fictions de Monique Wittig."

ERIKA OSTROVSKY was born in Austria but educated primarily in America and France. At New York University she met Germaine Brée, who became her inspiration and mentor. She received an M.A. in 1960 and a Ph.D. in

French literature in 1964. That same year she became a faculty member of the Department of French at New York University, retiring in 1992 as professor emerita. Among her publications are *Céline and His Vision; Voyeur Voyant: Portrait of L. F. Céline* (and its French version, *Céline le voyeur voyant*) and *Under the Sign of Ambiguity: Saint John Perse/Alexis Léger*. Her book *A Constant Journey: The Fiction of Monique Wittig* was the first on Wittig to be published in America. She is also author of numerous essays on a variety of modern French writers and has contributed to several volumes of *Cahiers de l'Herne, The Columbia Dictionary of Modern European Literature,* and *European Writers: The Twentieth Century.*

JEANNELLE LAILLOU SAVONA is professor emerita of French at Trinity College, University of Toronto, where she is also an Honorary Fellow of the Graduate Institute for Women's Studies and Gender Studies. She has published *Le Juif dans le roman Américain contemporain* and *Jean Genet;* coedited *Théâtralité, écriture et mise en scène* and two special issues of *Modern Drama:* "Theory of Drama and Performance" (1983) and "Women in the Theatre" (1989); and been editor of a special issue of *Études Littéraires* on "Theater and Theatricality." Her many articles on twentieth-century French theater, French female authors, and feminist and lesbian theories have appeared in *Feminine Focus: The New Women Playwrights; Hélène Cixous, chemins d'une écriture; Theatre and Feminist Aesthetics; Feminist Writers;* and *Hélène Cixous, croisées d'une oeuvre,* among other journals and anthologies. In 2002 the Canadian Association of University Professors of French awarded her first prize for the best learned article published in French in the year 2000. She has published an essay on the Québecois writer Nicole Brossard and writes on the work of contemporary Quebec lesbian playwrights.

NAMASCAR SHAKTINI teaches French literature and feminist theory as an associate professor at Florida Atlantic University. As a student in Paris, she met Monique Wittig in January 1970 and has written extensively on Wittig's work, beginning with her Ph.D. dissertation, "The Problem of Gender and Subjectivity Posed by the New Subject Pronoun j/e in the Writing of Monique Wittig," which includes an unpublished concordance of Wittig's *Le corps lesbien.* Her first publication on Monique Wittig, "Displacing the Phallic Subject: Wittig's Lesbian Writing," appeared in *Signs* and has been republished several times and translated into French. She has published widely on Wittig in both English and French publications. Her essay "'Marriage Is between a Man and a Woman' (Or Is It?)" is under review. She is also at work on the manuscript for a book: "The Straight Mind Meets the Lesbian Body: Reading Monique Wittig."

LINDA M. G. ZERILLI is a professor of political science at Northwestern University, where she teaches feminist theory and modern political theory. Among her articles on feminist theory and continental political thought are "This Universalism Which Is Not One," which appeared in *Diacritics;* "Doing without Knowing: Feminism's Politics of the Ordinary" in *Political Theory;* and "The Trojan Horse of Universalism: Language as a War Machine in the Writings of Monique Wittig," published in *Social Text.* She is also the author of *Signifying Woman: Culture and Chaos in Rousseau, Burke, and Mill* and *Feminism and the Abyss of Freedom.*

INDEX

Across the Acheron. See *Virgile, non*
Amazones d'Hier, Lesbiennes d'Aujourd'hui,
    193, 197n8
L'Arc de Triomphe, 4, 8, 20, 190
Arendt, Hannah: on philosophy, 87–88, 91–95,
    100, 102–3; mentioned, 107–13 passim
Aristotle, 37, 88, 105, 108n9, 110n24
Auerbach, Nina, 105, 107n2, 112n41, 113n41,
    114n57

Bakhtin, Mikhail, 163, 169, 178n2
Balzac, Honoré de, 79, 157
"Banlieues" (Wittig), 7
Barnes, Djuna, 9, 44, 82–83, 147n9, 186n3, 224
Barthes, Roland, 191
Baudelaire, Charles: *L'héautontimorouménos,*
    5; intertextual influence of, 45–47, 81, 118,
    171–72, 183; use of dialogism by, 164; use
    of lesbian by, 157, 173, mentioned, 129n5,
    165, 178n13
Beauvoir, Simone de: analysis of feminine
    condition, 2–5; philosophical influence of,
    53–56 passim, 64, 80, 181, 194; mentioned,
    8, 60n10, 148n16, 192
Benmussa, Simone, 134, 136, 142; mentioned,
    147nn2–5 passim
Benson, Margaret, 17, 31
Benveniste, Emile, 150–52, 156, 158n4,
    159nn11–12, 185
Bergson, Henri, 108n4, 111n28, 113n46
Bernheim, Cathy, 4. *See also* For a Movement
    of Women's Liberation
Bhabha, Homi K., 53; mentioned, 59n5
Bible, 24, 45–46, 119, 124–26, 174; Christ, 122,
    128, 151, 185
Bonnet, Marie-Jo, 178–79nn12–13

book-within-the-book, 42
Bourcier, Marie-Hélène, 11, 178, 187, 196n4
Bourque, Dominique, 163, 223
Bourroux, Monique, 4, 8. *See also* For a Move-
    ment of Women's Liberation
Braidotti, Rosi, 61n17
Brecht, Berthold, 37, 42, 85n33, 137–38, 142,
    146, 148nn12–24, 149n24, 152, 158
Brouillon pour un dictionnaire des amantes
    (Wittig and Zeig), 1, 8–9, 58, 71, 81, 84n16,
    85n44, 86n44, 124–27 passim, 137, 147n9
Brown, Rita Mae, 194
Bryant, Anita, 75
Butler, Judith: and theoretical misreadings, 57;
    60n17; on gender, 65–78 passim, 91, 109–11
    passim, 184, 186nn15–17 passim; men-
    tioned, 84n12, 86nn37–40 passim

Castoriadis, Cornelius, 89, 93, 103, 108nn6–10
    passim, 109n13, 110nn24–25
"The Category of Sex" (Wittig), 66, 68,
    110nn21–27 passim, 111n32, 187
Cervantes, Miguel de, 137, 143, 175, 177. See
    also *Quixote*
Chisholm, Diane, 154–55, 158n6
Christ. *See* Bible
Christian fantastic, 42. *See also* mythology
Cixous, Hélène, 9, 133, 146, 185, 188–89, 192,
    196n4. *See also* feminine writing
Cocteau, Jean, 137, 148n23
Colette, 45, 149n23
Combahee River Collective, 54, 60n7, 197n9
Combat pour la libération de la femme. *See*
    For a Movement of Women's Liberation
The Constant Journey, 9, 81, 86n42, 133–46
    passim, 148n13

Cope, Karin, 154–55, 158nn7–9, 159n10
Le corps lesbien. See The Lesbian Body
cross-dressing, 186
Crowder, Diane Griffin, 63, 110n8, 153, 224
Curtin Lesbian, Alternative, and Gay Collective
    (CLAG), 10

Dante, 2, 58, 73, 81, 126–28, 181
Dassin, Julie, 4, 8. *See also* For a Movement of
    Women's Liberation
Deleuze, Gilles, 114n51
Delphy, Christine, 8, 59n6, 64, 147nn7–8, 189,
    192, 197n7. *See also* For a Movement of
    Women's Liberation
Deroin, Jeanne, 26
Derrida, Jacques, 56–57, 61n20, 109n17,
    114n51
Descartes, René, 57, 151, 163, 180, 186n1
The Divine Comedy. See Dante
Dostoevsky, Fyodor, 164–65
Douglas, Sally, 6n10,
Duras Marguerite, 1, 116, 128, 129n2, 138

Ecarnot, Catherine Rognon, 224
Engels, Fredrick, 2–28 passim
Englebrecht, Penelope, 150–52, 155, 158n2
Eribon, Didier, 10
L'Esprit Créateur, 10, 43n1, 85n27, 86n44,
    147n9
essentialism, 152, 155–56, 180
ethnicity, 24, 32, 56, 60, 65–69, 197n9; *ma-
    ronnes*, 195, 197n17; minority writers, 3,
    82; racism, 3, 17, 54; slavery, 22, 26–27, 29,
    65–66, 68–72 passim, 102–3, 137, 145, 175

Fausto-Sterling, Anne, 92, 110n22
feminine writing, 189, 191
Feminist Issues, 4, 9, 192–93
For a Movement of Women's Liberation, 21
    passim, 84n10, 148n22, 158, 190–94 passim;
    militantes, 4, 6n11, 8, 15
Foucault, Michel, 56, 59, 113n45
Fouque, Antoinette, 189–90
Freud, Sigmund, 22, 39, 53, 59, 81, 84n16,
    169, 224
Friedan, Betty, 194, 197n12
Front of Radical Lesbians, 148n22
Fuss, Diana, 64–65, 70, 83nn2–3

gender, 65, 92, 111n31, 126, 128, 136, 184; in
    language, 46, 81, 116–23 passim, 127, 164,
    168–70, 196. *See also* Butler, Judith

Gide, André, 148n23
Gouges, Olympe de, 25
Gournay, Marie de, 41
Le Grand Robert de la langue Française, 4, 10.
    See also neologism
Grassi, Ernesto, 88–90 passim, 92, 105–14
    passim
Les guérillères (Wittig), 3 passim, 7, 158;
    critical assessment of, 68, 70, 72–73, 82,
    84nn9–15, 85n26; gender in 122–29 passim,
    137–45 passim, 164–74 passim, 178n1, 182,
    191, 195, 197n6; language and poetics in, 87,
    90, 98–113 passim; Wittig on, 37–61 passim
Guillaumin, Colette, 64–66, 83n8, 147n7, 193

Haraway, Donna J., 193
Heidegger, Martin, 109n13
heterosexuality. *See* sexuality
Hewitt, Leah D., 186n
homosexuality. *See* sexuality
"Homo Sum" (Wittig), 64, 112n34, 187

L'Idiot International, 5, 6n11, 7, 15, 84n10, 189
Irigaray, Luce, 57, 110n23, 192

Jagose, Annemarie, 70
"Le jardin" (Un jour mon prince viendra) (Wit-
    tig), 68, 84n15
Jesus Christ. *See* Bible

Kant, Immanuel, 87–88, 90, 107–10 passim
Kristeva, Julia, 38, 57, 178n3, 191–92

Labé, Louise, 44, 48, 121
Lacan, Jacques, 39, 69, 81, 84n16, 169, 190.
    See also phallogocentrism
Lakeland, Mary Jo, 4, 9, 192
Lauretis, Teresa de, 51, 59n3, 60n12, 61n20,
    110n18, 184, 186n16, 193, 224
Lautréamont, 46–47
Lavender Menace, 194, 197n12. *See also*
    Friedan, Betty
Le Vay, David. *See* translations
Lenin, 27–28
lesbianism, 52–62, 69–74, 79, 82, 145, 173–76,
    179n15, 180, 185, 188–89, 192–96. *See also*
    sexuality
The Lesbian Body (Wittig), 1, 6nn4–5, 8;
    remarks on, 44–48 passim, 51–59 passim,
    73, 84nn9–16 passim, 120–24; theoretical
    analysis of, 150–58 passim, 166, 171–32,
    183–85, 195

Lesbian Peoples: Material for a Dictionary (Wittig and Zeig). *See Brouillon pour un dictionnaire des amantes*

Lesseps, Emmanuelle de, 4, 8, 192. *See also* For a Movement of Women's Liberation

Lévi-Strauss, Claude, 39, 81, 190

Locke, John, 95, 109n12, 113n41

Lorde, Audre, 141, 148n19

Machiavelli, 95, 112nn35–39 passim, 114n51

Mallarmé, Stéphane, 43, 164, 171, 178n11

Manastabal, 74–78 passim, 126–27, 175–6, 181, 187–97 passim

Manifesto (Wittig et al.). *See* For a Movement of Women's Liberation

"The Mark of Gender" (Wittig), 10, 86n41, 104, 114nn53–55, 156

Marks, Elaine, 9, 58, 61n19, 84n14, 149n23, 159n14

maronnes. See ethnicity

Marx, Karl, 2–28 passim, 54, 56, 60n9, 64, 68–69, 80, 133, 168, 189–94 passim

materialist lesbianism, 4, 64–65

Mathieu, Nicole-Claude, 64–65, 83n6, 147n7, 192–93

McCartny, Mary, 85n22

Miller, Judith G., 147n2

minority writers. *See* ethnicity

MLF (Mouvement de Libération des Femmes). *See* For a Movement of Women's Liberation

Modern Language Association (MLA), 8, 188, 196n4

Moi, Toril, 105, 114n58

mythology, 42, 73, 102, 118–23 passim, 148n21, 157–58; Aphrodite, 124; Argos and Io, 173; Artemis, 185; Echo and Narcissus, 182; Eros, 59; Hermes, 119; Orpheus and Eurydice, 47, 118–22 passim, 172; Osiris, 122, 156; Prometheus, 119; Venus, 182; Zeus, 122, 184

National Organization for Women (NOW), 194

neologism, 4–5, 10, 118–19, 123, 127. See also *Le Grand Robert de la langue Française*

Nietzsche, Friedrich Wilhelm, 22, 25

nouveau roman literary movement, 38, 79, 177, 186n10. *See also* Sarraute, Nathalie

Nouvelles Questions Feministes, 148n22, 179n17, 190–94 passim, 197n15

"One Is Not Born a Woman" (Wittig), 9, 51, 69, 147n6

"On the Social Contract" (Sur le contrat social) (Wittig), 10, 69, 72, 109nn11–16, 110n19, 112n36, 187

L'opoponax (Wittig), 1, 7, 39–40, 70, 85n22, 114n56; gender in, 116–28 passim, 164–70, 178n1, 186n12, 187

Ostrovsky, Erika, 70, 79, 83; on language use, 100, 103, 112–14 passim, 129n1, 224–45; mentioned, 85nn22–35 passim

"Paradigm" (Wittig), 9, 158, 159n14

Paris-la-politique et autres histoires (Wittig), 10, 51, 58

Pascal, Blaise, 41

Pateman, Carole, 109n1

patriarchy, 196. *See also* heterosexuality

Père Lachaise Cemetery, 4, 11

phallogocentrism, 5, 150, 152, 158; phallic signifier, 158, 169

Plato, 42

"The Point of View: Universal or Particular?" (Wittig), 9, 112n38

Porter, Laurence, 99, 112n40, 113nn41–45 passim

Prix Médicis, 1, 187

pronouns, 1, 6n10, 114n55–56, 164, 171, 178n7, 185; *elles,* 38–39, 78, 85n27, 103–6, 119–20; *j/e,* 47, 150–51, 156, 166, 171–72, 178n7, 185; *on,* 117, 164–68, 178n6

Proust, Marcel, 46, 82–83, 148n23, 167, 191

queer theory, 56–57, 180, 191, 223

Questions Feministes, 4–9 passim, 133, 136, 147n6, 190, 192, 194

Quixote, 1, 58, 81, 137–46, 175, 177. *See also* Zeig, Sande

racism. *See* ethnicity

Rich, Adrienne, 195, 197n15

Rimbaud, Arthur, 43

Robichon, Suzette, 11, 223

Rochefort, Christiane, 4–16 passim. *See also* For a Movement of Women's Liberation

Rosenfeld, Marthe, 10, 179n14

Rothenburg, Marcia, 6n10, 7, 15, 21, 84n10, 190

Rousseau, Jean-Jacques, 95, 112n36

San Francisco, 181, 194

Sappho, 44–45, 81–82, 121–24, 157, 173, 184–85

Sarraute, Nathalie, 1, 4, 10, 45–46; dialogism

and, 164; *nouveau roman* and, 38, 79, 177; mentioned, 179n17

Sartre, Jean-Paul, 38, 79

Saussure, Ferdinand de, 151, 157, 159n13

Savona, Jeanelle Laillou, 133, 225

Scève, Maurice, 81, 118, 129n5, 167, 178n8, 183

Schor, Naomi, 64, 83n4, 86n38

Seal, Bobby, 3, 17, 29

The Second Sex (Beauvoir), 2, 60n10

Sert, Janine, 4. *See also* For a Movement of Women's Liberation

sexuality: heterosexuality, 47, 52–59 passim, 69–72, 75–82 passim, 85n36, 90–91, 99, 104–11 passim, 121, 133, 136, 145, 150, 154, 180–96 passim; homosexuality, 55, 71, 75, 82, 97, 133–36, 145, 182, 190

Shaktini, Namascar, 20–21, 59n4, 73, 84n17, 107n2, 110n18; mentioned, 85n29. *See also* Stephenson, Margaret

"The Site of Action" (Le lieu de l'action) (Wittig), 9, 108n7

slavery. *See* ethnicity

Stambolian, George, 6n4, 9, 61n19, 84n14, 149n23, 159n14

Stephenson, Margaret, 4–21 passim, 84n10, 190. *See also* For a Movement of Women's Liberation; Shaktini, Namascar

Stonewall, 194, 197n14

The Straight Mind and Other Essays (Wittig), 9–10, 47, 51, 57–69 passim, 84n16, 108–9, 111–12, 148n20, 158n1, 178n5, 179n15, 187–88, 192, 195–96

Straub, Jean-Marie, 37, 38, 4

"Les tchiches et les tchouches" (Wittig), 9, 68, 181, 186n6

Tomb of the Unknown Soldier. *See* L'Arc de Triomphe

translations: of David Le Vay 5–10 passim, 61n18, 84n15, 107, 158n3, 186nn4–7 passim; of Helen Weaver, 7, 186n12; of Marie-Hélène Bourcier, 186–88; of Marthe Rosenfeld, 10; of Monique Wittig, 7, 186nn3–12 passim, 189, 193; questions of, 103

travestissement, 186. *See also* cross-dressing

travesty 180–81, 185

Tristan, Flora, 26

"The Trojan Horse" (Wittig), 4, 9, 63, 70, 79, 95–97, 104, 111n27, 146, 154–55; mentioned, 107n2, 112n37, 129n6

Turcotte, Louise, 63, 146, 148n16

University of Vincennes, 4, 15

Verlaine, Paul, 45, 47, 173

Virgile, non (Wittig), 2, 10, 51, 58, 68–73 passim, 78, 81, 84n15, 126–29, 171, 174–77, 178n, 181–83, 186n14, 196n1

Vivien, Renée, 159n2, 49n23, 173

Vlasta, 10, 85n42, 86n42, 129n3, 147n1, 179n14

Le voyage sans fin. See The Constant Journey

Weaver, Helen. *See* translations

Wenzel, Hélène Vivienne, 107n2

Whatling, Clare, 152–55, 158n5

Wilde, Oscar, 173

Wittig, Gille, 6n11, 7, 15, 21, 84n10, 190

Wolf, Susan Ellis, 4, 9, 192

Zeig, Sande, 11, 71, 81, 84n16, 86n44, 124, 134–48 passim

Zelensky, Anne, 4, 8

Zerilli, Linda M. G., 8, 108n10, 112n34, 113n41, 226

The University of Illinois Press
is a founding member of the
Association of American University Presses.

University of Illinois Press
1325 South Oak Street
Champaign, IL 61820-6903
www.press.uillinois.edu